201

P!

WILLPOWER

WILLPOWER

REDISCOVERING OUR GREATEST STRENGTH

Roy F. Baumeister

and

John Tierney

ALLEN LANE
an imprint of
PENGUIN BOOKS

ALLEN LANE

Published by the Penguin Group

Penguin Books Ltd, 80 Strand, London WC2R 0RL, England
Penguin Group (USA) Inc., 375 Hudson Street, New York, New York 10014, USA
Penguin Group (Canada), 90 Eglinton Avenue East, Suite 700, Toronto, Ontario,
Canada M4P 2Y3 (a division of Pearson Penguin Canada Inc.)
Penguin Ireland, 25 St Stephen's Green, Dublin 2, Ireland (a division of Penguin Books Ltd)
Penguin Group (Australia), 250 Camberwell Road, Camberwell, Victoria 3124, Australia
(a division of Pearson Australia Group Pty Ltd)
Penguin Books India Pvt Ltd, 11 Community Centre, Panchsheel Park,
New Delhi – 110 017, India
Penguin Group (NZ), 67 Apollo Drive, Rosedale, Auckland 0632, New Zealand (a division of
Pearson New Zealand Ltd)
Penguin Books (South Africa) (Pty) Ltd, 24 Sturdee Avenue, Rosebank, Johannesburg 2196,
South Africa

Penguin Books Ltd, Registered Offices: 80 Strand, London WC2R 0RL, England

www.penguin.com

First published in the United States of America by The Penguin Press, a member of
Penguin Group (USA) Inc. 2011
First published in Great Britain by Allen Lane 2012
1

Printed in Great Britain by Clays Ltd, St Ives plc

A CIP catalogue record for this book is available from the British Library

Hardback ISBN: 978–1–846–14350–2
Trade Paperback ISBN: 978–1–846–14610–7

www.greenpenguin.co.uk

To our children,
Athena and Luke

CONTENTS

WILLPOWER

INTRODUCTION

However you define success—a happy family, good friends, a satisfying career, robust health, financial security, the freedom to pursue your passions—it tends to be accompanied by a couple of qualities. When psychologists isolate the personal qualities that predict "positive outcomes" in life, they consistently find two traits: intelligence and self-control. So far researchers still haven't learned how to permanently increase intelligence. But they have discovered, or at least rediscovered, how to improve self-control.

Hence this book. We think that research into willpower and self-control is psychology's best hope for contributing to human welfare. Willpower lets us change ourselves and our society in small and large ways. As Charles Darwin wrote in *The Descent of Man,* "The highest possible stage in moral culture is when we recognize that we ought to control our thoughts." The Victorian notion of willpower would later fall out of favor, with some twentieth-century psychologists and philosophers doubting it even existed. Baumeister himself started out as something of a skeptic. But then he observed willpower in the laboratory: how it gives people the strength to persevere, how they lose self-control as their willpower is depleted, how this mental energy is fueled by the glucose in the body's bloodstream. He and his collaborators discovered that willpower, like a muscle, becomes fatigued from overuse but can also be strengthened over the long term through exercise. Since Baumeister's experiments first demonstrated the existence of willpower, it has become one of the most intensively studied topics in social science (and those experiments now rank among the most-cited research in psychology). He and colleagues around the world have found that improving willpower is the surest way to a better life.

They've come to realize that most major problems, personal and social, center on failure of self-control: compulsive spending and borrowing, impulsive violence, underachievement in school, procrastination at work, alcohol and drug abuse, unhealthy diet, lack of exercise, chronic anxiety, explosive anger. Poor self-control correlates with just about every kind of individual trauma: losing friends, being fired, getting divorced, winding up in prison. It can cost you the U.S. Open, as Serena Williams's tantrum in 2009 demonstrated; it can destroy your career, as adulterous politicians keep discovering. It contributed to the epidemic of risky loans and investments that devastated the financial system, and to the shaky prospects for so many people who failed (along with their political leaders) to set aside enough money for their old age.

Ask people to name their greatest personal strengths, and they'll often credit themselves with honesty, kindness, humor, creativity, bravery, and other virtues—even modesty. But not self-control. It came in dead last among the virtues being studied by researchers who have surveyed more than one million people around the world. Of the two dozen "character strengths" listed in the researchers' questionnaire, self-control was the one that people were least likely to recognize in themselves. Conversely, when people were asked about their failings, a lack of self-control was at the top of the list.

People feel overwhelmed because there are more temptations than ever. Your body may have dutifully reported to work on time, but your mind can escape at any instant through the click of a mouse or a phone. You can put off any job by checking e-mail or Facebook, surfing gossip sites, or playing a video game. A typical computer user checks out more than three dozen Web sites a day. You can do enough damage in a ten-minute online shopping spree to wreck your budget for the rest of the year. Temptations never cease. We often think of willpower as an extraordinary force to be summoned to deal with emergencies, but that's not what Baumeister and his colleagues found when they recently monitored a group of more than two hundred men and women in central Germany. These Germans wore beepers that went off at random intervals seven times a day, prompting them to report whether they were currently experiencing some sort of desire or had recently felt such a desire. The painstaking study, led by Wilhelm Hofmann, collected more than ten thousand momentary reports from morning until midnight.

Desire turned out to be the norm, not the exception. About half the time, people were feeling some desire at the moment their beepers went off, and another quarter said a desire had just been felt in the past few minutes. Many of these desires were ones they were trying to resist. The researchers concluded that people spend about a quarter of their waking hours resisting desires—at least four hours per day. Put another way, if you tapped four people at any random moment of the day, one of them would be using willpower to resist a desire. And that doesn't even include all the instances in which willpower is exercised, because people use it for other things, too, such as making decisions.

The most commonly resisted desire in the beeper study was the urge to eat, followed by the urge to sleep, and then by the urge for leisure, like taking a break from work by doing a puzzle or game instead of writing a memo. Sexual urges were next on the list of most-resisted desires, a little ahead of urges for other kinds of interactions, like checking e-mail and social-networking sites, surfing the Web, listening to music, or watching television. To ward off temptation, people reported using various strategies. The most popular was to look for a distraction or to undertake a new activity, although sometimes they tried suppressing it directly or simply toughing their way through it. Their success was decidedly mixed. They were pretty good at avoiding sleep, sex, and the urge to spend money, but not so good at resisting the lure of television or the Web, or the general temptation to relax instead of work. On average, when they tried to resist a desire with willpower, they succeeded about half the time.

A 50 percent failure rate sounds discouraging, and it may well be pretty bad by historical standards. We have no way of knowing how much our ancestors exercised self-control in the days before beepers and experimental psychologists, but it seems likely that they were under less strain. During the Middle Ages, most people were peasants who put in long, dull days in the fields, frequently accompanied by prodigious amounts of ale. They weren't angling for promotions at work or trying to climb the social ladder, so there wasn't a premium on diligence (or a great need for sobriety). Their villages didn't offer many obvious temptations beyond alcohol, sex, or plain old sloth. Virtue was generally enforced by a desire to avoid public disgrace rather than by any zeal to achieve human perfection. In the medieval Catholic Church, salvation depended more on being part of the group and keeping up with the standard rituals than on heroic acts of willpower.

But as farmers moved into industrial cities during the nineteenth century, they were no longer constrained by village churches and social pressures and universal beliefs. The Protestant Reformation had made religion more individualistic, and the Enlightenment had weakened faith in any kind of dogma. Victorians saw themselves as living in a time of transition as the moral certainties and rigid institutions of medieval Europe died away. A popular topic of debate was whether morality could survive without religion. Many Victorians came to doubt religious principles on theoretical grounds, but they kept pretending to be faithful believers because they considered it their public duty to preserve morality. Today it's easy to mock their hypocrisy and prudery, like the little skirts they put on table legs—no bare ankles! Mustn't excite anyone! If you read their earnest sermons on

God and duty, or their battier theories on sex, you can understand why people of that era turned for relief to Oscar Wilde's philosophy: "I can resist everything except temptation." But considering all the new temptations available, it was hardly neurotic to be searching for new sources of strength. As Victorians fretted over moral decay and the social pathologies concentrated in cities, they looked for something more tangible than divine grace, some internal strength that could protect even an atheist.

They began using the term *willpower* because of the folk notion that some kind of force was involved—some inner equivalent to the steam powering the Industrial Revolution. People sought to increase their store of it by following the exhortations of the Englishman Samuel Smiles in *Self-Help,* one of the most popular books of the nineteenth century on both sides of the Atlantic. "Genius is patience," he reminded readers, explaining the success of everyone from Isaac Newton to Stonewall Jackson as the result of "self-denial" and "untiring perseverance." Another Victorian-era guru, the American minister Frank Channing Haddock, published an international bestseller titled simply *The Power of Will.* He tried to sound scientific by calling it "an energy which is susceptible of increase in quantity and of development in quality," but he had no idea—much less any evidence—of what it might be. A similar notion occurred to someone with better credentials, Sigmund Freud, who theorized that the self depended on mental activities involving the transfer of energy.

But Freud's energy model of the self was generally ignored by subsequent researchers. It wasn't until recently, in Baumeister's laboratory, that scientists began systematically looking for this source of energy. Until then, for most of the past century, psychologists and educators and the rest of the chattering classes kept finding one reason or another to believe it didn't exist.

The Decline of the Will

Whether you survey the annals of academe or the self-help books at the airport, it's clear that the nineteenth-century concept of "character building" has been out of fashion for quite a while. The fascination with willpower ebbed in the twentieth century partly in reaction to the Victorians' excesses, and partly due to economic changes and the world wars. The prolonged bloodshed of World War I seemed a consequence of too many stubborn gentlemen following their "duty" to senseless deaths. Intellectuals preached a more relaxed view of life in America and much of Western Europe—but not, unfortunately, in Germany, where they developed a "psychology of will" to guide their country during its bleak recovery from the war. That theme would be embraced by the Nazis, whose rally in 1934 was featured in Leni Riefenstahl's infamous propaganda film, *The Triumph of the Will.* The Nazi concept of mass obedience to a sociopath was hardly the Victorian concept of personal moral strength, but the distinction was lost. If the Nazis represented the triumph of the will . . . well, when it comes to bad PR, there's nothing quite like a personal endorsement from Adolf Hitler.

The decline of will didn't seem like such a bad thing, and after the war there were other forces weakening it. As technology made goods cheaper and suburbanites richer, stimulating consumer demand became vital to the economy, and a sophisticated new advertising industry urged everyone to buy now. Sociologists identified a new generation of "other-directed" people who were guided by their neighbors' opinions rather than by strong inner moral convictions. The stern self-help books of the Victorian era came to be seen as naïvely self-centered. The new bestsellers were cheery works like Dale Carnegie's *How to Win Friends and Influence People* and Norman Vincent Peale's *The Power of Positive Thinking.* Carnegie spent eight pages instructing readers how to smile. The right smile would make people feel good about you, he explained, and if they believed in you, success was assured. Peale and other authors came up with an even easier method.

"The basic factor in psychology is the realizable wish," Peale wrote. "The man who assumes success tends already to have success." Napoleon Hill sold millions of copies of *Think and Grow Rich* by telling readers to decide how much money they wanted, write the figure down on a piece of paper, and then "believe yourself already in possession of the money." These gurus' books would go on selling for the rest of the century, and the feel-good philosophy would be distilled to a rhyming slogan: "Believe it, achieve it."

The shift in people's characters was noticed by a psychoanalyst named Allen Wheelis, who in the late 1950s revealed what he considered a dirty little secret of his profession: Freudian therapies no longer worked the way they were supposed to. In his landmark book, *The Quest for Identity,* Wheelis described a change in character structure since Freud's day. The Victorian middle-class citizens who formed the bulk of Freud's patients had intensely strong wills, making it difficult for therapists to break through their ironclad defenses and their sense of what was right and wrong. Freud's therapies had concentrated on ways to break through and let them see why they were neurotic and miserable, because once those people achieved insight, they could change rather easily. By midcentury, though, people's character armor was different. Wheelis and his colleagues found that people achieved insight more quickly than in Freud's day, but then the therapy often stalled and failed. Lacking the sturdy character of the Victorians, people didn't have the strength to follow up on the insight and change their lives. Wheelis used Freudian terms in discussing the decline of the superego in Western society, but he was essentially talking about a weakening of willpower—and all this was *before* the baby boomers came of age in the 1960s with a countercultural mantra of "If it feels good, do it."

Popular culture kept celebrating self-indulgence for the "Me

Generation" of the 1970s, and there were new arguments against willpower from social scientists, whose numbers and influence soared during the late twentieth century. Most social scientists look for causes of misbehavior outside the individual: poverty, relative deprivation, oppression, or other failures of the environment or the economic and political systems. Searching for external factors is often more comfortable for everyone, particularly for the many academics who worry that they risk the politically incorrect sin of "blaming the victim" by suggesting that people's problems might arise from causes inside themselves. Social problems can also seem easier than character defects to fix, at least to the social scientists proposing new policies and programs to deal with them.

The very notion that people can consciously control themselves has traditionally been viewed suspiciously by psychologists. Freudians claimed that much of adult human behavior was the result of unconscious forces and processes. B. F. Skinner had little respect for the value of consciousness and other mental processes, except as needed to process reinforcement contingencies. In *Beyond Freedom and Dignity,* he argued that to understand human nature we must get beyond the outmoded values in the book's title. While many of Skinner's specific theories were discarded, aspects of his approach have found new life among psychologists convinced that the conscious mind is subservient to the unconscious. The will came to seem so unimportant that it wasn't even measured or mentioned in modern personality theories. Some neuroscientists claim to have disproved its existence. Many philosophers refuse to use the term. If they want to debate this classical philosophical question of freedom of the will, they prefer to speak of freedom of action, not of will, because they doubt there is any such thing as will. Some refer disdainfully to "the so-called will." Recently, some scholars have even begun to argue that the legal system must be revamped to eliminate outdated notions of free will and responsibility.

Baumeister shared the general skepticism toward willpower when he started his career as a social psychologist in the 1970s at Princeton. His colleagues were then focusing not on self-control but on self-esteem, and Baumeister became an early leader of this research, which showed that people with more confidence in their ability and their self-worth tended to be happier and more successful. So why not help everyone else succeed by finding ways to boost their confidence? It seemed a reasonable enough goal to psychologists as well as the masses, who bought pop versions of self-esteem and "empowerment" in best-sellers like *I'm OK— You're OK* and *Awaken the Giant Within*. But the eventual results were disappointing, both inside and outside the laboratory. While international surveys showed that U.S. eighth-grade math students had exceptionally high confidence in their own abilities, on tests they scored far below Koreans, Japanese, and other students with less self-esteem.

Meanwhile, in the 1980s, a few researchers started getting interested in self-regulation, the term that psychologists use for self-control. The resurrection of self-control wasn't led by theorists, who were still convinced that willpower was a quaint Victorian myth. But when other psychologists went into the laboratory or the field, they kept happening on something that looked an awful lot like it.

The Comeback of the Will

In psychology, brilliant theories are cheap. People like to think of the field advancing thanks to some thinker's startling new insight, but that's not how it usually works. Coming up with ideas isn't the hard part. Everyone has a pet theory for why we do what we do, which is why psychologists get sick of hearing their discoveries dismissed with "Oh, my grandmother knew *that*." Progress generally comes not from theories but from someone finding a clever way to *test* a theory, as Walter Mischel did. He and his colleagues weren't theorizing about self-regulation—in fact, they didn't even discuss their results in terms of self-control or willpower until many years later.

They were studying how a child learns to resist immediate gratification, and they found a creative new way to observe the process in four-year-old children. They would bring the children one at a time into a room, show them a marshmallow, and offer them a deal before leaving them alone in the room. The children could eat the marshmallow whenever they wanted to, but if they held off until the experimenter returned, they would get a second marshmallow to eat along with it. Some children gobbled the marshmallow right away; others tried resisting but couldn't hold out; some managed to wait out the whole fifteen minutes for the bigger reward. The ones who succeeded tended to do so by distracting themselves, which seemed an interesting enough finding at the time of the experiments, in the 1960s.

Much later, though, Mischel discovered something else thanks to a stroke of good fortune. His own daughters happened to attend the same school, on the Stanford University campus, where the marshmallow experiments took place. Long after he finished the experiments and moved on to other topics, Mischel kept hearing from his daughters about their classmates. He noticed that the children who had failed to wait for the extra marshmallow seemed to get in more trouble than the others, both in and out of school. To see if there was a pattern, Mischel and his colleagues tracked down hundreds of veterans of the experiments. They found that the ones who had shown the most willpower at age four went on to get better grades and test scores. The children who had managed to hold out the entire fifteen minutes went on to score 210 points higher on the SAT than the ones who had caved after the first half minute. The children with willpower grew up to become more popular with their peers and their teachers. They earned higher salaries. They had a lower body-mass index, suggesting that they were less prone to gain weight as middle age encroached. They were less likely to report having had problems with drug abuse.

These were stunning results, because it's quite rare for anything measured in early childhood to predict anything in adulthood at a statistically significant level. Indeed, this disconnect was one of the death blows against the Freudian psychoanalytic approach to psychology, which emphasized early childhood experiences as the foundation of adult personality. Surveying this literature in the 1990s, Martin Seligman concluded that there was hardly any convincing proof that episodes in early childhood have a causal impact on the adult personality, with the possible exceptions of severe trauma or malnutrition. The very few significant correlations he noted between childhood and adult measures could be explained as mostly reflecting genetic (inborn) tendencies, such as having a generally sunny or grumpy disposition. The willpower to resist a marshmallow may well have had a genetic component, too, but it also seemed amenable to nurture, producing that rare childhood advantage that could pay dividends throughout life. These dividends looked even more remarkable once the overall benefits of self-control were assessed, which Baumeister did in *Losing Control,* a scholarly book he wrote in 1994 with his wife, Dianne Tice, a fellow professor at Case Western Reserve University, and Todd Heatherton, a professor at Harvard.

"Self-regulation failure is the major social pathology of our time," they concluded, pointing to the accumulating evidence of its contribution to high divorce rates, domestic violence, crime, and a host of other problems. The book stimulated more experiments and studies, including the development of a scale for measuring self-control on personality tests. When researchers compared students' grades with nearly three dozen personality traits, self-control turned out to be the *only* trait that predicted a college student's grade-point average better than chance. Self-control also proved to be a better predictor of college grades than the student's IQ or SAT score. Although raw intelligence was obviously an advantage, the study showed that self-control was more important because it helped the students show up more reliably for classes, start their homework earlier, and spend more time working and less time watching television.

In workplaces, managers scoring high in self-control were rated more favorably by their subordinates as well as by their peers. People with good self-control seemed exceptionally good at forming and maintaining secure, satisfying attachments to other people. They were shown to be better at empathizing with others and considering things from other people's perspectives. They were more stable emotionally and less prone to anxiety, depression, paranoia, psychoticism, obsessive-compulsive behavior, eating disorders, drinking problems, and other maladies. They got angry less often, and when they did get angry, they were less likely to get aggressive, either verbally or physically. Meanwhile, people with poor self-control were likelier to hit their partners and to commit a variety of other crimes—again and again, as demonstrated by June Tangney, who worked with Baumeister to develop the self-control scale on personality tests. When she tested prisoners and then tracked them for years after their release, she found that the ones with low self-control were most likely to commit more crimes and return to prison.

The strongest evidence yet was published in 2010. In a painstaking long-term study, much larger and more thorough than anything done previously, an international team of researchers tracked one thousand children in New Zealand from birth until the age of thirty-two. Each child's self-control was rated in a variety of ways (through observations by researchers as well as in reports of problems from parents, teachers, and the children themselves). This produced an especially reliable measure of children's self-control, and the researchers were able to check it against an extraordinarily wide array of outcomes through adolescence and into adulthood. The children with high self-control grew up into adults who had better physical health, including lower rates of obesity, fewer sexually transmitted diseases, and even healthier teeth. (Apparently, good self-control includes brushing and flossing.) Self-control was irrelevant to adult depression, but its lack made people more prone to alcohol and drug problems. The children with poor self-control tended to wind up poorer financially. They worked in relatively low-paying jobs, had little money in the bank, and were less likely to own a home or have money set aside for retirement. They also grew up to have more children being raised in single-parent households, presumably because they had a harder time adapting to the discipline required for a long-term relationship. The children with good self-control were much more likely to wind up in a stable marriage and raise children in a two-parent home. Last, but certainly not least, the children with poor self-control were more likely to end up in prison. Among those with the lowest levels of self-control, more than 40 percent had a criminal conviction by the age of thirty-two, compared with just 12 percent of the people who had been toward the high end of the self-control distribution in their youth.

Not surprisingly, some of these differences were correlated with intelligence and social class and race—but all these results remained significant even when those factors were taken into account. In a follow-up study, the same researchers looked at brothers and sisters from the same families so that they could compare children who grew up in similar homes. Again, over and over, the sibling with the lower self-control during childhood fared worse during adulthood. They ended up sicker, poorer, and were more likely to spend time in prison. The results couldn't be clearer: Self-control is a vital strength and key to success in life.

Evolution and Etiquette

As psychologists were identifying the benefits of self-control, anthropologists and neuroscientists were trying to understand how it evolved. The human brain is distinguished by large and elaborate frontal lobes, giving us what was long assumed to be the crucial evolutionary advantage: the intelligence to solve problems in the environment. After all, a brainier animal could presumably survive and reproduce better than a dumb one. But big brains also require lots of energy. The adult human brain makes up 2 percent of the body but consumes more than 20 percent of its energy. Extra gray matter is useful only if it enables an animal to get enough extra calories to power it, and scientists didn't understand how the brain was paying for itself. What, exactly, made ever-larger brains with their powerful frontal lobes spread through the gene pool?

One early explanation for the large brain involved bananas and other calorie-rich fruits. Animals that graze on grass don't need to do a lot of thinking about where to find their next meal. But a tree that had perfectly ripe bananas a week ago may be picked clean today or may have only unappealing, squishy brown fruits left. A banana eater needs a bigger brain to remember where the ripe stuff is, and the brain could be powered by all the calories in the bananas, so the "fruit-seeking brain theory" made lots of sense—but only in theory. The anthropologist Robin Dunbar found no support for it when he surveyed the brains and diets of different animals. Brain size did not correlate with the type of food. Dunbar eventually concluded that the large brain did not evolve to deal with the physical environment, but rather with something even more crucial to survival: social life. Animals with bigger brains had larger and more complex social networks. That suggested a new way to understand Homo sapiens. Humans are the primates who have the largest frontal lobes because we have the largest social groups, and that's apparently why we have the most need for self-control. We tend to think of willpower as a force for personal betterment—adhering to a diet, getting work done on time, going out to jog, quitting smoking—but that's probably not the primary reason it evolved so fully in our ancestors. Primates are social beings who have to control themselves in order to get along with the rest of the group. They depend on one another for the food they need to survive. When the food is shared, often it's the biggest and strongest male who gets first choice in what to eat, with the others waiting their turn according to status. For animals to survive in such a group without getting beaten up, they must restrain their urge to eat immediately. Chimpanzees and monkeys couldn't get through meals peacefully if they had squirrel-sized brains. They might expend more calories in fighting than they'd consume at the meal.

Although other primates have the mental power to exhibit some rudimentary etiquette at dinner, their self-control is still quite puny by human standards. Experts surmise that the smartest nonhuman primates can mentally project perhaps twenty minutes into the future—long enough to let the alpha male eat, but not long enough for much planning beyond dinner. (Some animals, like squirrels, instinctively bury food and retrieve it later, but these are programmed behaviors, not conscious savings plans.) In one experiment, when monkeys were fed only once a day, at noon, they never learned to save food for the future. Even though they could take as much as they wanted during the noon feeding, they would simply eat their fill, either ignoring the rest or wasting it by getting into food fights with one another. They'd wake up famished every morning because it never occurred to them to stash some of their lunch away for an evening snack or breakfast.

Humans know better thanks to the large brain that developed in our Homo ancestors two million years ago. Much of self-control operates unconsciously. At a business lunch, you don't have to consciously restrain yourself from eating meat off your boss's plate. Your unconscious brain continuously helps you avoid social disaster, and it operates in so many subtly powerful ways that some psychologists have come to view it as the real boss. This infatuation with unconscious processes stems from a fundamental mistake made by researchers who keep slicing behavior into thinner and briefer units, identifying reactions that occur too quickly for the conscious mind to be directing. If you look at the cause of some movement in a time frame measured in milliseconds, the immediate cause will be the firing of some nerve cells that connect the brain to the muscles. There is no consciousness in that process. Nobody is aware of nerve cells firing. But the will is to be found in connecting units across time. Will involves treating the current situation as part of a general pattern. Smoking one cigarette will not jeopardize your health. Taking heroin once will not make you addicted. One piece of cake won't make you fat, and skipping one assignment won't ruin your career. But in order to stay healthy and employed, you must treat (almost) every episode as a reflection of the general need to resist these temptations. That's where conscious self-control comes in, and that's why it makes the difference between success and failure in just about every aspect of life.

Why Will Yourself to Read This?

The first step in self-control is to set a goal, so we should tell you ours for this book. We hope to combine the best of modern social science with some of the practical wisdom of the Victorians. We want to tell how willpower—or the lack thereof—has affected the lives of the great and the not-so-great. We'll explain why corporate leaders pay $20,000 a day to learn the secrets of the to-do list from a former karate instructor, and why Silicon Valley's entrepreneurs are creating digital tools to promote nineteenth-century values. We'll see how a British nanny tamed a team of howling triplets in Missouri, and how performers like Amanda Palmer, Drew Carey, Eric Clapton, and Oprah Winfrey applied willpower in their own lives. We'll look at how David Blaine fasted for forty-four days and how the explorer Henry Morton Stanley survived for years in the African wilderness. We want to tell the story of scientists' rediscovery of self-control and its implications outside the laboratory.

Once psychologists began observing the benefits of self-control, they were faced with a new mystery: What exactly is willpower? What did it take for the self to resist a marshmallow? When Baumeister took up these questions, his understanding of the self was still pretty much in line with the then-conventional view, called the information-processing model. He and his colleagues talked about the mind as if it were a little computer. These information models of the human mind generally ignored concepts like power or energy, which were so out of fashion that researchers weren't even opposed to them anymore. Baumeister didn't expect to suddenly change his own view of the self, let alone anyone else's. But once he and his colleagues began experimenting, the old ideas didn't seem so dated.

The result, after dozens of experiments in Baumeister's lab and hundreds elsewhere, is a new understanding of willpower and of the self. We want to tell you what's been learned about human behavior, and how you can use it to change yourself for the better. Acquiring self-control isn't as magically simple as the techniques in modern self-help books, but neither does it have to be as grim as the Victorians made it out to be. Ultimately, self-control lets you relax because it removes stress and enables you to conserve willpower for the important challenges. We're confident that this book's lessons can make your life not just more productive and fulfilling but also easier and happier. And we can guarantee that you will not have to endure any sermons against bare ankles.

1.

IS WILLPOWER MORE
THAN A METAPHOR?

Sometimes we are devils to ourselves
When we will tempt the frailty of our powers,
Presuming on their changeful potency.

— Troilus, in Shakespeare's *Troilus and Cressida*

If you have a casual acquaintance with Amanda Palmer's music, if you know about her banned-in-Britain abortion song or the "Backstabber" video of her running down a hall naked holding an upraised knife while chasing the equally naked guy in lipstick who was just in bed with her, you probably don't think of her as a paragon of self-control.

She has been described in a lot of ways — an edgier Lady Gaga, a funnier Madonna, a gender-bending provocateur, the high priestess of "Brechtian punk cabaret" — but the words *Victorian* and *repressed* generally don't come up. Her persona is Dionysian. When she accepted a marriage proposal from Neil Gaiman, the British fantasy novelist, Palmer's idea of a formal announcement was a morning-after confession on Twitter that she might have gotten engaged "but also might have been drunk."

Yet an undisciplined artist could never have written so much music or sold out so many concerts around the world. Palmer couldn't have gotten to Radio City Music Hall without practicing. It took self-control to create her uncontrolled persona, and she credits her success partly to what she calls "the ultimate Zen training ground": posing as a living statue. She performed on the street for six years and started a company hiring out living statues for corporate gigs, like holding platters of organic produce at the opening of a Whole Foods supermarket.

Palmer took up this calling in 1998, when she was twenty-two and living in her hometown, Boston. She made videos describing herself as an "aspiring rock star," but that occupation didn't pay the rent, so she went into Harvard Square and introduced a form of street theater she'd seen in Germany. She called herself the Eight Foot Bride. With her face painted white, wearing a formal wedding dress and a veil, holding a bouquet in her formal white gloves, she would stand on top of a box. If someone put money in her tips basket, she would hand the person a flower, but otherwise she remained utterly motionless.

Some people would insult her or throw things at her. They tried to make her laugh. They grabbed her. Some yelled at her to get a real job and threatened to steal her money. Drunks tried to pull her down off the pedestal or to tip her over.

"It was not pretty," Palmer recalls. "Once I had a frat boy rub his head drunkenly in my crotch as I looked skyward thinking, *Good Lord, what have I done to deserve this?* But in six years I broke character maybe twice. You literally don't react. You don't even flinch. You just let it pass through you."

The crowds would marvel at her stamina, and people routinely assumed it must be grueling to hold the body in a rigid pose for so long. But Palmer didn't find it a strain on her muscles. She realized there was a physical aspect to the task—she learned not to drink coffee, for instance, because it produced a slight but uncontrollable quiver in her body. But the challenge seemed to be mainly in her mind.

"Standing still isn't really that difficult," she says. "The discipline in being a living statue is much more in the nonreactivity department. I couldn't move my eyes, so I couldn't look at interesting, intriguing things that were passing me by. I couldn't engage with people who were trying to engage me. I couldn't laugh. I couldn't wipe my nose if a piece of snot started to dribble down my upper lip. I couldn't scratch my ear if I had an itch. If a mosquito landed on my cheek, I couldn't swat at it. Those were the real challenges."

But even though the challenge was mental, she also noticed that it eventually took a physical toll. As much as she liked the money, usually about fifty dollars an hour, she found she couldn't do it for long. She would typically work for ninety minutes, take an hour break, get back on the box for another ninety minutes, then call it a day. Sometimes on a Saturday in peak tourist season she would supplement her street work by going to a Renaissance festival and posing as a wood nymph for a few hours, but it left her exhausted.

"I'd get home barely alive, barely able to feel my body," she says. "I would put myself into the bathtub, and my brain would be completely blank."

Why? She hadn't been expending energy to move her muscles. She hadn't been breathing harder. Her heart hadn't been beating faster. What was so hard about doing nothing? She would have said that she'd been exercising willpower to resist temptation, but that folk concept from the nineteenth century had been mostly abandoned by modern experts. What would it even mean to say that a person was exercising willpower? How could it be shown to be anything more than a metaphor?

The answer, as it turned out, was to start with warm cookies.

The Radish Experiment

Sometimes social scientists have to be a little cruel with their experiments. When the college students walked into Baumeister's laboratory, they were already hungry because they'd been fasting, and now they were in a room suffused with the aroma of chocolate chip cookies that had just been baked in the lab. The experimental subjects sat down at a table with several culinary choices: the warm cookies, some pieces of chocolate, and a bowl of radishes. Some students were invited to eat the cookies and candy. The unlucky ones were assigned to "the radish condition": no treats, just raw radishes.

To maximize temptation, the researchers left the students alone with the radishes and the cookies, and observed them through a small, hidden window. The ones in the radish condition clearly struggled with the temptation. Many gazed longingly at the cookies before settling down to bite reluctantly into a radish. Some of them picked up a cookie and smelled it, savoring the pleasure of freshly baked chocolate. A couple accidentally dropped a cookie on the floor and then hastened to put it back in the bowl so no one would know of their flirtation with sin. But nobody actually bit into the forbidden food. The temptation was always resisted, if in some cases by the narrowest of margins. All this was to the good, in terms of the experiment. It showed that the cookies were really quite tempting and that people needed to summon up their willpower to resist them.

Then the students were taken to another room and given geometry puzzles to work on. The students thought they were being tested for cleverness, although in fact the puzzles were insoluble. The test was to see how long they'd work before giving up. This has been a standard technique that stress researchers and others have used for decades because it's a reliable indicator of overall perseverance. (Other research has shown that someone who keeps trying one of these insoluble puzzles will also work longer at tasks that are actually doable.)

The students who'd been allowed to eat chocolate chip cookies and candy typically worked on the puzzles for about twenty minutes, as did a control group of students who were also hungry but hadn't been offered food of any kind. The sorely tempted radish eaters, though, gave up in just eight minutes—a huge difference by the standards of laboratory experiments. They'd successfully resisted the temptation of the cookies and the chocolates, but the effort left them with less energy to tackle the puzzles. The old folk wisdom about willpower appeared to be correct after all, unlike the newer and fancier psychological theories of the self.

Willpower looked like much more than a metaphor. It seemed to be like a muscle that could be fatigued through use, just as Shakespeare had recognized in *Troilus and Cressida*. The Trojan warrior Troilus, convinced that Cressida will be tempted "most cunningly" by the charms of Greek suitors, tells her that he trusts her desire to remain faithful but is worried that she will yield under strain. It's folly to presume that our power of resolution is constant, he explains to her, and warns of what happens when it becomes frail: "Something will be done that we will not." Sure enough, Cressida falls for a Greek warrior.

When Troilus speaks of the "changeful potency" of willpower, he's describing the sort of fluctuations observed in the students tempted by the cookies. After this concept was identified in the radish study and other experiments, it made immediate sense to clinical psychologists like Don Baucom, a veteran marital therapist in Chapel Hill, North Carolina. He said the Baumeister research crystallized something that he had sensed in his practice for years but never fully understood. He'd seen many marriages suffer because the two-career couples fought over seemingly trivial issues every evening. He sometimes advised them to go home from work early, which might sound like odd advice—why give them more time to fight with each other? But he suspected that the long hours at work were draining them. When they got home after a long, hard day, they had nothing left to help them overlook their partner's annoying habits, or to be kind and considerate out of the blue, or to hold their tongue when their partner said something that made them want to respond in a mean, sarcastic manner. Baucom recognized that they needed to leave work while they still had some energy. He saw why marriages were going bad just when stress at work was at its worst: People were using up all their willpower on the job. They gave at the office—and their home suffered the consequences.

After the radish experiment, similar results were observed over and over again in different groups of subjects. Researchers looked for more complex emotional effects and for other ways to measure them, like observing people's physical stamina. A sustained exercise like running a marathon takes more than just conditioning: No matter how fit you are, at some point your body wants to rest, and your mind has to tell it to run, run, run. Similarly, it takes more than just physical strength to grip a hand exerciser and keep squeezing it against the force of the spring. After a short time, the hand grows tired and then gradually starts to feel muscle pain. The natural impulse is to relax, but you can will yourself to keep squeezing—unless your mind has been too busy suppressing other feelings, as in an experiment involving a sad Italian film.

Before watching the movie, the subjects were told that their facial expressions would be recorded by a camera as they watched the movie. Some people were asked to suppress their feelings and show no emotions. Others were asked to amplify their emotional reactions so that their facial expressions would reveal their feelings. A third group, the control condition, got to watch the movie normally.

Everyone then watched an excerpt from the movie *Mondo Cane* ("A Dog's World"), a documentary about the effects of nuclear waste on wildlife. One memorable sequence showed giant sea turtles losing their sense of direction, wandering into the desert, and pathetically dying as they flapped their flippers aimlessly and feebly, unable to find the sea. It was unquestionably a tearjerker, but not everyone was allowed to cry. Some remained stoic, as instructed; some deliberately let the waterworks flow as much as possible. Afterward they all took the stamina test by squeezing the hand exerciser, and researchers compared the results.

The movie had no effect on the stamina of the control group: The people squeezed the handles just as long as they had in a test before the film. But the two other groups quit much sooner, and it didn't matter whether they'd been suppressing their feelings or venting their grief over the poor turtles. Either way, the effort to control their emotional reactions depleted their willpower. Faking it didn't come free.

Neither did a classic mental exercise: the white bear challenge. The white bear has been something of a mascot for psychologists ever since Dan Wegner heard the legend about how the young Tolstoy—or, depending on the version, the young Dostoyevsky—bet that his younger brother couldn't go five minutes without thinking about a white bear. The brother had to pay up, having made a disconcerting discovery about human mental powers. We like to think we control our thoughts, but we don't. First-time meditators are typically shocked at how their minds wander over and over, despite earnest attempts to focus and concentrate. At best, we have partial control over our streams of thought, as Wegner, who is now at Harvard, demonstrated by asking people to ring a bell whenever a white bear intruded on their thoughts. Some tricks and distraction techniques and incentives could briefly keep the creature at bay, he found, but eventually the bell tolled for everyone.

This sort of experiment might sound frivolous. Of all the traumas and psychoses afflicting humans, "unwanted white bear thoughts" doesn't rank very high. Yet that distance from everyday life is precisely what makes it a useful tool to researchers. To understand how well people control their thoughts, it's best not to pick ordinary thoughts. When a graduate student tried a version of Wegner's experiment in which people were told not to think about their mothers, the experiment failed in its purpose, and served to demonstrate only that college students are remarkably skilled at not thinking about their mothers.

What makes Mom different from a white bear? Perhaps the students are trying to separate themselves emotionally from their parents. Perhaps they often want to do things that their mothers would disapprove of, and so they need to put Mom out of their minds. Or perhaps they wish to avoid feeling guilty for not calling their mother as often as she would like. But notice that all these possible explanations for the difference between Mom and the white bear are things about Mom. That's exactly the problem, at least as a researcher would see it. Mothers are not good topics for pure research, because there is so much baggage—so many mental and emotional associations. The reasons you do or don't think about your mother are many, variable, and highly specific, so they would not easily generalize. In contrast, if people have trouble suppressing thoughts of white bears—creatures that presumably play essentially no role in the daily life or personal history of the average American college student and research participant—then the explanation is likely to apply to a wide range of topics.

For all those reasons, the white bear appealed to self-control researchers studying how people manage their thoughts. Sure enough, after people spent a few minutes trying not to think of a white bear, they gave up sooner on puzzles (compared with people who'd been free to ponder anything). They also had a harder time controlling their feelings in another slightly cruel experiment: being forced to remain stoic while watching classic skits from *Saturday Night Live* and a Robin Williams stand-up routine. The audience's facial reactions were recorded and later systematically coded by researchers. Once again, the effects were obvious on the people who'd earlier done the white bear exercise: They couldn't resist giggling, or at least smiling, when Williams went into one of his riffs.

You might keep that result in mind if you have a boss prone to making idiotic suggestions. To avoid smirking at the next meeting, refrain from any strenuous mental exercises beforehand. And feel free to think about all the white bears you want.

Name That Feeling

Once the experiments showed that willpower existed, psychologists and neuroscientists had a new set of questions. Exactly what *was* willpower? Which part of the brain was involved? What was happening in the neural circuits? What other physical changes were taking place? What did it feel like when willpower ebbed?

The most immediate question was what to call this process—something more precise than "changeful potency" or "weak will" or the "The devil made me do it." The recent scientific literature didn't offer much help. Baumeister had to go all the way back to Freud to find a model of the self that incorporated concepts of energy. Freud's ideas, as usual, turned out to be both remarkably prescient and utterly wrong. He theorized that humans use a process called sublimation to convert energy from its basic instinctual sources into more socially approved ones. Thus, Freud posited, great artists channel their sexual energy into their work. It was clever speculation, but the energy model of the self didn't catch on with psychologists in the twentieth century, and neither did the specific theory about the sublimation mechanism. When Baumeister and colleagues tested a list of Freud's theoretical mechanisms against the modern research literature, they found that sublimation fared the worst of all. There was essentially no evidence for it, and lots of reasons to think the opposite was true. For example, if the theory of sublimation was correct, then artists' colonies should be full of people sublimating their erotic urges, and therefore there should be relatively little sexual activity. Have you ever heard of an artists' colony known for its *lack* of sex?

Still, Freud was onto something with his energy model of the self. Energy is an essential element in explaining the liaisons at artists' colonies. Restraining sexual impulses takes energy, and so does creative work. If you pour energy into your art, you have less available to restrain your libido. Freud had been a bit vague about where this energy came from and how it operated, but at least he had assigned it an important place in his theory of self. As a kind of homage to Freud's insights in this direction, Baumeister elected to use Freud's term for the self: *ego*. Thus was born "ego depletion," Baumeister's term for describing people's diminished capacity to regulate their thoughts, feelings, and actions. People can sometimes overcome mental fatigue, but Baumeister found that if they had used up energy by exerting willpower (or by making decisions, another form of ego depletion that we'll discuss later), they would eventually succumb. This term would later appear in thousands of scientific papers, as psychologists came to understand the usefulness of ego depletion for explaining a wide assortment of behaviors.

How ego depletion occurs inside the brain, initially a mystery, became clearer when two researchers at the University of Toronto, Michael Inzlicht and Jennifer Gutsell, observed people who were wearing a cap that covered the skull with a dense network of electrodes and wires. This method, called electroencephalographic recording (EEG), enables scientists to detect electrical activity inside the brain. It can't exactly read someone's mind, but it can help map out how the brain deals with various problems. The Toronto researchers paid special attention to the brain region known as the anterior cingulate cortex, which watches for mismatches between what you are doing and what you intended to do. It's commonly known as the conflict-monitoring system or the error-detection system. This is the part of the brain that sounds the alarm if, say, you're holding a hamburger in one hand and a cell phone in the other, and you start to take a bite out of the cell phone. The alarm inside the brain is a spike in electrical activity (called event-related negativity).

With their skulls wired, the people in Toronto watched some upsetting clips from documentaries showing animals suffering and dying. Half the people were told to stifle their emotional reactions, thereby putting themselves into a state of ego depletion. The rest simply watched the movies carefully. Then everyone went on to a second, ostensibly unrelated activity: the classic Stroop task (named after psychologist James Stroop), requiring them to say what color some letters are printed in. For example, a row of *XXX*s might appear in red, and the correct response would be "Red," which is easy enough. But if the word *green* is printed in red ink, it takes extra effort. You have to override the first thought occasioned by reading the letters ("Green") and force yourself to identify the color of the ink, "Red." Many studies have shown that people are slower to answer under these circumstances. In fact, the Stroop task became a tool for American intelligence officials during the cold war. A covert agent could claim not to speak Russian, but he'd take longer to answer correctly when looking at Russian words for colors.

Picking the right color proved to be especially difficult for the people in the Toronto experiment who had already depleted their willpower during the sad animal movie. They took longer to respond and made more mistakes. The wires attached to their skulls revealed notably sluggish activity in the conflict-monitoring system of the brain: The alarm signals for mismatches were weaker. The results showed that ego depletion causes a slowdown in the anterior cingulate cortex, the brain area that's crucial to self-control. As the brain slows down and its error-detection ability deteriorates, people have trouble controlling their reactions. They must struggle to accomplish tasks that would get done much more easily if the ego weren't depleted.

That ego depletion results in slower brain circuitry is fascinating to neuroscientists, but for the rest of us it would be more useful to

detect ego depletion without covering your skull with wires and electrodes. What are the noticeable symptoms—something to warn you
that your brain is not primed for control *before* you get into a fight
with your partner or polish off the quart of Häagen-Dazs? Until recently, researchers couldn't offer much help. In dozens of studies,
they looked unsuccessfully for telltale emotional reactions, turning
up either contradictory results or nothing at all. Being depleted didn't
seem to consistently make people feel depressed or angry or discon-
tented. In 2010, when an international team of researchers combed
through the results of more than eighty studies, they concluded that
ego depletion's effects on behavior were strong, large, and reliable,
but that the effects on subjective feelings were considerably weaker.
People in depleted condition reported more fatigue and tiredness and
negative emotions, but even those differences weren't large. The results made ego depletion seem like an illness with no symptoms, a
condition that didn't "feel" like anything.

But now it turns out that there are signals of ego depletion, thanks
to some new experiments by Baumeister and a team headed by his
longtime collaborator, Kathleen Vohs, a psychologist at the University of Minnesota. In these experiments, while depleted persons (once
again) didn't show any single telltale emotion, they did react more
strongly to all kinds of things. A sad movie made them extra sad.
Joyous pictures made them happier, and disturbing pictures made
them more frightened and upset. Ice-cold water felt more painful to
them than it did to people who were not ego-depleted. Desires inten-
sified along with feelings. After eating a cookie, the people reported
a stronger craving to eat another cookie—and they did in fact eat
more cookies when given a chance. When looking at a gift-wrapped
package, they felt an especially strong desire to open it.

So if you'd like some advance warning of trouble, look not for
a single symptom but rather for a change in the overall intensity of
your feelings. If you find yourself especially bothered by frustrating
events, or saddened by unpleasant thoughts, or even happier about

some good news — then maybe it's because your brain's circuits aren't controlling emotions as well as usual. Now, intense feelings can be quite pleasurable and are an essential part of life, and we're not suggesting that you strive for emotional monotony (unless you aspire to Mr. Spock's Vulcan calm). But be aware of what these feelings can mean. If you're trying to resist temptation, you may find yourself feeling the forbidden desires more strongly just when your ability to resist them is down. Ego depletion thus creates a double whammy: Your willpower is diminished *and* your cravings feel stronger than ever.

The problem can be particularly acute for people struggling with addiction. Researchers have long noticed that cravings are especially strong during withdrawal. More recently they've noticed that lots of other feelings intensify during withdrawal. During withdrawal, the recovering addict is using so much willpower to break the habit that it's likely to be a time of intense, prolonged ego depletion, and that very state will make the person feel the desire for the drug all the more strongly. Moreover, other events will also have an unusually strong impact, causing extra distress and creating further yearnings for the cigarette or drink or drug. It's no wonder relapses are so common and addicts feel so weird when they quit. Long before psychologists identified ego depletion, the British humorist Sir A. P. Herbert nicely described the conflicting set of symptoms:

> "Thank heaven, I have given up smoking again!" he announced. "God! I feel fit. Homicidal, but fit. A different man. Irritable, moody, depressed, rude, nervy, perhaps; but the lungs are fine."

The Mystery of the Dirty Socks

In the 1970s, the psychologist Daryl Bem set about trying to distinguish conscientious people from others by making up a list of behaviors. He assumed he'd find a positive correlation between "turns in school assignments on time" and "wears clean socks," because both would stem from the underlying trait of conscientiousness. But when he collected data from students at Stanford, where he taught, he was surprised to find a hefty negative correlation.

"Apparently," he joked, "the students could either get their homework done or change their socks every day, but not both."

He didn't give it much further thought, but decades later other researchers wondered if there was something to the joke. Two Australian psychologists, Megan Oaten and Ken Cheng, considered the possibility that the students were suffering from the sort of ego depletion revealed in the radish experiment. These psychologists started by administering laboratory self-control tests to the students at different times during the semester. As hypothesized, the students performed relatively badly near the end of the term, apparently because their willpower had been depleted by the strain of studying for exams and turning in assignments. But the deterioration wasn't limited to arcane laboratory tests. When asked about other aspects of their lives, it became clear that Bem's dirty-sock finding hadn't been a fluke. All sorts of good habits were forsaken as the students' self-control waned during exam period.

They stopped exercising. They smoked more cigarettes. They drank so much coffee and tea that their caffeine intake doubled. The extra caffeine might have been excused as a study aid, but if they were really studying more, you'd expect them to be drinking less alcohol, and that didn't happen. Even though there were fewer parties during exam time, the students drank as much as ever. They abandoned healthy diets and increased their consumption of junk food by 50 percent. It wasn't that they suddenly convinced themselves that potato chips were a brain food. They simply stopped worrying about unhealthy, fattening food when they were focused on exams. They also became less concerned about returning phone calls, washing dishes, or cleaning floors. Final-exam time brought declines in every aspect of personal hygiene that was studied. The students became less diligent about brushing and flossing their teeth. They skipped washing their hair and shaving. And, yes, they wore dirty socks and other unwashed clothes.

Could all of this merely reflect a practical, if slightly unhealthy, shift in priorities? Were they sensibly saving time so that they could study more? Not quite. During exams, students reported an increase in the tendency to spend time with friends instead of studying—precisely the opposite of what would be sensible and practical. Some students even reported that their study habits got worse during exam time, which couldn't have been their intention. They must have been devoting much of their willpower to making themselves study harder, and yet they ended up studying less. Likewise, they reported an increase in oversleeping, and in spending money impulsively. Shopping sprees made no practical sense during exam period, but the students had less discipline to restrain their spending. They were also more grumpy, irritable, and prone to anger or despair. They may have blamed their outbursts on the stress of exam period, because there's a common misperception that stress causes those kinds of emotions. What stress really does, though, is deplete willpower, which diminishes your ability to control those emotions.

The effects of ego depletion were recently demonstrated even more precisely in the beeper study in Germany that we mentioned earlier. By using beepers to query people about their desires throughout the day, Baumeister and his colleagues could see how much willpower was being exerted as the day went on. Sure enough, the more willpower people expended, the more likely they became to yield to the next temptation that came along. When faced with a new desire that produced some I-want-to-but-I-really-shouldn't sort of inner conflict, they gave in more readily if they'd already fended off earlier temptations, particularly if the new temptation came soon after a previous one.

When they eventually yielded to temptation, the German adults as well as the American college students probably blamed their lapses

on some flaw in their character: *I just don't have enough willpower.* But earlier in the day, or earlier in the semester, they'd all had
enough willpower to resist similar temptations. What had happened
to it? Was it really all gone? Perhaps, but there was also another way
to interpret the research on ego depletion. Maybe people didn't simply run out of willpower. Maybe they consciously or unconsciously
hoarded it. One of Baumeister's graduate students, Mark Muraven,
took up the question of conservation and kept studying it until he
was well established as a tenured professor at the State University of
New York at Albany. He began, as usual, with a round of exercises
to deplete the subjects' willpower. Then, when he prepared them
for the second round, testing their perseverance, he warned them that
there would later be an additional third round featuring more tasks
to perform. People reacted by slacking off on the second round.
Consciously or unconsciously, they were conserving energy for the
final push.

Then Muraven tried another variation in the second round of the
experiment. Before testing people's perseverance, he informed them
that they could win money by doing well. The cash worked wonders.
People immediately found reserves to perform well. Watching the
experimental subjects persevere, you'd never have known that their
willpower had been depleted earlier. They were like marathoners
who found a second wind once they caught sight of the prize waiting
for them at the finish line.

But suppose, upon reaching that prize, the marathoners were
suddenly informed that the finish line was actually another mile down
the road. That's essentially what Muraven did to the people who won
cash for their perseverance in the second round. He waited until after
their stellar performance to inform them that they weren't quite done
yet—there'd be another round of perseverance tests. Since they hadn't
been warned ahead of time, they hadn't conserved any energy, and it
showed in their exceptionally bad performances. In fact, the better
they had done in the second round, the worse they did in the third

round. Now they were like marathoners who had started their closing kick too soon and were passed by everyone else as they limped toward the finish line.

Lessons from the Street and the Lab

For all her bohemian transgressiveness, Amanda Palmer is thoroughly bourgeois in one respect. Ask her about willpower, and she will tell you that she has never had enough. "I don't consider myself a disciplined person at all," she says. But if you press her, she will concede that her six years as a living statue did strengthen her resolve.

"The street performing gave me balls of steel," she says. "Those hours on the box trained me to stay focused. Being a performer is about tying yourself to the post of the present moment and staying focused. I'm pretty much the worst when it comes to long-term strategic planning, but I have a really strong brand of work ethic and I'm a very disciplined one-thing person. If it's just one project at a time, I can focus on it for hours."

That's more or less what researchers discovered after studying thousands of people inside and outside the laboratory. The experiments consistently demonstrated two lessons:

1. You have a finite amount of willpower that becomes depleted as you use it.
2. You use the same stock of willpower for all manner of tasks.

You might think you have one reservoir of self-control for work, another for dieting, another for exercise, and another for being nice to your family. But the radish experiment showed that two completely unrelated activities—resisting chocolate and working on geometry puzzles—drew on the same source of energy, and this phenomenon has been demonstrated over and over. There are hidden connections among the wildly different things you do all day. You use the same supply of willpower to deal with frustrating traffic, tempting food, annoying colleagues, demanding bosses, pouting children. Resisting dessert at lunch leaves you with less willpower to praise your boss's awful haircut. The old line about the frustrated worker going home and kicking the dog jibes with the ego-depletion experiments, although modern workers generally aren't so mean to their pets. They're more likely to say something nasty to the humans in the household.

Ego depletion affects even your heartbeat. When people in laboratory experiments exercise mental self-control, their pulse becomes more erratic; conversely, people whose normal pulse is relatively variable seem to have more inner energy available for self-control, because they do better on laboratory tests of perseverance than do people with steadier heartbeats. Other experiments have shown that chronic physical pain leaves people with a perpetual shortage of willpower because their minds are so depleted by the struggle to ignore the pain.

We can divide the uses of willpower into four broad categories, starting with the control of thoughts. Sometimes it's a losing struggle, whether you're fruitlessly trying to ignore something serious ("Out, damn'd spot!") or can't get rid of an annoying ear worm ("I got you babe, I got you babe"). But you can also learn to focus, particularly when the motivation is strong. People often conserve their willpower by seeking not the fullest or best answer but rather a predetermined conclusion. Theologians and believers filter the world to remain consistent with the nonnegotiable principles of their faith. The best salesmen often succeed by first deceiving themselves. Bankers packaging subprime loans convinced themselves that there was no problem giving mortgages to the class of unverified borrowers classified as NINA, as in "no income, no assets." Tiger Woods convinced himself that the rules of monogamy didn't apply to him—and that somehow nobody would notice the dalliances of the world's most famous athlete.

Another broad category is the control of emotions, which psychologists call affect regulation when it's focused specifically on mood. Most commonly, we're trying to escape from bad moods and unpleasant thoughts, although we occasionally try to avoid cheeriness (like when we're getting ready for a funeral, or preparing to deliver bad news), and we occasionally try to hang on to feelings of anger (so that we're in the right state to lodge a complaint). Emotional control is uniquely difficult because you generally can't alter your mood by an act of will. You can change what you think about or how you behave, but you can't force yourself to be happy. You can treat your in-laws politely, but you can't make yourself rejoice over their month-long visit. To ward off sadness and anger, people use indirect strategies, like trying to distract themselves with other thoughts, or working out at the gym, or meditating. They lose themselves in TV shows and treat themselves to chocolate binges and shopping sprees. Or they get drunk.

A third category is often called impulse control, which is what most people associate with willpower: the ability to resist temptations like alcohol, tobacco, Cinnabons, and cocktail waitresses. Strictly speaking, "impulse control" is a misnomer. You don't really control the impulses. Even someone as preternaturally disciplined as Barack Obama can't avoid stray impulses to smoke a cigarette. What he can control is how he reacts: Does he ignore the impulse, or chew a Nicorette, or sneak out for a smoke? (He has usually avoided lighting up, according to the White House, but there have been slips.)

Finally, there's the category that researchers call performance control: focusing your energy on the task at hand, finding the right combination of speed and accuracy, managing time, persevering when you feel like quitting. In the rest of the book, we'll discuss strategies for improving performance at work and at home, and we'll look at techniques for improving self-control in all the other categories, too—thoughts, emotions, impulses.

But before we get into specific advice, we can offer one general bit of guidance based on the ego-depletion studies, and it's the same approach taken by Amanda Palmer: Focus on one project at a time. If you set more than one self-improvement goal, you may succeed for a while by drawing on reserves to power through, but that just leaves you more depleted and more prone to serious mistakes later.

When people have to make a big change in their lives, their efforts are undermined if they are trying to make other changes as well. People who are trying to quit smoking, for example, will have their best shot at succeeding if they aren't changing other behaviors at the same time. Those who try to quit smoking while also restricting their eating or cutting back on alcohol tend to fail at all three—probably because they have too many simultaneous demands on their willpower. Research has likewise found that people who seek to control their drinking tend to fail on days when they have other demands on their self-control, as compared with days when they can devote all their willpower to limiting the booze.

Above all, don't make a list of New Year's resolutions. Each January 1, millions of people drag themselves out of bed, full of hope or hangover, resolved to eat less, exercise more, spend less money, work harder at the office, keep the home cleaner, and still miraculously have more time for romantic dinners and long walks on the beach.

By February 1, they're embarrassed to even look at the list. But instead of lamenting their lack of willpower, they should put the blame where it belongs: on the list. No one has enough willpower for that list. If you're going to start a new physical exercise program, don't try to overhaul your finances at the same time. If you're going to need your energy for a new job—like, say, the presidency of the United States—then this probably isn't the ideal time to go cold turkey on cigarettes. Because you have only one supply of willpower, the different New Year's resolutions all compete with one another. Each time you try to follow one, you reduce your capacity for all the others.

A better plan is to make one resolution and stick to it. That's challenge enough. There will be moments when that will still seem like one resolution too many, but perhaps you can persevere by thinking of Amanda Palmer heroically frozen in place on her pedestal. She may not consider herself a disciplined person, but she did learn something inspiring about her species even during her days surrounded by drunken hecklers and gropers.

"You know, humans are capable of incredible things," she says. "If you simply decide that you're not going to move, you just don't move."

2.

WHERE DOES THE POWER IN WILLPOWER COME FROM?

Whether or not ingestion of food stuffs with preservatives and sugar in high content causes you to alter your personality somehow, or causes you to act in an aggressive manner, I don't know. I'm not going to suggest to you for a minute that that occurs. But there is a minority opinion in psychiatric fields that there is some connection.

—Defense's closing argument in the trial of Dan White,
the murderer whose taste for junk food inspired
the term "Twinkie defense"

I have terrible PMS, so I just went a little crazy.

—Actress Melanie Griffith, explaining why she had filed
for divorce from Don Johnson only to
immediately withdraw it

If willpower isn't just a metaphor, if there is a power driving this virtue, where does it come from? The answer emerged by accident from a failed experiment inspired by Mardi Gras and the other carnivals held on the eve of Lent. Mardi Gras means Fat Tuesday, the day before Ash Wednesday, when people prepare for a season of fasting and self-sacrifice by shamelessly indulging their desires. In some places it's known as Pancake Day and begins with all-you-can-eat flapjack breakfasts at churches. Bakers honor the occasion by producing special treats—the names of the delicacies vary from culture to culture, but the recipes generally involve gargantuan quantities of sugar, eggs, flour, butter, and lard. And the gluttony is just the beginning.

From Venice to New Orleans to Rio de Janeiro, revelers move on to more interesting vices, sometimes under the cover of traditional masks, but often just letting it all hang out. It's the one day you can strut down the street with a beaded headdress and nothing else, proudly parading to cheers from drunks. Losing self-control becomes a virtue. In Mexico, married men are officially granted one day of liberty from their obligations on what's called El Dia del Marido Oprimido—the day of the oppressed husband. On the eve of Lent, even the sternest Anglo-Saxon churchgoers are in a forgiving mood. They call it Shrove Tuesday, derived from the verb *shrive*, which means "to receive absolution for sins."

It's all rather confusing from a theological standpoint. Why would the clergy encourage public vice with a package of preapproved absolution? Why reward premeditated sinning? Why would a merciful, benevolent god encourage so many already overweight mortals to stuff themselves with deep-fried dough?

But to psychologists there was a certain logic to it: By relaxing before Lent, perhaps people could store up the willpower necessary to sustain themselves through weeks of self-denial. The Mardi Gras theory, as it was known, was never as popular with scientists as it was with pancake eaters in peacock headdresses, but it seemed worth an experiment. In place of a Fat Tuesday breakfast, the chefs in Baumeister's lab whipped up lusciously thick ice cream milkshakes for a group of subjects who were resting in between two laboratory tasks requiring willpower. Meanwhile, the less fortunate subjects in other groups had to spend the interval reading dull, out-of-date magazines or drinking a large, tasteless concoction of low-fat dairy glop that was rated even less enjoyable than the old magazines.

Just as predicted by the Mardi Gras theory, the ice cream did seem to strengthen willpower by helping people perform better than expected on the next task. Fortified by the milkshake, they had more self-control than did the unlucky subjects who'd been stuck reading the old magazines. So far, so good. But it turned out that the joyless drink of glop worked just as well, which meant that building will-power didn't require happy self-indulgence. The Mardi Gras theory looked wrong. Besides tragically removing an excuse for romping through the streets of New Orleans, the result was embarrassing for the researchers. Matthew Gailliot, the graduate student who had run the study, stood looking glumly at his shoes as he told Baumeister about the fiasco.

Baumeister tried to be optimistic. Maybe the study wasn't a failure. Something *had* happened, after all. They'd succeeded in elim-inating the ego-depletion effect. The problem was that they'd suc-ceeded too well. Even the tasteless milkshake had done the job, but how? The researchers began to consider another possible explanation for the boost in self-control. If it wasn't the pleasure, could it be the calories?

At first the idea seemed a bit daft. Why should drinking some low-fat dairy concoction improve performance on a lab task? For decades, psychologists had been studying performance on mental tasks without worrying about its being affected by a glass of milk. They liked to envision the human mind as a computer, focusing on the way it processed information. In their eagerness to chart the human equivalent of the computer's chips and circuits, most psy-chologists neglected one mundane but essential part of the machine: the power cord.

Chips and circuit boards are useless without a source of energy. So is the brain. It took psychologists a while to realize this, and the realization came not from computer models but from biology. The transformation of psychology based on ideas from biology was one of the major developments of the late twentieth century. Some researchers found that genes had important effects on personality and intelligence. Others began to show that sexual and romantic behavior conformed to predictions from evolutionary theory and resembled aspects of behavior in many animal species. Neuroscientists began to map out brain processes. Others found out how hormones altered behavior. Psychologists were reminded over and over that the human mind exists in a biological body.

This newly emerging emphasis on biology made the milkshake experimenters think twice before dismissing their results. Before writing off that dairy glop, they figured, maybe they should take a look at its ingredients, and start paying attention to stories from people like Jim Turner.

Brain Fuel

The comedian Jim Turner has played dozens of roles in films and television series, like the football-star-turned-sports-agent on HBO's *Arliss* series, but his most dramatic performance was reserved for his wife. It occurred the night he had a dream in which he was responsible for righting all the world's wrongs. It was an exhausting duty, even in a dream, but then he discovered teleportation. To travel anywhere, all he had to do was think of the place, and he'd magically appear there. He went back to his old home in Iowa, to New York, to Greece, even to the moon. When he woke up, he was convinced he still possessed this power. He generously tried to teach it to his wife by shouting over and over, "You think it, you go there and you be there!"

His wife had a better plan. Knowing he was diabetic, she tried to get him to drink some fruit juice. He was still so crazed that he poured some of it over his face, got up, and then demonstrated his power by doing a somersault in the air and landing back on the bed. Finally, much to her relief, the juice kicked in, and he calmed down— or at least that was how it looked to his wife, as if the manic frenzy had subsided. But in fact he hadn't been sedated. Quite the reverse: The juice's sugar had given him extra energy.

More precisely, the energy in the juice was converted to glucose, the simple sugar manufactured in the body from all kinds of foods, not just sweet ones. The glucose produced by digestion goes into the bloodstream and is pumped throughout the body. The muscles, not surprisingly, use plenty of glucose, as do the heart and liver. The immune system uses large quantities, but only sporadically. When you're relatively healthy, your immune system may use only a relatively small amount of glucose. But when your body is fighting off a cold, it may consume gobs of it. That's why sick people sleep so much: The body uses all the energy it can to fight the disease, and it can't spare much for exercising, making love, or arguing. It can't even do much thinking, a process that requires plentiful glucose in the bloodstream. The glucose itself doesn't enter the brain, but it's converted into neurotransmitters, which are the chemicals that your brain cells use to send signals. If you ran out of neurotransmitters, you'd stop thinking.

The link between glucose and self-control appeared in studies of people with hypoglycemia, the tendency to have low blood sugar. Researchers noted that hypoglycemics were more likely than the average person to have trouble concentrating and controlling their negative emotions when provoked. Overall, they tended to be more anxious and less happy than average. Hypoglycemia was also reported to be unusually prevalent among criminals and other violent persons, and some creative defense attorneys brought the low-blood-sugar research into court.

The issue became notorious during the 1979 trial of Dan White for the assassination of two city officials in San Francisco, Mayor George Moscone and Harvey Milk, a member of the board of supervisors and the most prominent openly gay politician in America. When a psychiatrist testifying for the defense cited White's consumption of Twinkies and other junk food in the days before the murders, journalists mocked White for trying to excuse himself with a "Twinkie defense." In fact, White's chief defense wasn't based on the argument that the Twinkies turned him murderous by causing his blood-sugar levels to quickly spike and then crash. His attorneys argued that he deserved mercy because he suffered from "diminished capacity" due to severe depression, and they presented his junk-food consumption (along with other changes in habits) as evidence of his depression, not as the cause of it. But when White received a relatively light sentence, the popular wisdom became that the Twinkie defense had worked, and the public was understandably outraged.

Other defense attorneys actually did argue, with limited success, that their clients' blood-sugar problems should be taken into account. Whatever the legal or moral merits of that argument, there certainly was scientific data showing a correlation between blood sugar and criminal behavior. One study found below-average glucose levels in 90 percent of the juvenile delinquents recently taken into custody. Other studies reported that people with hypoglycemia were more likely to be convicted of a wide variety of offenses: traffic violations, public profanity, shoplifting, destruction of property, exhibitionism, public masturbation, embezzlement, arson, spouse abuse, and child abuse.

In one remarkable study, researchers in Finland went into a prison to measure the glucose tolerance of convicts who were about to be released. Then the scientists kept track of which ones went on to commit new crimes. Obviously there are many factors that can influence whether an ex-con goes straight: peer pressure, marriage, employment prospects, drug use. Yet just by looking at the response to the glucose test, the researchers were able to predict with greater than 80 percent accuracy which convicts would go on to commit violent crimes. These men apparently had less self-control because of their impaired glucose tolerance, a condition in which the body has trouble converting food into usable energy. The food gets converted into glucose, but the glucose in the bloodstream doesn't get absorbed as it circulates. The result is often a surplus of glucose in the bloodstream, which might sound beneficial, but it's like having plenty of firewood and no matches. The glucose remains there uselessly, rather than being converted into brain and muscle activity. If the excess glucose reaches a sufficiently high level, the condition is labeled diabetes.

Most diabetics aren't criminals, obviously. Most keep themselves and their glucose levels under control by monitoring themselves and using insulin when necessary. Like Jim Turner, one of the rare actors to make a good living in Hollywood, they can succeed in the most difficult endeavors. But they do face above-average challenges, particularly if they don't monitor themselves carefully. Researchers testing personality have found that diabetics tend to be more impulsive and have more explosive temperaments than other people their age. They're more likely to get distracted while working on a time-consuming task. They have more problems with alcohol abuse, anxiety, and depression. In hospitals and other institutions, diabetics throw more tantrums than other patients. In everyday life, stressful conditions seem to be harder on diabetics. Coping with stress typically takes self-control, and that's difficult if your body isn't providing your brain with enough fuel.

Jim Turner deals with his self-control problems directly—and hilariously—in a one-man show titled "Diabetes: My Struggles with Jim Turner." He recalls moments like the argument with his teenage son that ended with him, ostensibly the adult, getting so mad that he went outside and kicked a permanent dent into the family car. "There are many times," Turner says, "when my son can see that I am not in control, when he has to force me to drink some juice, when he is afraid that I am just not there."

Turner doesn't use any version of the Twinkie defense to excuse the dent, and he doesn't feel sorry for himself, either. On the whole, he keeps his diabetes under control, and says the disease hasn't stopped him from being happy and fulfilling his dreams (except for that one about teleportation). But he also recognizes the emotional consequences of glucose. "There are so many little moments of connection that I have missed," he says, "that I wasn't available to my son because I was busy dealing with a low-blood-sugar episode and too overwhelmed trying to figure out what was going on. It's the single biggest heartbreak of this disease."

What exactly happens to Turner during those moments? You can't draw definitive conclusions from any anecdote or even from the large studies showing above-average problems with self-control among diabetics and other groups of people. Correlation is not causation. In social science, the strongest conclusions are permitted only when researchers use experiments that randomly assign people among different treatment conditions, so that individual differences even out. Some people arrive at the experiment happier than others, or more aggressive, or more preoccupied and distracted. There is no way to guarantee that the average person in one experimental condition is the same as the average person in another experimental condition, except by counting on the law of averages. If the researchers randomly assign people among treatment and control groups, the differences tend to average out.

For example, if you wanted to test the effects of glucose on aggression, you would have to consider that some people are already aggressive while others are peaceful and gentle. To show that glucose caused the aggressiveness, you'd want about an equal number of aggressive people in the glucose and in the no-glucose conditions, and also equal numbers of pacifists. Random assignment usually does this pretty well. Once you've got representative groups of people, you can see how they're affected by different treatments.

Nutritionists used this method during food experiments at elementary schools. All the children in a class were told to skip breakfast one morning, and then, by random assignment, half of the children were given a good breakfast at school. The others got nothing. During the first part of the morning, the children who got breakfast learned more and misbehaved less (as judged by monitors who didn't know which children had eaten). Then, after all the students were given a healthy snack in the middle of the morning, the differences disappeared as if by magic.

The magic ingredient was isolated in other experiments by measuring glucose levels in people before and after doing simple tasks, like watching a video in which a series of words flashed at the bottom of the screen. Some people were told to ignore the words; others were free to relax and watch however they wanted. Afterward, glucose levels were measured again, and there was a big difference: Levels remained constant in the relaxed viewers but dropped significantly in the people who'd been trying to avoid the words. That seemingly small exercise of self-control was associated with a big drop in the brain's fuel of glucose.

To establish cause and effect, the researchers tried refueling the brain in a series of experiments involving lemonade mixed either with sugar or with a diet sweetener. The strong taste of the lemon made it hard for the tasters to know whether real sugar or diet sweetener was used. The sugar gave them a quick burst of glucose (though not for long, so the experimenters needed to get to the point pretty soon). The diet sweetener didn't furnish any glucose or, indeed, any nutrition at all.

The effects of the drinks showed up clearly in a study of aggression among people playing a computer game. At first, the game seemed reasonable, but it soon became impossibly difficult. Everyone got frustrated as the game went on, but the one who got a sugar-filled drink managed to grumble quietly and keep playing. The others started cursing aloud and banging the computer. And when by prearranged script the experimenter made an insulting remark about their performance, the glucose-deprived people were much more likely to get angry.

No glucose, no willpower: The pattern showed up time and again as researchers tested more people in more situations. They even tested dogs. While self-control is a distinctively human trait, in the sense that we've developed it so extensively in the process of becoming cultural animals, it's not unique to our species. Other social animals require at least some degree of self-control to get along with one another. And dogs, because they live with humans, must often learn to bring their behavior into line with what must seem to them to be absurd and arbitrary rules, like the ban on sniffing the crotches of houseguests (at least the human ones).

To mimic the human studies, the experimenters first depleted the willpower of one group of dogs by having each dog obey "sit" and "stay" commands from its owner for ten minutes. A control group of dogs was simply left alone for ten minutes in cages, where they had no choice but to remain and therefore didn't have to exercise any self-control. Then all the dogs were given a familiar toy with a sausage treat inside it. All the dogs had played with this toy in the past and successfully extracted the treat, but for the experiment the toy was rigged so that the sausage could not be extracted. The control group of dogs spent several minutes trying to extract it, but the dogs who'd had to obey the commands gave up in less than a minute. It was the familiar ego-depletion effect, and the canine cure turned out to be familiar, too. In a follow-up study, when the dogs were given different drinks, the drinks with sugar restored the willpower of the dogs who'd had to obey the commands. Newly fortified, they persisted with the toy just as long as the dogs who'd been in cages. The artificially sweetened drink had no effect, as usual.

Despite all these findings, the growing community of brain researchers still had some reservations about the glucose connection. Some skeptics pointed out that the brain's overall use of energy remains about the same regardless of what one is doing, which doesn't square easily with the notion of depleted energy. Among the skeptics was Todd Heatherton, who had worked with Baumeister early in his career and eventually wound up at Dartmouth, where he became a pioneer of what is called social neuroscience: the study of links between brain processes and social behavior. He believed in ego depletion, but the glucose findings just didn't seem to add up.

Heatherton decided on an ambitious test of the theory. He and his colleagues recruited dieters and measured their reactions to pictures of food. Then ego depletion was induced by asking everyone to refrain from laughing while watching a comedy video. After that, the researchers again tested how their brains reacted to pictures of food (as compared with nonfood pictures). Earlier work by Heatherton and Kate Demos had shown that these pictures produce various reactions in key brain sites, such as the nucleus accumbens and the amygdala. These same reactions were found again. Among dieters, depletion caused an increase in activity in the nucleus accumbens and a corresponding decrease in the amygdala. The crucial change in this experiment involved a manipulation of glucose. Some people drank lemonade sweetened with sugar, which sent glucose flooding through the bloodstream and presumably into the brain.

Dramatically, Heatherton announced the results during his speech accepting the leadership of the Society for Personality and Social Psychology, the world's largest group of social psychologists. In his presidential address at the annual meeting in 2011 in San Antonio, Heatherton reported that the glucose reversed the brain changes wrought by depletion—a finding, he said, that thoroughly surprised him. (Baumeister, sitting in the audience to watch his protégé enjoy the moment of glory as society president, recalled his own surprise when his own lab had first found the links to glucose.) Heatherton's results did much more than provide additional confirmation that glucose is a vital part of willpower. They helped resolve the puzzle over how glucose could work without global changes in the brain's total energy use. Apparently ego depletion shifts activity from one part of the brain to another. Your brain does not stop working when glucose is low. It stops doing some things and starts doing others. That may help explain why depleted people feel things more intensely than normal: Certain parts of the brain go into high gear just as others taper off.

As the body uses glucose during self-control, it starts to crave sweet things to eat—which is bad news for people hoping to use their self-control to avoid sweets. When people have more demands for self-control in their daily lives, their hunger for sweets increases. It's not a simple matter of wanting all food more—they seem to be specifically hungry for sweets. In the lab, students who have just performed a self-control task eat more sweet snacks but not other (salty) snacks. Even just expecting to have to exert self-control seems to make people hungry for sweet foods.

All these results don't offer a rationale for providing sugar fixes to anyone, human or canine, outside the laboratory. The body may crave sweets as the quickest way to get energy, but low-sugar, high-protein foods and other nutritious fare work just as well (albeit more slowly). Still, the discovery of the glucose effect does point to some useful techniques for self-control. It also offers a solution to a long-standing human mystery: Why is chocolate so appealing on certain days of the month?

Inner Demons

Whatever you think of Jennifer Love Hewitt's acting ability, you have to give her credit for originality when she was cast in a film version of "The Devil and Daniel Webster." She shared star billing with Anthony Hopkins and Alec Baldwin, which would have been a daunting enough proposition for any young actress, but she also had the challenge of playing the Devil. If your goal, as drama coaches say, is to "inhabit the character," a demon poses more difficulties than, say, a police officer. You can't do field research by riding around in a squad car with Satan. But Hewitt came up with an alternative method of role prep.

"I started paying close attention to myself and how I felt when I had PMS," she said. "That's what formed my basis for playing Satan."

If that strikes you as a singularly dark view of premenstrual syndrome, you haven't spent much time at PMSCentral.com and the other Web sites where women swap remedies and stories. They joke that PMS stands for Psychotic Mood Shift, or simply Pass My Shotgun. Or they share genuine PMS stories like this one:

> It ruins a large portion of my life. I have swollen, puffy eyes, I can't think straight, I make wrong decisions, ugly emotional outbursts, irrational thinking, purchases I have to return, overspending, quit jobs, extremely tired, cranky, crying, extreme emotional sensitivity, body aches all over, nerve pain, blank staring, that "not here" feeling.

PMS has been blamed for everything from chocolate binges (it also stands for Provide Me with Sweets) to murder. After Marg Helgenberger, a star on the *CSI* television show, was photographed at an awards dinner with oddly colored hair, she explained: "That shade was known as 'PMS Pink.' I was totally PMSing that day. I was crazy! What did I think, I was gonna get away with pink hair on *CSI*?" The word *crazy* was also used by Melanie Griffith in diagnosing the PMS state that drove her to file for divorce and then abruptly change her mind, although her publicist preferred to use more clinical terms, calling it "an impulsive act that occurred during a moment of frustration and anger." Over and over, women describe being mysteriously overcome by impulses that seem weirdly alien.

These dark mood swings have also mystified scientists. To evolutionary psychologists, it seems especially counterproductive for a woman in her childbearing years not to get along with the people around her. Isn't empathy a crucial skill for raising children? Isn't it useful to maintain good relations with a mate providing child support? Some scientists, noting that a woman reaches this premenstrual phase of the cycle only if she wasn't impregnated during the earlier ovulation phase, have speculated that natural selection favored women who became dissatisfied with infertile men, thereby liberating themselves to seek another mate. That hypothesis certainly jibes with another name that women give to PMS: Pack My Stuff. But it's not clear that the evolutionary benefits would have outweighed the costs, or that such selective pressures even operated on the ancient savanna. For our hunter-gatherer ancestors, PMS was presumably less of a problem because women spent more of their lives either being pregnant or breast-feeding children.

In any case, there's now a solid physiological explanation for PMS that doesn't involve any mysterious alien impulses. During this premenstrual part of the cycle, which is called the luteal phase, the female body starts channeling a high amount of its energy to the ovaries and to related activities, like producing extra quantities of female hormones. As more energy and glucose are diverted to the reproductive system, there's less available for the rest of the body, which responds by craving more fuel. Chocolate and other sweets are immediately appealing because they provide instant glucose, but any kind of food can help, which is why women report more food cravings and tend to eat more. One study found that the average woman eats about 810 calories at lunch during this time, which is about 170 calories more than what she eats at lunch during the rest of the month.

But most women still aren't getting enough extra calories. The typical woman in a modern thin-conscious society like America does not take in enough extra food to supply the body's increased demands for glucose during these few days each month. When there isn't enough energy to go around, the body has to ration it, and the reproductive system takes priority, leaving less glucose available for willpower. As a general rule, women are less likely than men to suffer from lapses of self-control, but their self-control problems do worsen during the luteal phase, as studies have repeatedly shown.

During this phase, women spend more money and make more impulsive purchases than at other times. They smoke more cigarettes. They drink more alcohol, and not just because they enjoy drinks more. The increase is especially likely for women who have a drinking problem or a family history of alcoholism. During this luteal phase, women are more liable to go on drinking binges or abuse cocaine and other drugs. PMS is not a matter of one specific behavior problem cropping up. Instead, self-control seems to fail across the board, letting all sorts of problems increase.

One drug that isn't used more frequently is marijuana, and that exception is revealing. Unlike cocaine and opiates, marijuana is not a drug of escape or euphoria. Marijuana merely intensifies what you're already feeling. PMS feels bad, and a drug that intensifies the feeling isn't going to be attractive. Moreover, marijuana doesn't produce the same sort of addictive cravings as nicotine, alcohol, cocaine, and other drugs, so a lessening of overall self-control wouldn't make a marijuana user more vulnerable to those kinds of temptations.

Researchers have found that women who are prone to PMS miss twice as many days of work as other women do. Some of those missed days are due, no doubt, to the physical pain associated with PMS, but some of the absenteeism is probably related to self-control. Following rules is harder when your body is short of glucose. Inside women's prisons, disciplinary problems based on breaking prison rules are highest among women who are at the luteal phase of their cycle. Violent, aggressive acts—legal or illegal—reach a peak among PMS sufferers during the luteal phase. To be sure, only a few women turn violent at any time, but many report emotional changes during the luteal phase. Studies have repeatedly documented increases in emotional outbursts and distress at this time. Women have more conflicts with spouses and other relationship partners, as well as with colleagues at work. They become less sociable and often prefer to be alone—which may be an effective strategy of avoiding conflicts that would arise from interacting.

The standard explanation for PMS has been that the luteal phase directly causes negative emotions, but that explanation doesn't really fit the data. Women aren't uniformly affected by negative emotions. When Amanda Palmer was posing as a living statue in Harvard Square, she found that PMS weakened her self-control because it liberated both positive and negative feelings.

"I'm prone to being way more sensitive and likely to cry when I'm PMSing, and that translated right into my statue work if something emotional happened," Palmer recalls. "Something emotional could be as simple as nobody walked by and looked at me for ten minutes, and therefore the world was a cold and lonely place and no one loved me. The other extreme would be a ninety-five-year-old man hobbling up to me at the rate of one mile per hour and taking five minutes to get a folded five-dollar bill out of his wallet and put it into my can and look up at me with his wizened lonely old eyes. I would just lose it. I would try to transmit the largest concentration of love I could possibly transmit without speaking or moving my face."

Her experience is fairly typical of what other women report during the luteal phase: They're affected by a variety of feelings, and their problems often arise from a strong reaction to some event. They say they don't want to get upset but can't seem to stop themselves from getting worked up over minor things. They're not consciously aware that their body has abruptly cut the fuel supply for self-control, so they're surprised that normal controls don't work as usual.

It feels to many women as if life stresses increase: They report more negative events and fewer positive events occurring during this luteal phase. But the outside world doesn't predictably change for a few days every month. If a woman feels less capable than usual of handling her problems, she'll be more stressed out. If PMS weakens her control over her emotions, then the same misfortune is more upsetting. The same task at work is more of a challenge if she doesn't have as much energy available to focus her attention. In carefully controlled laboratory tests requiring concentration, women in the luteal phase performed worse than women at other stages of the menstrual cycle, and these effects were found for a general sample of women, not just PMS sufferers. Whether or not they felt the acute symptoms of PMS, their bodies were short of glucose.

We don't want to exaggerate these problems, because most women cope quite well with PMS at work and at home, and we certainly don't want to suggest that women have weaker willpower than men. To repeat, women on the whole have *fewer* problems with self-control than men: They commit fewer violent crimes and are less likely to become alcoholics or drug addicts. Girls' superior self-control is probably one reason they get better grades in school than boys do. The point is only that self-control is tied in to the body's rhythms and the fluctuations in its energy supply. A woman with the self-control of a saint may become a tiny bit less saintly during the luteal phase. PMS, like hypoglycemia and diabetes, makes a conveniently clear-cut example of what happens when the body is short of glucose—and everyone, male or female, diabetic or nondiabetic, runs low on glucose at times. We all succumb to frustration and anger. We all sometimes feel beset by insoluble problems and overcome by impulses that seem alien, if not satanic.

Usually, though, the problem is within. It's not that the world has suddenly turned cruel. It's not that Lucifer is tormenting us with dark new temptations and impulses. It's that we're less capable of dealing with ordinary impulses and long-standing problems. The provocations can be real enough—you may well have reason to get angry at your boss or reconsider your marriage. (Melanie Griffith eventually did get divorced from Don Johnson.) But you won't make much progress on those other problems until you control your own emotions, and that starts with controlling your glucose.

Eat Your Way to Willpower

Now that we've surveyed the problems caused by lack of glucose, we can turn to solutions and to cheerier topics, like good meals and long naps. Here are some lessons and strategies for putting glucose to work for you:

Feed the beast. By beast, we don't mean Beelzebub. We mean the potential demon inside you or anyone spending time with you. Glucose depletion can turn the most charming companion into a monster. The old advice about eating a good breakfast applies all day long, particularly on days when you're physically or mentally stressed. If you have a test, an important meeting, or a vital project, don't take it on without glucose. Don't get into an argument with your boss four hours after lunch. Don't thrash out serious problems with your partner just *before* dinner. When you're on a romantic trip across Europe, don't drive into a walled medieval town at seven P.M. and try to navigate to your hotel on an empty stomach. Your car can probably survive the cobblestone maze, but your relationship might not.

Above all, don't skimp on calories when you're trying to deal with more serious problems than being overweight. If you're a smoker, don't try quitting while you're also on a diet. In fact, to quit you might even consider adding some calories, because part of what seems to be a craving for a cigarette may actually be a craving for food once you're no longer suppressing your appetite with nicotine. When researchers have given sugar tablets to smokers trying to quit, sometimes the extra glucose has led to higher rates of success, particularly when the sugar tablets were combined with other therapies, like the nicotine patch.

Sugar works in the lab, not in your diet. It's a bit ironic that self-control researchers are so fond of giving sugar to experimental subjects, given how many of those people wish for the willpower to resist sweets. But the scientists are doing it just for short-term convenience. A sugar-filled drink provides a quick rise in energy that enables experimenters to observe the effects of glucose in a short period of time. Neither the researchers nor their experimental subjects want to wait around an hour for the body to digest something more complex, like protein.

There might be times when you could use sugar to boost your self-control right before a brief challenge, like a math test or a track meet. If you've just quit smoking, you might use a sweet lozenge as an emergency stopgap against a sudden craving for a cigarette. But a sugar spike is promptly followed by a crash that leaves you feeling more depleted, so it's not a good long-term strategy. We're certainly not recommending that you switch from diet sodas to sugar-filled drinks, or to sweet snacks in general. It may be true, as researchers found, that drinks with sugar in them will temporarily diminish the symptoms of PMS. But outside the lab, you're better off heeding the observation made by the singer Mary J. Blige when discussing her PMS and its attendant mood swings and shopping sprees: "Sugar makes it worse."

When you eat, go for the slow burn. The body converts just about all sorts of food into glucose, but at different rates. Foods that are converted quickly are said to have a high glycemic index. These include starchy carbohydrates like white bread, potatoes, white rice, and plenty of offerings on snack racks and fast-food counters. Eating them produces boom-and-bust cycles, leaving you short on glucose and self-control—and too often unable to resist the body's craving for quick hits of starch and sugar from doughnuts and candy. Those all-you-can-eat pancake breakfasts on Fat Tuesday may make for wilder parades, but they're not all that useful the rest of the year.

To maintain steady self-control, you're better off eating foods with a low glycemic index: most vegetables, nuts (like peanuts and cashews), many raw fruits (like apples, blueberries, and pears), cheese, fish, meat, olive oil, and other "good" fats. (These low-glycemic foods may also help keep you slim.) The benefits of the right diet have shown up in studies of women with PMS, who report fewer symptoms when they're eating healthier food. There has also been a successful series of experiments carried out with thousands of teenagers in correctional institutions. After the institutions replaced some of the sugary foods and refined carbohydrates with fruits, vegetables, and whole grains, there was a sharp decline in escape attempts, violence, and other problems.

When you're sick, save your glucose for your immune system. The next time you're preparing to drag your aching body to work, here's something to consider: Driving a car with a bad cold has been found to be even more dangerous than driving when mildly intoxicated. That's because your immune system is using so much of your glucose to fight the cold that there's not enough left for the brain.

If you're too glucose-deprived to do something as simple as driving a car, how much use are you going to be in the office (assuming you make it there safely)? Sometimes the job has to be muddled through, but don't trust the glucose-deprived brain for anything important. If you simply can't miss a meeting at work, try to avoid any topics that will strain your self-control. If there's a make-or-break project under your supervision, don't make any irrevocable decisions. And don't expect peak performance from others who are under the weather. If your child has a cold the day of the SAT test, reschedule it.

When you're tired, sleep. We shouldn't need to be told something so obvious, but cranky toddlers aren't the only ones who resist much-needed naps. Adults routinely shortchange themselves on sleep, and the result is less self-control. By resting, we reduce the body's demands for glucose, and we also improve its overall ability to make use of the glucose in the bloodstream. Sleep deprivation has been shown to impair the processing of glucose, which produces immediate consequences for self-control—and, over the long term, a higher risk of diabetes.

A recent study found that workers who were not getting enough sleep were more prone than others to engage in unethical conduct on the job, as rated by their supervisors and others. For example, they were more likely than others to take credit for work done by somebody else. In a laboratory experiment offering test takers the chance to win cash, students who had not slept enough were more likely than others to take advantage of an opportunity to cheat. Not getting enough sleep has assorted bad effects on mind and body. Hidden among these is the weakening of self-control and related processes like decision making. To get the most out of your willpower, use it to set aside enough time to sleep. You'll behave better the next day — and sleep more easily the next night.

3.

A BRIEF HISTORY OF THE TO-DO LIST, FROM GOD TO DREW CAREY

In the beginning God created the heavens and the earth;
and the earth was without form and empty,
and darkness was upon the face of the deep;
and the Spirit of God was brooding upon the face of the waters.

—Genesis 1:1

In the beginning was the list.

Creation, as the Bible tells it, was not a simple job, not even for an omnipotent deity. The project required divine brooding, which did not mean that God was unhappily mulling it over. It meant that the heavens and earth, like an egg, required a period of incubation. The project had to be broken down into a schedule of daily tasks, starting with Monday's to-do list:

1. Let there be light.
2. Observe light.

   3. Confirm light is good.
   4. Divide light from darkness.
   5. Give name to light (Day).
   6. Give name to darkness (Night).

Thus was writ the weekly calendar: Tuesday for firmament-making chores, Wednesday for creating land and trees, Thursday for stars, Friday for fish and fowl, Saturday for man and woman, Sunday for R&R. The tasks were checked off one at a time, then reviewed at the end of the week: "And God saw every thing that He had made, and, behold, it was very good."

Does that restful weekend sound anything like yours? At first glance, the Genesis strategy seems ridiculously obvious: Set a goal; make a list of the steps to reach it; do them; relax. But how many mortals actually cross off all the items on their weekly list? Our failure rate keeps climbing as the lists keep getting longer. At any one time, a person typically has at least 150 different tasks to be done, and fresh items never stop appearing on our screens. How do we decide what goes on the list and what to do next? The good news is that there are finally some practical answers, but it's hardly been a straightforward process to discover these strategies. Only after decades of research by psychologists and neuroscientists, after centuries of self-help books and millennia of trial and error, can we recognize the essential components of the Genesis to-do list.

The first step in self-control is to set a clear goal. The technical term researchers use for self-control is self-regulation, and the "regulation" part highlights the importance of a goal. Regulating means changing, but only a particular kind of intentional, meaningful changing. To regulate is to guide toward a specific goal or standard: the speed limit for cars on a highway, the maximum height for an office building. Self-control without goals and other standards would be nothing more than aimless change, like trying to diet without any idea of which foods are fattening.

For most of us, though, the problem is not a lack of goals but rather too many of them. We make daily to-do lists that couldn't be accomplished even if there were no interruptions during the day, which there always are. By the time the weekend arrives, there are more unfinished tasks than ever, but we keep deferring them and expecting to get through them with miraculous speed. That's why, as productivity experts have found, an executive's daily to-do list for Monday often contains more work than could be done the entire week.

We can be even more unrealistic in setting longer-term goals. When that great self-help pioneer Benjamin Franklin wrote his autobiography late in life, he recalled with some amusement the mission he had set for himself in his twenties: "I conceiv'd the bold and arduous project of arriving at moral perfection. I wish'd to live without committing any fault at any time; I would conquer all that either natural inclination, custom, or company might lead me into." Soon enough, he noticed a problem. "While my care was employ'd in guarding against one fault, I was often surprised by another. Habit took the advantage of inattention; inclination was sometimes too strong for reason."

So Franklin tried a divide-and-conquer approach. He drew up a list of virtues and wrote a brief goal for each one, like this one for Order: "Let all your things have their places; let each part of your business have its time." There were a dozen more virtues on his list— Temperance, Silence, Resolution, Frugality, Industry, Sincerity, Justice, Moderation, Cleanliness, Tranquility, Chastity, and Humility— but he recognized his limits. "I judg'd it would be well not to distract my attention by attempting the whole at once," Franklin explained, "but to fix it on one of them at a time." The result was what he called a "course," and what today would be marketed as *13 Weeks to Total Virtue.* Long before Steven Covey's seven habits and leather-bound organizers and planners, long before the Daily Affirmations recited by the likes of Stuart Smalley, Franklin devised a regimen complete with a "table of virtues" and an inspirational prayer:

Father of light and life, thou Good Supreme!

O teach me what is good; teach me Thyself!

Save me from folly, vanity, and vice,

From every low pursuit; and fill my soul

With knowledge, conscious peace, and virtue pure;

Sacred, substantial, never-fading bliss!

In a paper notebook, Franklin drew lines of red ink to make thirteen weekly charts, one for every virtue. Each chart had columns for the days and rows for all the virtues, starting with the virtue of the week. At the end of the day, he would go down the column and put a black pencil mark in the row of any virtue that he'd failed to uphold. In one chart, compiled during a week devoted to Temperance, he gave himself black marks for other virtues: not enough Silence and Order on Sunday, more disorder and too little Industry on Tuesday, a breakdown in Resolution and Frugality on Friday. But he met his weekly goal by keeping the row for Temperance blank every day. Encouraged by that progress, he could then move on to a different virtue the next week, with the hope that the first week had left him with a "habitude" for Temperance that would persist even as he concentrated on different virtues. Franklin compared himself to a gardener removing the weeds from one of thirteen flower beds at a time, and then returning to repeat the course again, each time finding fewer weeds: "So should I have, I hoped, the encouraging pleasure of seeing on my pages the progress I made in virtue, by clearing successively my lines of their spots, till in the end, by a number of courses, I should be happy in viewing a clean book, after a 13 weeks' daily examination."

It didn't quite work out that way. The marks kept appearing on the pages. In fact, as he kept repeating the course, erasing the black pencil marks from the paper to make a fresh start, he eventually wore holes in the paper. So he drew his red-ink charts again, in a sturdier notebook with leaves made of ivory (which spread open like a fan).

After completing a course, he could wipe off the pencil marks with a wet sponge, and the ivory charts proved remarkably durable. Nearly half a century later, when he was a diplomat flirting with ladies in Paris, he still had the charts and liked to show them off, causing one French friend to marvel at touching "this precious booklet." Unlike his self-help successors (including the ones who borrowed his name for the FranklinCovey 31-Day Planner), Franklin never tried marketing an international line of notebook organizers, perhaps because he was too busy in Paris trying to get help for George Washington's army. Or maybe because his fondness for female company made it difficult for him to promote virtues like Chastity. Besides those lapses, Franklin had a terrible time keeping the papers on his desk in Order, which meant more black marks. As he put it in *Poor Richard's Almanack:*

> 'Tis easy to frame a good bold resolution;
> But hard is the Task that concerns execution.

No matter how hard he tried, Franklin never could have kept that notebook clean, because some of the goals were bound to conflict at times. When, as a young journeyman printer, he tried to practice Order by drawing up a rigid daily work schedule, he kept getting interrupted by unexpected demands from his clients—and Industry required him to ignore the schedule and meet with them. If he practiced Frugality ("Waste nothing") by always mending his own clothes and preparing all his own meals, there'd be less time available for Industry at his job—or for side projects like flying a kite in a thunderstorm or editing the Declaration of Independence. If he promised to spend an evening with his friends but then fell behind his schedule for work, he'd have to make a choice that would violate his virtue of Resolution: "Perform without fail what you resolve."

Still, Franklin's goals seem fairly consistent by comparison with modern ones. He focused on the old Puritan virtues of hard work and didn't aim for much fun (at least not on paper). He didn't resolve to enjoy long walks on the beach, volunteer with a nonprofit group, promote recycling in his community, and spend more quality time playing with his children. He didn't have a bucket list of tourist destinations or dreams of retiring to Florida. He didn't resolve to learn golf while negotiating the Treaty of Paris. Today there are more temptations—including the temptation to want them all at once.

When asked by researchers to list their personal goals, most people have no trouble coming up with at least fifteen separate ones. Some can dovetail well and support each other, like a goal to quit smoking and a goal to spend less money. But there are inevitably conflicts between work and family goals. Even within a family, the demands of taking care of children may clash with those of maintaining a good relationship with one's spouse, which may help explain why marital satisfaction declines when a couple gives birth to their first child and goes back up when the last child finally moves out. Some goals bring conflict all by themselves, like Franklin's virtue of Moderation: "Forbear resenting injuries so much as you think they deserve." Many people have the goal of holding their temper if they are wronged. When something unfair happens to them, they manage to restrain themselves from saying or doing anything, but then afterward they may feel bad because they failed to make their point or stand up for themselves, or because the original problem remains unresolved. By practicing Moderation they violate another of Franklin's virtues, Justice.

The result of conflicting goals is unhappiness instead of action, as the psychologists Robert Emmons and Laura King demonstrated in a series of studies. They had people list their fifteen main goals and mark which ones conflicted with which others. In one study, the subjects kept daily logs of their emotions and physical symptoms for three weeks, and they gave researchers access to their health records for the previous year. In another study, they wore beepers that went off at random points during the day, prompting them to answer questions about what they were doing and feeling. They also returned to the lab a year later to furnish additional information on what they had accomplished and how their health had fared. By asking people about their goals and then monitoring them, the researchers identified three main consequences of conflicting goals:

First, you worry a lot. The more competing demands you face, the more time you spend contemplating these demands. You're beset by rumination: repetitive thoughts that are largely involuntary and not especially pleasant.

Second, you get less done. It might seem that people who think more about their goals would also take more steps to reach them, but instead they replace action with rumination. The researchers found that people with clear, unconflicting goals tended to forge ahead and make progress, but the rest were so busy worrying that they got stuck.

Third, your health suffers, physically as well as mentally. In the studies, people with conflicting goals reported fewer positive emotions, more negative emotions, and more depression and anxiety. They had more psychosomatic complaints and symptoms. Even just plain physical sickness, measured both by the number of visits to the doctor and by the number of self-reported illnesses over the course of a year, was higher among the people with conflicting goals. The more the goals conflicted, the more the people got stuck, and the more unhappy and unhealthy they became.

They paid the price for too much brooding—in the most common modern use of the word, not the one in Genesis. The old term for incubation would eventually come to be associated with mental distress, no doubt because so many people could see the same problems later measured by psychologists. A hen might brood contentedly, but humans suffer when their conflicting goals leave them sitting around doing nothing. And they can't resolve those conflicts until they decide which kinds of goals will do them the most good.

Which Goals?

> Joe is having a cup of coffee in a restaurant. He's thinking of the time to come when . . .

Suppose, as a storytelling exercise, you finish that story about Joe any way you like. Quickly imagine what might be going through Joe's mind.

Now try a similar exercise. Finish a story that begins with these words:

> After awakening, Bill began to think about his future. In general he expected to . . .

Once again, you have complete freedom. Complete the story about Bill, and don't worry about polishing your mental prose. Rough ideas are fine.

Finished?

Now consider the actions described in your story. In each story, over how long a period do those actions take place?

This is not, of course, a literary test for aspiring novelists. It's an experiment that was previously conducted by psychiatrists among heroin addicts at a treatment center in Burlington, Vermont. The researchers also gave the exercises to a control group of adults who were demographically similar to the addicts (no college degree, annual income of less than twenty thousand dollars, etc.). When Joe sat in the coffee shop thinking of the "time to come," that time typically covered about a week in the stories from the control group, but in the heroin addicts' stories it covered only an hour. When the control group wrote about "the future" for Bill, they tended to mention long-term aspirations, like earning a promotion at work or getting married, while the addicts wrote about upcoming events, like a doctor's appointment or a visit with relatives. The typical person in the control group contemplated the future over four and a half years, while the typical addict's vision of the future extended only nine days.

This shortened temporal horizon has been demonstrated over and over in addicts of all kinds. When drug addicts play games of cards in the laboratory, they prefer risky strategies with quick big payoffs, even if they could make more money in the long run by settling for a series of smaller payoffs. Given a choice between getting $375 today or $1,000 a year from now, the addicts are more likely to take the quick money, and so are alcoholics and smokers. The psychiatrist Warren Bickel, who tested those addicts in Vermont and has continued research at the University of Arkansas, says that in studies of heavy users of tobacco, alcohol, and other drugs, a preference for short-term payoffs has been observed again and again. (The only exception was, once again, marijuana; being far less addictive than other substances, it seems not to require the destructive short-term mind-set that goes with addiction.) A short-term perspective can make you more likely to become addicted, and then the addiction can further shrink your horizons as you focus on quick rewards. If you can manage to eliminate or moderate your addiction, your future horizon is liable to expand, as Bickel and his colleagues have found in experiments with smokers and opioid users.

In the lab, as in life, the alcoholics and addicts and smokers are exemplars of the hazards of short-term goals. Ignoring the long term is hazardous to your health, both physically and fiscally. In another experiment with those stories about Joe and Bill, researchers found that people with high incomes tended to look further into the future than people with low incomes. That difference is partly due to necessity: If you're scrambling to pay the rent, you don't have the luxury of comparing 401(k) retirement plans. Yet being unable to pay the rent can also be a consequence of short-term thinking. As in Aesop's fable, the farsighted ant is better prepared for the winter than the live-for-the-moment grasshopper.

Still, Aesop isn't the last word on setting goals. For decades, psychologists have been debating the merits of proximal goals (which are short-term objectives) versus distal goals (which are long-term objectives). One of the classic experiments was conducted by Albert Bandura, a legendary figure in the field (one survey of citations ranked him in fourth place behind Freud, Skinner, and Piaget). He and Dale Schunk studied children between the ages of seven and ten who were having difficulty with math. The children took a course featuring self-directed learning, with many arithmetic exercises. Some of the students were told to set themselves proximal goals of trying to do at least six pages' worth of problems in each session. Others were told to set only one distal goal of completing forty-two pages by the end of seven sessions. The pace was thus the same for both goals. A third group did not set goals, and a fourth group did not even do the exercises.

The group with the proximal goals outperformed everyone else when the program was over and competence was tested. They succeeded, apparently, because meeting these daily goals gradually built their confidence and self-efficacy. With their focus on a specific goal for each session, they learned better and faster than the others. Even though they spent less time per session, they got more done, thus progressing through all the material faster. At the end, when faced with hard problems, they persevered longer and were less likely to give up. It turned out that the distal goals were no better than having no goals at all. Only the proximal goals produced improvements in learning, self-efficacy, and performance.

But soon after that study was published in the *Journal of Person-*

ality and Social Psychology (the most prestigious and rigorous journal for those fields), the same journal published a paper by Dutch researchers demonstrating the virtues of distal goals, at least for the high school boys being studied. The boys who cared more about long-term objectives—finding an interesting career, making plenty of money, having a good family life, achieving high social status—tended to do better in school. Those who were relatively indifferent to such distal goals tended to be worse students. Focusing on far-off goals seemed to be more effective than focusing on intermediate goals, like getting good grades, going on holidays, or earning a diploma. Those distal goals also seemed to be more useful than present-oriented goals, like aiming to help others or acquire knowledge. Why did the long-term objectives work with these high school students but not in the earlier study with the arithmetic lessons? One reason is that the high school students could clearly see a connection between their daily tasks and their long-term goals. The superior students not only emphasized distal goals but were also more likely than the lesser students to see their current studies and work as vital steps leading toward those goals. Another reason is that older children are better able than younger ones to think about the future.

Regardless of whether those boys ever reached their distal goals, they moved forward by seeing the connection between their distant dreams and the drudgery of daily life. And they presumably reaped the same kind of reward that Ben Franklin did. Late in life, he cheerfully acknowledged that he had failed to ever reach his proximal goal of a clean weekly notebook, much less his distal goal of moral perfection. But the link between the two goals had inspired him along the way, and he took solace from the results. "On the whole," Franklin concluded, "tho' I never arrived at the perfection I had been so ambitious of obtaining, but fell far short of it, yet I was, by the endeavour, a better and a happier man than I otherwise should have been if I had not attempted it."

Fuzzy Versus Fussy

To reach a goal, how specific should your plans be? In one carefully controlled experiment, researchers monitored college students taking part in a program to improve their skills at studying. In addition to receiving the usual instructions on how to use time effectively, the students were randomly assigned among three planning conditions. One group was instructed to make daily plans for what, where, and when to study. Another made similar plans, only month by month instead of day by day. And a third group, the controls, did not make plans.

The researchers felt they were on solid ground in predicting that the day-by-day plans would work best. But they were wrong. The monthly planning group did the best, in terms of improvements in study habits and attitudes. Among the weaker students (though not among the good ones), monthly planning led to much bigger improvements in grades than did the daily planning. Monthly planners also kept it up much longer than the daily planners, and the continued planning thus was more likely to carry over into their work after the program ended. A year after the program ended, the monthly planners were still getting better grades than the daily planners, most of whom by this point had largely abandoned planning, daily or otherwise.

Why? Daily plans do have the advantage of letting the person know exactly what he or she should be doing at each moment. But their preparation is time-consuming, because it takes much longer to make thirty daily plans than a broad plan for the month without any daily details. Another drawback of daily plans is that they lack flexibility. They deprive the person of the chance to make choices along the way, so the person feels locked into a rigid and grinding sequence of tasks. Life rarely goes exactly according to plan, and so the daily plans can be demoralizing as soon as you fall off schedule. With a monthly plan, you can make adjustments. If a delay arises one day, your plan is still intact.

The most extensive experiments in fuzzy-versus-fussy planning have been the uncontrolled ones run by military leaders on the battlefields of Europe. Napoleon once summarized his idea of strategic military planning: "You engage, and then you wait and see." By making contact with the enemy and then improvising, he triumphed and made his armies the envy (and the scourge) of Europe. His rivals to the north, the Prussians, groped for some advantage to make sure they didn't keep losing to the French, and they came up with more planning. The officer class of other countries ridiculed the idea that soldiers should sit at tables with pens and paper, making plans. But the plans turned out to be a genuine advantage, and the next time the two nations fought, the Prussians won a resounding victory.

By World War I, everyone was planning. By World War II, military leaders had the bureaucratic skills for what has been called the most complicated logistical exercise in history: the invasion of Normandy. The Allied force of 160,000 that landed on the beaches wasn't large by the standards of Napoleon, who had marched into Russia with more than 400,000 troops. But the operation was orchestrated so precisely that planners invented their own calendar for a landing on D-day at precisely H-Hour (1.5 hours after nautical twilight). The to-do list had detailed instructions covering the preparations (like the bombing runs on day D-3) and then the invasion itself. It continued all the way to day D+14, specifying where reinforcements would arrive a full two weeks after the beginning of the battle. The military planners' confidence might have seemed presumptuous to Napoleon, but their success raised everyone's faith in their powers.

After the war, corporate America had new planning heroes, like the Whiz Kids, a group of World War II veterans who reorganized the Ford Motor Company. Their leader was Robert S. McNamara, who before the war had taught accounting at Harvard Business School. He used his mathematical skills to analyze bombing missions in the Army Air Force's Office of Statistical Control, and his success there led to the job at Ford. Then he went back to the military to become secretary of defense, introducing the Pentagon to elaborate new planning tools based on principles of "systems analysis" and reams of data. He seemed the very model of a modern warrior until his plans for the Vietnam War turned out so badly. While he sat in the Pentagon plotting the demise of the enemy based on the casualty statistics he saw, soldiers in the jungle were discovering that they couldn't put any faith in those statistics or plans. The Vietnam debacle gave military leaders a new respect for the need for flexibility, and that lesson was reinforced by the plans that went awry in Iraq and Afghanistan. Sometimes, as Napoleon said, you just have to engage and improvise.

So how exactly does a modern general plan for the future? That question was put to a group of them recently by a psychologist who had been invited to give a talk at the Pentagon about managing time and resources. To warm up the elite group of generals, he asked them all to write a summary of their approach to managing their affairs. To keep it short, he instructed each to do this in twenty-five words or less. The exercise stumped most of them. None of the distinguished men in uniform could come up with anything.

The only general who managed a response was the lone woman in the room. She had already had a distinguished career, having worked her way up through the ranks and been wounded in combat in Iraq. Her summary of her approach was as follows: "First I make a list of priorities: one, two, three, and so on. Then I cross out everything from three on down."

The other generals might have objected to her approach, arguing that everyone has more than two goals, and that some projects—like, say, D-day—require more than two steps. But this general was on to something. Hers was a simple version of a strategy for reconciling the long-term with the short-term, the fussy with the fuzzy. She was aiming, as we will see, for a mind like water.

Drew Carey's Dream In-Box

One day in Hollywood, when faced with the usual dispiriting sight of his desk, Drew Carey had a fantasy. He looked at the mounds of paper and thought: *What would David Allen do?* Or, more precisely: *What if I could get David Allen to come here and deal with this stuff?*

Until that point, Carey was a fairly typical victim of information overload, if a celebrity can ever be called typical. He'd starred in his own hit sitcom, run improv-comedy shows on television, written a bestselling memoir, hosted game shows, led philanthropic and political causes, owned a soccer team—but none of those challenges was as daunting as his in-box or to-do list. Even with an assistant, he couldn't keep up with the phone calls to return, the scripts to read, the meetings to juggle, the charity dinners to emcee, the dozens of e-mails every day requiring an immediate answer. The desk of his home office was littered with unpaid bills, unanswered letters, unfinished tasks, unfulfilled promises.

"I have self-control in some ways, but not in others," Carey says. "It depends on what's at stake. I just got so fed up with the mess in my office. I had boxes of paperwork and a desk I couldn't get through. Both sides of my computer were piled up with crap and old mail. You know, it was at a point where I couldn't think. I always felt out of control. I always knew I had stuff to do. You can't read a book and enjoy yourself because in the back of your mind you feel like, *I should go through those e-mails I have.* You're never really at rest."

Carey had picked up a copy of David Allen's book *Getting Things Done: The Art of Stress-Free Productivity,* yet the subtitle's bliss continued to elude him. "I was reading the book and doing some of the stuff in it, but not all of it. I was so desperate. I finally said, 'Shit, man, I'm rich,' and I called him up directly. I contacted his organization and asked how much it would cost if David Allen came out and worked with me personally. He said, 'For x amount of money, I'll work with you for a whole year.' And I said, 'Done.' It cost me a lot of money, but I didn't even think about it."

However large x was, Carey's decision makes perfect sense to devotees of GTD, the acronym for Allen's book that has become the name for a system of working and living. But it's not the usual personality-driven cult of self-help gurus and motivational speakers. Allen doesn't offer seven simple rules of life or rouse crowds into frenzies of empowerment. He doesn't offer vague wisdom like "Begin with the end in mind," or exhortations like "Awaken the giant within." He focuses on the minutiae of to-do lists, folders, labels, in-boxes.

It's a system involving a mental phenomenon that psychologists recognized decades ago—your inner nag—but that wasn't really understood until some recent experiments in Baumeister's laboratory testing ways to silence that inner voice. The experimenters and Allen independently arrived at the same technique, but they took very different paths. Allen did not operate from any psychological theory. He worked strictly by trial and error, starting, in his own life, with lots of trials and a good deal of error. Coming of age in the 1960s, he studied Zen and Sufi texts, started grad school in history at Berkeley, dropped out, experimented with drugs (punctuated by a brief mental breakdown), taught karate, and worked for a company offering personal-growth seminars. Along the way, he paid the bills by being a moped salesman, magician, landscaper, travel agent, glassblower, cab driver, U-Haul dealer, waiter, vitamin distributor, gas station manager, construction worker, and chef.

"If you had told me in 1968 that I'd end up being a personal productivity consultant," he says, "I would have told you that you're out of your mind." He drifted from job to job—he counted thirty-five by his thirty-fifth birthday—until his skill at running seminars led to invitations to work with executives at Lockheed and other corporations. As weird as this résumé path sounds, Allen sees a certain consistency in the progression from philosophy, mind-altering drugs, and karate to personal-growth trainer and corporate consultant. He describes it all as a quest for mental peace, for a "mind like water," the phrase he borrows from his karate lessons: "Imagine throwing a pebble into a still pond. How does the water respond? The answer is, totally appropriately to the force and mass of the input; then it returns to calm. It doesn't overreact or underreact."

You can get a sense of this philosophy by visiting his office, which will produce a severe case of desk envy. You would expect an efficiency expert to be orderly, but it's still a shock to arrive at his company's headquarters in Ojai, a small town in the mountains of Southern California near Santa Barbara, and see the complete absence of paperwork or any kind of clutter. On the right side of his L-shaped desk are three stacked wooden trays, all utterly empty, including his in-box. On the left side are another two trays with a dozen books and magazines, which are his to-read pile for airplane trips. Otherwise, his desk is immaculate. In accordance with the four Ds of his system, everything that has not been done, delegated, or dropped has been deferred to a half dozen two-drawer file cabinets, which contain his alphabetized plastic folders with labels printed by the little machine next to his computer. You might dismiss this all as evidence of dreary anal-retentiveness, but Allen could not be less dour or more relaxed.

When he began working with overtaxed executives, he saw the problem with the traditional big-picture type of management planning, like writing mission statements, defining long-term goals, and setting priorities. He appreciated the necessity of lofty objectives, but he could see that these clients were too distracted to focus on even the simplest task of the moment. Allen described their affliction with another Buddhist image, "monkey mind," which refers to a mind plagued with constantly shifting thoughts, like a monkey leaping wildly from tree to tree. Sometimes Allen imagined a variation in which the monkey is perched on your shoulder jabbering into your ear, constantly second-guessing and interrupting until you want to scream, "Somebody, shut up the monkey!"

"Most people have never tasted what it's like to have nothing on their mind except whatever they're doing," Allen says. "You could tolerate that dissonance and that stress if it only happened once a month, the way it did in the past. Now people are just going numb and stupid, or getting too crazy and busy to deal with the anxiety."

Instead of starting with goals and figuring out how to reach them, Allen tried to help his clients deal with the immediate mess on their desks. He could see the impracticality of traditional bits of organizational advice, like the old rule about never touching a piece of paper more than once—fine in theory, impossible in practice. What were you supposed to do with a memo about a meeting next week? Allen remembered a tool from his travel-agent days, the tickler file. The meeting memo, like an airplane ticket, could be filed in a folder for the day it was needed. That way the desk would remain uncluttered, and the memo wouldn't distract you until the day it was needed. Allen's tickler file—thirty-one folders for each day of the current month, twelve folders for each of the months—would become so widely copied that his followers used it for the name of a popular lifehacker Web site: 43folders.com.

Besides getting paperwork off the desk, the tickler file also removed a source of worry: Once something was filed there, you knew you'd be reminded to deal with it on the appropriate day. You weren't nagged by the fear that you'd lose it or forget about it. Allen looked for other ways to eliminate that mental nagging by closing the "open loops" in the mind. "One piece I took from the personal-growth world was the importance of the agreements you make with yourself," he recalls. "When you make an agreement and you don't keep it, you undermine your own self-trust. You can fool everybody but yourself, and you're going to pay for that, so you should be aware of the agreements you make. We developed a workshop for writing down those agreements."

There was, of course, nothing revolutionary about the strategy of listing one's commitments and goals. The make-a-list strategy had been in every self-help program since Noah's Ark and the Ten Commandments. But Allen made refinements with the help of a veteran management consultant named Dean Acheson (not the former secretary of state). To help his clients eliminate distractions, Acheson started off by having them write down everything that had their attention, large and small, professional and personal, distal and proximal, fuzzy and fussy. They didn't have to analyze or organize or schedule anything, but in each case they did have to identify the specific next action to be taken.

"Dean sat me down and had me empty my head," Allen says. "I'd done a lot of meditating and considered myself highly organized, so I thought I already had my shit together. But I was blown away by the results. I thought, *Look at what this does!*" As Allen went on to work with his own clients, he preached the importance of the Next Action, or NA, as GTDers call it. The to-do list was not supposed to have items like "Birthday gift for Mom" or "Do taxes." It had to specify the very next action, like "Drive to jewelry store" or "Call accountant."

"If your list has 'Write thank-you notes,' that's a fine Next Action, as long as you have a pen and cards," Allen says. "But if you don't have the cards, you'll know subliminally that you can't write the notes, so you'll avoid the list and procrastinate." That distinction might sound easy enough to learn, but people get it wrong all the time. When Allen hears that John Tierney has been inspired by the book to install a GTD organizer on his smartphone, Allen promptly offers to bet that most of the items on the Next Action list won't be immediately doable. Sure enough, he finds the list dominated by imperatives like "Contact mint.com researchers" or "Consult Esther Dyson about self-control"—much too vague for GTD standards.

"How are you going to contact or consult them?" Allen asks. "Do you already have the phone number or e-mail address? Have you decided whether to call or e-mail? That dumb little distinction matters. Everything on that list is either attracting or repulsing you. If you say 'Consult Esther' because you haven't finished thinking exactly what you're going to do next, there's a part of you that doesn't want to look at the list. You're walking around with this subliminal anxiety. But if you put down "E-mail Esther,' you think, *Oh, I can do that*, and you move forward and feel you've finished something."

A few years ago, when the technology writer Danny O'Brien sent a questionnaire asking seventy of the most "sickeningly over-prolific" people he knew for their organizational secrets, most said they didn't use special software or other elaborate tools. But a good many did say they followed the GTD system, which doesn't re-quire anything more complicated than pen, paper, and folders. As yet there's no body of peer-reviewed research comparing GTDers with a control group. But there is evidence in the psychological literature of the mental stress that Allen observed. Psychologists have also been studying how to eliminate the monkey mind. They just use a differ-ent term for it.

The Zeigarnik Effect

The discovery began, according to the legend among psychologists, with a lunch in the mid-1920s near the University of Berlin. A large group from the university went to a restaurant and placed their or-ders with a single waiter, who didn't bother writing anything down. He simply nodded. Yet he served everyone's food correctly, a feat of memory that impressed the group. They finished eating and left the restaurant, whereupon one person (the legend is unclear on exactly who) returned to retrieve an item that had been left behind. The person spotted the waiter and asked for help, hoping to benefit from his obviously excellent memory.

But the waiter looked back blankly. He had no idea who the patron was, much less where the person had sat. When asked how he could have forgotten everything so quickly, the water explained that he remembered each order only until it was served.

One of the scholars, a young Russian psychology student named Bluma Zeigarnik, and her mentor, the influential thinker Kurt Lewin, pondered this experience and wondered if it pointed to a more general principle. Did the human memory make a strong distinction between finished and unfinished tasks? They began observing people who were interrupted while doing jigsaw puzzles. This research, and many studies in the following decades, confirmed what became known as the Zeigarnik effect: Uncompleted tasks and unmet goals tend to pop into one's mind. Once the task is completed and the goal reached, however, this stream of reminders comes to a stop.

A good way to appreciate the Zeigarnik effect is to listen to a randomly chosen song and shut it off halfway through. The song is then likely to run through your mind on its own, at odd intervals. If you get to the end of the song, the mind checks it off, so to speak. If you stop it in the middle, however, the mind treats the song as unfinished business. As if to keep reminding you that there is a job to be done, the mind keeps inserting bits of the song into your stream of thought. That's why when Bill Murray in *Groundhog Day* keeps shutting off "I Got You Babe" on his clock radio, the tune keeps going through our minds (and keeps driving him crazy). And that's why this kind of ear worm is so often an awful tune rather than a pleasant one. We're more likely to turn off the bad one in midsong, so it's the one that returns to haunt us.

Why would the mind inflict "I Got You Babe" on itself? Psychologists have generally assumed that earworms are an unfortunate byproduct of an otherwise useful function: the completion of tasks.

How the Zeigarnik effect works has been explained by various theories over the years, including two rival hypotheses that dominated the debate. One hypothesis was that the unconscious mind is keeping track of your goals and working to make sure they're accomplished, so these stray conscious thoughts are actually a reassuring sign that your unconscious will stay on the case until the job is done. The rival hypothesis was that the unconscious mind is seeking help from the conscious mind: Like a small child tugging at the sleeve of an adult to get attention and help, the unconscious mind is telling the conscious mind to finish the task.

But now there's a newer and better explanation for the Zeigarnik effect, thanks to some recent experiments conducted by E. J. Masicampo, a graduate student at Florida State working with Baumeister. In one study, he assigned some students to think about their most important final examination. Others, in a control condition, thought about the most important party pending on their social calendar. Among the ones who thought about the exam, half were also told to make specific plans of what, where, and when they would study. But nobody did any actual studying during the experiment.

Then everyone performed a task that contained a subtle measure of the Zeigarnik effect. They were given word fragments and instructed to complete them. The fragments were artfully constructed so that they could be completed with words relevant to studying— but also with alternative, irrelevant words. For instance, the item re_ _ could be completed as *read* but also be made into *real, rest, reap,* and *reek*. Likewise, *ex_ _* could be completed as *exam* but also as *exit*. If thoughts of the unfulfilled task of studying for the exam were on the person's mind, he or she would be expected to generate more exam-related words due to the Zeigarnik effect. And indeed, Masicampo found that these words popped more often into the minds of some people: the ones who had been reminded of the exam but hadn't made plans to study for it. But no such effect was observed among the students who'd made a study plan. Even though they, too, had been reminded of the exam, their minds had apparently been cleared by the act of writing down a plan.

In another experiment, participants were asked to reflect on important projects in their lives. Some were told to write about some tasks they had recently completed. Others were told to write about tasks that were unfulfilled and needed to be done soon. A third group was also told to write about unfulfilled tasks, but also to make specific plans for how they would get these done. Then everyone went on to what they were told was a separate and unrelated experiment. They were assigned to read the first ten pages of a novel. As they read, they were checked periodically to ascertain whether their minds were wandering from the novel. Afterward, they were asked how well they had focused and where, if anywhere, their minds had wandered. They also were tested on how well they understood what they'd read.

Once again, making a plan made a difference. Those who'd written about unfulfilled tasks had more trouble keeping their minds focused on the novel—unless they'd made a specific plan to complete the task, in which case they reported relatively little mind wandering and scored quite well on the reading comprehension test. Even though they hadn't finished the task or made any palpable progress, the simple act of making a plan had cleared their minds and eliminated the Zeigarnik effect. But the Zeigarnik effect remained for the students without a plan. Their thoughts wandered from the novel to their undone tasks, and afterward they scored worse on the comprehension test.

So it turns out that the Zeigarnik effect is not, as was assumed for decades, a reminder that continues unabated until the task gets done. The persistence of distracting thoughts is not an indication that the unconscious is working to finish the task. Nor is it the unconscious nagging the conscious mind to finish the task right away. Instead, the unconscious is asking the conscious mind to *make a plan*. The unconscious mind apparently can't do this on its own, so it nags the conscious mind to make a plan with specifics like time, place, and opportunity. Once the plan is formed, the unconscious can stop nagging the conscious mind with reminders.

That's how Allen's system deals with the problem that he calls monkey mind. If, like his typical client, you've got at least 150 items on your to-do list, the Zeigarnik effect could leave you leaping from task to task, and it won't be sedated by vague good intentions. If you've got a memo that has to be read before a meeting Thursday morning, the unconscious wants to know exactly what needs to be done next, and under what circumstances. But once you make that plan—once you put the meeting memo in the tickler file for Wednesday, once you specify the very next action to be taken on the project—you can relax. You don't have to finish the job right away. You've still got 150 things on the to-do list, but for the moment the monkey is still, and the water is calm.

Zero Euphoria

Upon arriving at Drew Carey's office, David Allen began where he always begins: the collection of *stuff*. This is a broadly encompassing term. Stuff, as defined in *Getting Things Done,* is "anything you have allowed into your psychological or physical world that doesn't belong where it is, but for which you haven't yet determined the desired outcome and the next action step." Or, as Carey defined it, all the crap in his office.

Then came the second phase of the GTD system, the processing of the stuff, when Carey had to decide whether to do it, delegate it, defer it, or drop it. If something didn't require action, it could be either thrown out or filed away for future reference. Stuff requiring action that was part of a multistep project, like Carey's preparations to emcee a charity benefit dinner honoring Archbishop Desmond

Tutu, had to be grouped together in a project list or in a folder on the computer or in a file cabinet. By going through all the paperwork, all the unanswered e-mails, all the other unfinished tasks in his computer or on his mind, Carey identified dozens of personal and business projects, which was typical. Allen's clients usually have between thirty and one hundred projects, each with at least a couple of tasks, and they spend a full day or two to complete the great initial purging and sorting and processing. After Carey identified the projects, he had to single out the specific Next Action for each project. What was the very next thing to do for the charity dinner? As Carey worked through all the stuff, Allen sat in his office all day long.

"He'd honestly sit there and watch me do my-emails," Carey says. "Whenever I'd get stuck he'd say, 'What's going on?' And I'd tell him, and he'd go, 'Do this.' And I would do it. He was very decisive about it. There would be only a few times when he'd say, 'It could be a this or a that. What are you going to do with it?'" Allen taught him to set up separate folders for phone calls and e-mails, to put vague projects in a "Someday/Maybe" folder, and to follow the Two-Minute Rule: If something will take less than two minutes, don't put it on a list. Get it out of the way immediately.

"Before, I'd see a pile of papers and wouldn't know what the hell was in them and just be like, *Oh, my God,*" Carey says. "The day I got to zero, which is GTD talk for having nothing in your in-box— no phone messages, no e-mails, nothing, not a piece of paper—when I got to that point, I felt like the world got lifted off my shoulders. I felt like I had just come out of meditating in the desert, not a care in the world. I just felt euphoric."

Since that day, with the help of monthly visits from Allen, Carey says he has kept fairly close to zero. He falters sometimes, and if he's been traveling, stuff will build up, but at least he knows what's there and feels sure he'll get to it. He can read a book or take a yoga class without feeling guilty. With the mundane out of the way, he can focus on the important stuff, like writing comedy. "There's nothing worse than sitting down to write when you've got a blinking phone and a pile of letters and a ton of e-mails in your face," Carey says. "You're not going to do your very best work. But if you know the other stuff is taken care of, you can concentrate on your writing. You can be more creative." Ultimately, that's the selling point of GTD in corporate offices and far beyond. That's the reason that comedians and artists and rock musicians rhapsodize about Allen's lists and folders.

"Whether you're trying to garden or take a picture or write a book," Allen says, "your ability to make a creative mess is your most productive state. You want to be able to throw ideas all over the place, but you need to be able to start with a clear deck. One mess at a time is all you can handle. Two messes at a time, you're screwed. You may want to find God, but if you're running low on cat food, you damn well better make a plan for dealing with it. Otherwise the cat food is going to take a whole lot more attention and keep you from finding God."

But why is it so hard to put cat food on a list? Why, even after paying Allen's twenty-thousand-dollars-a-day fee to sit by their side, do his corporate clients still look for any excuse to flee from the stuff on their desks? He sometimes has to hunt them down in the men's room and drag them back. After watching so many clients agonize over the most trivial decisions and Next Actions, Allen has come to appreciate why *decide* has the same etymological root as *homicide:* the Latin word *caedere,* meaning "to cut down" or "to kill."

"When we're trying to decide what to do with our stuff or what movie to see," Allen says, "we don't think to ourselves, *Look at all these cool choices.* There's a powerful thing inside that says, *If I decide to do that movie, I kill all the other movies.* You can pretend all the way up to that point that you know the right thing to do, but once you're faced with a choice, you have to deal with this open loop in your head: *You're wrong, you're right, you're wrong, you're right.*

Every single time you make a choice, you're stepping into an existential void."

An existential void is not, ordinarily, very easy for psychologists to observe in the lab. But when people spend a lot of time in that void, the consequences can start to show up in ways that are easier to measure. A person might, as we shall see, start behaving like Eliot Spitzer.

4.

DECISION FATIGUE

Man who man would be,
Must rule the empire of himself; in it
Must be supreme, establishing his throne
On vanquished will, quelling the anarchy
Of hopes and fears, being himself alone.

—From Shelley's sonnet "Political Greatness"

Before we get to the science of decisions, let's start with a political exercise. Suppose you are a married man who is the governor of a large state in the American Northeast. You've put in a long day at the office, and you're relaxing late in the afternoon by surfing the Web. You happen upon—well, it's not exactly by happenstance—a site that describes itself as "the most preferred international social introduction service for those accustomed to excellence." It is named the Emperors Club VIP.

"Our goal," the club explains, "is to make life more peaceful, balanced, beautiful and meaningful." Toward these purposes, the club displays pictures of young women, many in transparent lingerie, each rated by a certain number of diamonds. Each woman happens to be available to spend time with you in return for an "introduction fee." A decision must be made. Which of these options would bring the most "balance" to your life?

    a. Arrange to contemplate Impressionist paintings at a museum in the company of Savannah, "an artist by profession and creative beauty at heart," for $1,000 per hour, to be paid in cash.

    b. Make a dinner date with Renee, an "Italian/Greek fashion model" who "delights in Tuscan wines, black espresso, and the cool fresh scent of men's perfume," for $1,500 per hour, to be paid with an anonymous money order.

    c. Book an evening in a hotel room with Kristen, a twenty-three-year-old who describes herself as having "a lot of depth, a lot of layers," in addition to a tattoo in Latin, for $1,000 per hour, to be covered by a wire transfer from your personal bank account.

    d. Schedule an entire day with Maya, rated at seven diamonds with "her incomparable look and electrifying presence," for $31,000, to be billed to your gubernatorial expense account under the heading of "Personal Balance Consultant."

    e. Ask your chief political adviser which woman would be most suitable for you.

    f. Close the Web page, turn on C-SPAN, and take a cold shower.

Not a very tough call, is it? So why did Eliot Spitzer have such a tough time with it when he was the governor of New York? By choosing *c* (Kristen), he joined the long list of famously shrewd politicians and corporate executives who have destroyed their careers with an inexplicably dumb decision. Spitzer, who had targeted prostitution in his days as a prosecutor, not only arranged a hotel tryst with Kristen but even sent money to the Emperor's Club VIP with a traceable transfer from his own bank account. He knew the scrutiny he was under as governor; he had seen firsthand the risks and legal dangers of prostitution. In his long quest to become governor, he'd built a reputation for political savvy, firm discipline, and moral righteousness. Why, once he got his dream job, did he lose his bearings? Did power so warp his judgment that he felt invincible, or was he a narcissist all along? Did he subconsciously want to sabotage his career? Deep down, did he feel unworthy? Or, after all the perks of power, did he simply feel entitled to whatever he wanted?

Any of those answers might or might not be right, and we won't try to sort them out or psychoanalyze Spitzer. But we can suggest one other factor that certainly contributed to his downfall—and to the mistakes that have wrecked the careers and families of so many other executives. When Spitzer hired a hooker, when the governor of South Carolina snuck off to Buenos Aires to see his girlfriend, when Bill Clinton took up with an intern, they were all subject to the occupational hazard that comes with being, as President George W. Bush once described himself, "the decider." The problem of decision fatigue affects everything from the careers of CEOs to the prison sentences of felons appearing before weary judges. It influences the behavior of everyone, executive and nonexecutive, every day. Yet few people are even aware of it. When asked whether making decisions would deplete their willpower and make them vulnerable to temptation, most people say no. They don't realize that decision fatigue helps explain why ordinarily sensible people get angry at their colleagues and families, splurge on clothes, buy junk food at the supermarket, and can't resist the car dealer's offer to rustproof their new sedan.

This hazard was first identified at Baumeister's lab by Jean Twenge, a postdoctoral student who took up self-control research at the same time that she was planning her wedding. As she read up on the lab's previous experiments, like the one showing how self-control was depleted by the act of resisting chocolate chip cookies, she was reminded of a recent and quite draining personal experience: registering for wedding gifts, that odd tradition of enlisting a corporation to help with extorting gifts from family and friends. Although it's ordinarily considered rude for anyone beyond the Santa Claus years to demand specific gifts, listing your wishes on a bridal registry has been rationalized as a social ritual that eases the stress on everyone. The guests don't have to bother shopping; the couple doesn't have to worry about ending up with thirty-seven soup tureens and no ladles. But that doesn't mean it's stress-free, as Twenge discovered on the evening that she and her fiancé sat down with the store's wedding specialist to decide exactly what items to put on their registry. How ornate did they want their china to be? Which brand of knives? What kind of towels? Which color? Precisely how many threads per square inch of their sheets?

"By the end," Twenge told her colleagues in the lab, "you could have talked me into anything." She thought the experience of having one's willpower depleted must be something like the way she felt that evening. She and the other psychologists wondered how to test that idea. They remembered that a nearby department store was going out of business and holding a clearance sale, which made plenty of products affordable on the laboratory budget. The researchers went shopping and filled their car trunks with simple products—not exactly posh wedding gifts, but sufficiently appealing to college students.

For the first experiment, participants were shown a table loaded with these products. They were told they would get to keep one at the end of the experiment. Then some of the students were told to make choices, which would supposedly determine which product they eventually received. They went through a series of choices, each time between two items. Would they prefer a pen or a candle? A vanilla-scented candle or an almond-scented one? A candle or a T-shirt? A black T-shirt or a red T-shirt? Meanwhile, a control group—call them the nondeciders—spent an equally long period of time contemplating all these same products without having to make any choices. They were asked just to rate their opinion of each product and report how often they had used such a product in the last six months. Afterward, everyone was given one of the classic tests of self-control: holding your hand in ice water for as long as you can. The water is uncomfortable and the impulse is to pull the hand out, so self-discipline is needed to keep the hand under water. It turned out that the deciders gave up significantly sooner than the nondeciders. Making all those choices had apparently sapped their willpower, and the effect showed up again in other decision-making exercises.

In some experiments, students had to go through a college catalog and choose courses for themselves. In another experiment, designed to be immediately relevant to students enrolled in a psychology course, they had to make a series of choices about how they wanted their course to be taught for the remainder of the semester: which films to watch, how many quizzes to have. After making the choices, some students were given puzzles to solve. Some were told that they were about to take a math test that would be an important measure of their intelligence, and that they could improve their score if they spent fifteen minutes practicing for it—but in addition to being given practice materials for the test, they were left in a room with magazines and handheld video games as tempting distractions. Again and again, the decision making took a toll on the students. Compared with the nondeciders, who'd spent just as much time evaluating the same kind of information without making choices, the deciders gave up sooner on the puzzles. Instead of using their time to practice for the math test, they goofed off by reading magazines and playing video games.

As the ultimate real-world test of their theory, researchers went into that great modern arena of decision making: the mall. Shoppers in a suburban mall were interviewed about their experiences in the stores that day and then asked to solve some simple arithmetic problems. The researchers politely asked them to do as many as possible but said they could quit at any time. Sure enough, the shoppers who'd already made the most decisions in the stores gave up the quickest on the math problems. When you shop till you drop, your willpower drops, too. On a practical level, the experiment demonstrated the perils of marathon shopping. On a theoretical level, the results of all these experiments raised a new question: What kinds of decisions deplete the most willpower? Which choices are the hardest?

Crossing the Rubicon

Psychologists distinguish two main types of mental processes, automatic and controlled. Automatic processes, like multiplying 4 times 7, can be done without exertion. If someone says "4 times 7," *28* probably pops into your head whether you want it to or not—that's why the process is called automatic. In contrast, computing 26 times 30 requires mental effort as you go through the steps of multiplying to come up with 780. Difficult mathematical calculations, like other logical reasoning, require willpower as you follow a set of systematic rules to get from one set of information to something new. You often go through steps like these in making a decision, through a process that psychologists call the Rubicon model of action phases, in honor of the river that separated Italy from the Roman province of Gaul. When Caesar reached it, he knew that a general returning to Rome was forbidden to bring his legions across the Rubicon. He realized that crossing it with his army would start a civil war. Waiting on the Gaul side of the river, he was in the "predecisional phase" as he contemplated his goals and possibilities along with the potential costs and benefits. Then he stopped calculating and crossed the Rubicon, reaching the "postdecisional phase," which Caesar defined much more felicitously: "The die is cast."

The whole process could deplete anyone's willpower, but which part is most fatiguing? Could the depletion be due mainly to all the calculations before the decision? By this point, Twenge and several other researchers had been depleted by this long-running project, but the reviewers who decided whether the work could be published in the field's top journal wanted more answers. Kathleen Vohs, a veteran "closer" who knew how to bring embattled projects to final success, took over and masterminded the project through its final stages. She designed an experiment using the self-service sales site of the Dell computer company. At dell.com, shoppers could research and configure their own customized computer by choosing the size of the hard drive, the type of screen, and a series of other features. In the experiment, participants went through some of the same processes as Dell's shoppers (except that nobody bought a computer at the end).

By random assignment, each participant in the study was given one of three tasks. Some were told to look at several features relevant to a computer but not make a decision. They were instructed to think about the options and prices and to form preferences and opinions, but not to make a definite selection. The purpose of this condition was to duplicate the predecision thinking without the actual deciding.

Another group was handed a list of selections and told to configure the computer. They had to go through the laborious, step-by-step process of locating the specified features among the arrays of options and then clicking on the right ones. The purpose was to duplicate everything that happens in the postdecisional phase, when the choice is implemented. The third group had to choose which features they wanted on their customized computers. They didn't simply ponder options or implement others' choices. They had to cast the die, and that turned out to be the most fatiguing task of all. When self-control was measured afterward by asking people to solve as many anagrams as they could, the people who had actually made decisions gave up sooner than the others. Crossing the Rubicon appeared to be tough mental work, whether it involved deciding the fate of an empire or the size of a computer drive.

But suppose the choice involved options easier and more appealing than starting a civil war or contemplating the innards of a computer. Suppose it involved a process that you found entertaining. Would those choices still deplete willpower? Researchers investigated by conducting another version of the bridal-registry experiment, but this time the subjects included people with widely assorted attitudes toward the task. Some of the young men and women were much more enthusiastic than Jean Twenge at the prospect of choosing wedding gifts for themselves. They said they looked forward to making the choices, and afterward they reported that they enjoyed the experience. Meanwhile, other subjects in the same experiment utterly detested the whole process of picking china and silverware and appliances.

As you might expect, the process wasn't as depleting for the ones who enjoyed it—but only up to a point. If the participants were given a short list of choices to be made in four minutes, then the ones who liked picking gifts could zip through without depleting any of their willpower, whereas the registry-dreading group was predictably depleted even by that short exercise. But when the list was longer and the process went on for twelve minutes, both groups were equally depleted (meaning that they exhibited less self-control on tests than did a control group that hadn't made any choices about wedding gifts). A few pleasant decisions are apparently not all that depleting, but in the long run, there seems to be no such thing as a free choice, at least when it comes to making it for yourself.

Choosing for others, though, isn't always so difficult. While you may agonize over just the right furniture to put in your own living room, you probably wouldn't expend all that much energy if you were asked to make decorating decisions for a casual acquaintance. When researchers put a series of home decor questions to people and then tested their willpower afterward, the results showed that it was much less depleting to decide for a casual acquaintance than for oneself. Even though it might seem difficult to choose a sofa for an acquaintance whose taste you don't know, that difficulty is apparently offset by not caring a great deal about the outcome. After all, you won't have to look at the sofa every day. The other side of the Rubicon looks less scary when you know someone else is going to end up there.

The Judge's Dilemma
(and the Prisoner's Distress)

Four men serving time in Israeli prisons recently asked to be released on parole. Their cases were heard by a board, consisting of a judge, a criminologist, and a sociologist, that periodically met for a daylong session to consider prisoners' appeals. There were certain similarities to the four cases. Each of the prisoners was a repeat offender, having served a previous term in prison for a separate offense. Each man had served two-thirds of his current sentence, and each would have been able to participate in a rehabilitation program if released. But there were also differences, and the board granted parole to only two of the four men. From the list of the four cases, try guessing which two men were denied parole and had to remain in prison:

> Case 1 (heard at 8:50 A.M.): An Arab-Israeli male serving a
>   30-month sentence for fraud.
> Case 2 (heard at 1:27 P.M.): A Jewish-Israeli male serving
>   a 16-month sentence for assault.
> Case 3 (heard at 3:10 P.M.): A Jewish-Israeli male serving a
>   16-month sentence for assault.
> Case 4 (heard at 4:25 P.M.): An Arab-Israeli male serving
>   a 30-month sentence for fraud.

There's a pattern to the board's decisions, but it's not one you'll find by looking at the men's ethnic backgrounds or crimes or sentences. In looking for it, you might keep in mind a long-running debate about the nature of the legal system. One traditional school of scholars treats it as a system of rules to be administered impartially: the classic image of a blindfolded Lady Justice weighing the scales. Another school emphasizes the importance of human foibles, not abstract rules, in determining verdicts. These legal realists, as they're known, are often caricatured as defining *justice* to be "what the judge ate for breakfast."

Now their definition has been tested by a team of psychologists led by Jonathan Levav of Columbia University and Shai Danziger of Ben-Gurion University. They reviewed more than one thousand decisions made over the course of ten months by judges who took turns presiding over the parole board of an Israeli prison system. Each judge, after hearing prisoners' appeals and getting advice from the criminologist and sociologist on the parole board, would decide whether to release the criminal on parole. By awarding parole, the judge could please the prisoner and the prisoner's family, and save the taxpayers' money. But there was also the risk that the paroled prisoner would go on to commit another crime.

On average, each judge approved parole for only about one of every three prisoners, but there was a striking pattern to the decisions of all the judges, as the researchers found. The prisoners who appeared early in the morning received parole about 65 percent of the time. Those who appeared late in the day won parole less than 10 percent of the time. Thus, the odds favored the prisoner in our Case 1, who appeared at 8:50 A.M., the second case of the day—and he did in fact receive parole. But even though the prisoner in Case 4 was serving the same sentence for the same crime—fraud—the odds were against him when he appeared (on a different day) at 4:25 P.M. Like most of the other prisoners who appeared late in the afternoon, he was denied parole.

The change from the morning to the afternoon didn't occur at a steady rate, though. There were other striking patterns during the day. In midmorning, usually a little before 10:30, the parole board would take a break, and the judges would be served a sandwich and a piece of fruit. That would replenish the glucose in their bloodstreams. (Remember the studies about how children who skipped breakfast would suddenly start to behave and learn better after the midmorning snack?) The prisoners who happened to appear just before the break had only about a 15 percent chance of getting parole, which means that only about one out of seven would get to leave the prison. In contrast, the ones who came right after the food break had around a 65 percent chance—about two out of three.

The same pattern happened with lunch. At 12:30 P.M., just before lunch, the chances of getting parole were only 20 percent, but if you came up right after lunch, the chances were more than 60 percent. The prisoner in Case 2 was lucky enough to be the first one to appear after the lunch break, and he did indeed receive parole. The prisoner in Case 3 was serving the same sentence for the same crime, assault, and he also appeared in the afternoon—but later, at 3:10 P.M. Instead of being the first prisoner to appear after the lunch break, he was the twelfth, and he suffered the usual fate at that late hour: Parole was denied.

Judging is hard mental work. As the judges made one decision after another, their brains and bodies used up glucose, that crucial component of willpower that we discussed earlier. Whatever their personal philosophy—whether they were known for being tough on crime or sympathetic to the potential for rehabilitation—they had fewer available mental resources to make further decisions. And so, apparently, they tended to go for the less risky choice (for themselves, anyway). As horribly unfair as it was for the prisoner—why should he linger in jail just because the judge hadn't yet had his midmorning snack?— such bias is not an isolated phenomenon. It occurs naturally in all kinds of situations. The link between willpower and decision making works both ways: Decision making depletes your willpower, and once your willpower is depleted, you're less able to make decisions. If your work requires you to make hard decisions all day long, at some point you're going to be depleted and start looking for ways to conserve energy. You'll look for excuses to avoid or postpone decisions. You'll look for the easiest and safest option, which often is to stick with the status quo: Leave the prisoner in prison.

Denying parole can also seem like the easier call to the judge because it leaves more options open: The judge retains the option of paroling the prisoner at a future date without sacrificing the option of keeping him securely in prison right now. Part of the resistance against making decisions comes from the fear of giving up options. The more you give up by deciding, the more you're afraid of cutting off something vital. Some students choose double majors in college not because they're trying to prove something or because they have some grand plan for a career integrating, say, political science and biology. Rather, they just can't bring themselves to say no to either option. To choose a single major is to pronounce judgment on the other and kill it off, and there's abundant research showing that people have a hard time giving up options, even when the options aren't doing them any good. This reluctance to give up options becomes more pronounced when willpower is low. It takes willpower to make decisions, and so the depleted state makes people look for ways to postpone or evade decisions.

In one experiment, people were invited to choose which, if any, of several items they'd like to buy. The people whose willpower had been depleted by previous acts of self-control were much more likely than the others to duck the decision by not buying anything. In another study, people were asked to imagine that they had ten thousand dollars that they did not need in a savings account. Then they were presented with an investment opportunity described as average risk and above-average rate of return. That combination defines a good investment, because usually risk and return rates are in step. When people were not depleted of willpower, most of them said they would make the investment. Depleted people, in contrast, said to leave the money where it was. Their decision didn't make sense financially, because they were essentially losing money by leaving it in the low-yield savings account, but it was easier than making a decision.

This form of procrastination helps explain why so many people put off the biggest choice of their lives: picking a mate. In the middle of the twentieth century, most people married by their early twenties. But then more options opened for both sexes. More men and women

stayed in school longer and pursued careers that took long preparation. Thanks to the birth control pill and changing social values,
people could enjoy the option of having sex without deciding to get
married. As more people settled in large metropolitan areas, they had
more choices in potential mates, and hence more options than ever
to fear losing. For a column in 1995, Tierney did a semiscientific survey to investigate a New York phenomenon: the huge number of
intelligent and attractive people who complained that it was impossible to find a romantic partner. Manhattan had the highest percent-
age of single people of any county in America except for an island in
Hawaii originally settled as a leper colony.

What was keeping New Yorkers apart? Tierney surveyed a sampling of personal ads in the city magazines of Boston, Baltimore,
Chicago, Los Angeles, and New York. He found that singles in the
biggest city, New York, not only had the most choices but were also
the pickiest in listing the attributes of their desired partners. The
average personal ad in *New York* magazine listed 5.7 criteria required
in a partner, significantly more than second-place Chicago's average
(4.1 criteria) and about twice the average for the other three cities.
As one woman in New York put it in her ad: "Not willing to settle?
Neither am I!" She claimed to be someone who "loves all NY has
to offer," but her definition of "all" did not include any male New
Yorkers who were not handsome, successful, over five feet nine, and
between the ages of twenty-nine and thirty-five. Another New Yorker
demanded a man over five feet ten who played polo. A lawyer who
listed twenty-one requisite qualities in his "princess" professed to be
"astonished" to find himself unattached.

That survey of personal ads was just an informal study, but recently several teams of researchers have reached a similar conclusion
from a far more rigorous analysis of people's romantic pickiness.
They've monitored tens of thousands of people seeking love through
either an online dating service or speed-dating events. At the online
dating service, customers filled out an extensive questionnaire about

their attributes. In theory, that detailed profile should have helped people find just the right mate, but in practice it produced so much information and so many choices that people became absurdly picky. The researchers—Gunter Hitsch and Ali Hortacsu of the University of Chicago, and Dan Ariely of Duke—found that the online customers typically go out with fewer than 1 percent of the people whose profiles they check out. Romance seekers have much better luck at speed-dating events, which are generally limited to a dozen or two dozen people. Each person spends several minutes talking to each of the potential partners. Then all the participants turn in scorecards indicating which people they'd like to see again, and those with mutual interest are matched up. The average participant makes a match with at least one in ten of the people they meet, and some studies have found the ratio to be two or three in ten. Faced with fewer options in mates and an immediate deadline, the speed daters quickly pick out potential partners. But because the online seekers have so many choices, Ariely says, they just go on browsing.

"When you have all these criteria to consider, and so many people to choose from, you start striving for perfection," he says. "You don't want to settle for someone who's not ideal in height, age, religion, and forty-five other dimensions." Ariely further studied this reluctance to give up options by watching people play a computer game in which they earned real cash by opening doors to find rewards inside rooms. The best strategy was to open each of the three doors on the computer screen, find the one with the most lucrative rewards, and then stay in that room. But even after players learned that strategy, they had a hard time following it when an additional feature was introduced: If they stayed out of any room for a while, its door would start shrinking and eventually disappear, effectively closing the door permanently. That prospect so bothered players that they would jump back into a room to keep the door open even though the move reduced their overall earnings.

"Closing a door on an option is experienced as a loss, and people are willing to pay a price to avoid the emotion of loss," Ariely says. Sometimes that makes sense, but too often we're so eager to keep options open that we don't see the long-term price that we're paying—or that others are paying. When you won't settle for less than a perfect mate, you end up with no one. When parents can never say no to projects at the office, their children suffer at home. When a judge can't bring himself to make a hard decision about parole, he's quite literally closing the door on the prisoner's cell.

Lazy Choices

To compromise is human. In the animal kingdom, you don't see a lot of protracted negotiations between predators and their victims. The ability to compromise is a particularly advanced and difficult form of decision making—and therefore one of the first abilities to decline when our willpower is depleted, particularly when we take our depleted selves shopping.

Shoppers face continual compromises between quality and price, which don't always change in the same proportions at the same time. Often, price goes up much faster than quality. A wine selling for $100 a bottle is usually better than a $20 wine, but is it five times better? Is a $1,000-per-night hotel room five times nicer than a $200-per-night room? There's no objectively correct answer—it all depends on your taste and your budget—but the relative paucity of $100 wines and $1,000 hotel rooms indicates that most people don't find the extra quality worthwhile. Above a certain point, increases in price are not worth the gains in quality. Choosing that point is the optimal decision. But it requires the difficult task of figuring out just where that point is.

When your willpower is low, you're less able to make these trade-offs. You become what researchers call a "cognitive miser," hoarding your energy by avoiding compromises. You're liable to look at only one dimension, like price: *Just give me the cheapest.* Or you indulge yourself by looking at quality: *I want the very best* (an especially easy strategy if someone else is paying).

Decision fatigue leaves us vulnerable to marketers who know how to time their sales, as was demonstrated by Jonathan Levav, the Columbia psychologist, in experiments involving tailored suits and new cars. The idea for these experiments, like Jean Twenge's, also happened to come during the preparations for a wedding. At his fiancée's suggestion, Levav visited a tailor to have a bespoke suit made and began going through the choices of fabric, type of lining, style of buttons, and so forth.

"By the time I got through the third pile of fabric swatches, I wanted to kill myself," Levav recalls. "I couldn't tell the choices apart anymore. After a while my only response to the tailor became: 'What do you recommend?' I just couldn't take it."

Levav ended up not buying any kind of bespoke suit (the two-thousand-dollar price tag eventually made that decision easy), but he put the experience to use in a couple of experiments conducted with Mark Heitmann of Christian-Albrechts University in Germany, Andreas Hermann at the University of St. Gallen in Switzerland, and Sheena Iyengar of Columbia. One involved asking MBA students in Switzerland to choose a bespoke suit; the other was conducted at German car dealerships by discreetly observing customers ordering options for their new sedans. The car buyers—and these were real customers spending their own money—had to choose, for instance, among four styles of gearshift knobs, thirteen kinds of tires and rims, twenty-five configurations of the engine and gearbox, and a palette of fifty-six different colors for the interior of the sedan.

As they started picking features, customers would carefully weigh the choices, but as decision fatigue set in they'd start settling for whatever the default option was. And the more tough choices they encountered early in the process—like going through those fifty-six colors to choose the precise shade of gray or brown for the sedan's interior—

the quicker people got fatigued and settled for the path of least resistance by taking the default option. By manipulating the order of the car buyers' choices, the researchers found that the customers would end up settling for different kinds of options, and the average difference totaled more than fifteen hundred euros per car (about two thousand dollars at the time). Whether the customers paid a little extra for fancy tire rims or a lot extra for a more powerful engine depended on when the choice was offered (early or late) and how much willpower was left in the customer. Similar results were found in the experiment with custom-made suits: Once decision fatigue set in, people tended to settle for the recommended option. When they were confronted early on with the toughest decisions—the ones with the most options, like the one hundred fabrics for the suit—they became fatigued more quickly and also reported enjoying the shopping experience less than if they started off with easier decisions before moving on to the tough ones.

Sometimes shoppers get so tired of making choices that they simply stop buying, but clever marketers can often find ways to exploit decision fatigue, and you don't have to go any farther than your supermarket to see their strategy. After you navigate the aisles and deplete your willpower by choosing among thousands of nutritious foods and practical products, what greets you as you wait in line at the cash register? Gossipy tabloids and chocolate bars. Not for nothing are they called impulse purchases. It's no accident that the candy is presented just at the moment when your impulse control is weakest—and just when your decision-fatigued brain is desperate for a quick hit of glucose.

Choose Your Prize

Suppose, as a reward for finishing this chapter, we offered you a choice of two checks that have been filled out and dated. One is for

$100 and can be cashed tomorrow. The other is for $150 and cannot be cashed until a month from tomorrow. Which would you choose?

To an economist, the now-or-later money question is a classic test of self-control. There are generally no reliable investments (at least not legal ones) that will increase your money by 50 percent in a single month. Unless you have a rare opportunity to double your money in a month, or an immediate financial emergency and no other source of funds, you'd be better off turning down the $100 in quick cash and waiting a month to receive $150. Hence, in general, the right answer to the payment question is to take the larger, later reward. Being able to resist short-term temptations in favor of long-term pay-offs is the secret not just to wealth but to civilization itself. It took singular willpower for the first farmers to go out and plant seeds instead of treating themselves to an immediate meal.

So why do their better-fed descendants grab the $100 now instead of waiting for the $150 in a month, as many people do in experiments? One reason is that it's another example of the irrational short-cuts taken by people whose self-control has been depleted by too many previous decisions or other exertions. A quick dose of glucose can counteract this short-term thinking, as researchers demonstrated by giving people a soft drink just before asking them to make choices between quick-but-small versus larger-but-later rewards.

Another reason for choosing the quick cash emerged in an inge-nious study by Margo Wilson and Martin Daly of McMaster Univer-sity. These evolutionary psychologists began the experiment by asking young men and women to choose between a check dated to-morrow versus a check for a larger amount that could be cashed on a later date. Then, ostensibly as part of an experiment to measure pref-erences, the subjects were asked to rate photographs of people and cars. The photos of people were taken from hotornot.com, the Web site where people submit photos of themselves and are then rated for attractiveness on a 10-point scale. Some of the young men and women saw photos of the opposite sex who had already been rated on the

Web site as very hot (above 9); some of the participants saw not-hot photos (around 5). Other participants rated pictures of cars, with some seeing hot cars and others looking at clunkers.

Then everyone was asked once again to make choices between getting an immediate reward versus a larger reward later, and the researchers compared the answers to see if looking at the photos had changed any of the subjects' preferences for rewards. The car pictures had no effect on the young men and only a slight effect on some of the women: Women who saw the hot cars became a little more likely to opt for the quick reward. One might speculate that seeing the shiny sports car made the young women a bit more eager for instant gratification, but the change was so small that the researchers declined to draw any conclusions from it. The women in the experiment were even less influenced by looking at photos of men. Their decision making didn't change after looking at either the hot men or the not-so-hot men. Nor did the men's decision making change after looking at pictures of not-hot women.

But there was one group that changed dramatically: Men who saw photos of hot women shifted toward getting an immediate reward instead of waiting for a larger payoff in the future. Apparently, the sight of an attractive woman makes men want cash right away. They focus on the present rather than the future. This effect is probably deeply rooted in the psyche and in the evolutionary past. Modern DNA research has revealed that most men in the past did not leave a line of descendants—their odds of reproducing were only half as high as the typical woman's. (For every prolific patriarch like Genghis Khan, there were lots of other men whose genetic lines died out.) Men today are therefore descended from the minority of men who managed to reproduce, and their brains seem primed for a quick response to any opportunity to improve their reproductive odds. Other studies have shown that the sight of an attractive woman (but not an unattractive woman) activates the male brain's nucleus accumbens, which is connected to the part of the brain activated by rewards like cash and sweet-tasting foods. In the past, there might well have been some evolutionary advantage in going for a quick display of resources upon seeing an attractive female; today, it might still be useful on occasions, especially if you think the woman's decision might be affected by your owning a hot car. Clearly that's the strategy of marketers of upscale cars and other goods. Advertising agencies figured out long ago that men are more likely to splurge on a luxury product if it's shown next to a beautiful woman.

But in general, nowadays this sort of short-term thinking is not a great strategy for life—and not even for attracting resource-conscious mates. As Madonna advised in "Material Girl": "Only boys who save their pennies/Make my rainy day." So if you are a male about to make any important financial decisions, focus on numerical figures, not female ones. And if you are an image-conscious executive whose willpower has already been depleted by making decisions all day long, you should definitely not make any plans for the evening—or for anything longer-term—after scanning the photos at the Emperors Club VIP.

5.

WHERE HAVE ALL THE DOLLARS GONE?

The Quantified Self Knows

I have never known a man who was too idle to attend to his affairs & accounts, who did not get into difficulties; & he who habitually is in money difficulties, very rarely keeps scrupulously honourable, & God forbid that this should ever be your fate.

> —Charles Darwin, in a letter to his son accompanying a check to pay off the young man's debts

People just don't want to have to be accountants.

> —Aaron Patzer, founder of Mint.com

Not long ago, a spendthrift sought help for his credit card debt from a team of researchers who called themselves neuroeconomists. They were monitoring the brains of people in the act of shopping—or at least as close to that as you can get inside a functional MRI machine in a lab at Stanford University. The researchers measured activity in the brain's insula region as people contemplated spending money on gadgets, books, and assorted tchotchkes. This brain region ordinarily lights up when you see or hear something distasteful, and that's just what happened when the tightwads in the study saw the prices of the items. But when a typical spendthrift went shopping for the same items, the insula didn't register the same sort of disgust—not even when the brain considered spending a good chunk of hard-earned money on a color-changing "mood clock."

The one bit of hope for fiscal rectitude came in a separate experiment conducted at the request of this one particularly remorseful spendthrift. In the interest of full disclosure, we should note that this spendthrift was Tierney, before Baumeister began teaching him about self-control. Sure enough, the MRI test confirmed his spendthrift tendencies by revealing just how blasé his insula remained as he prepared to spend money for gizmos he didn't need. But then the researchers tried an intervention. They flashed an image of Tierney's most recent Visa bill—and got a reaction! At last, there was some sign of disgust: The researchers reported a "little spot of insula activation" when he contemplated the unpaid balance of $2,178.23. Apparently he wasn't completely brain-dead when it came to money.

That was reassuring, but how could this finding be put to use? How, short of having Stanford researchers follow him through a mall waving his Visa bill, could a spendthrift be forced to contemplate the effects of his spending? The obvious solution was for him to set a budget and monitor his own spending, just as Charles Darwin had advised his spendthrift son. But this was much easier said than done, until Aaron Patzer came along.

Patzer was the kind of son Darwin would have liked—a fastidious bookkeeper who kept his checkbook balanced as a teenager and then went on to spend his Sundays dutifully categorizing all his purchases with Quicken software. But at one point, while working for a software start-up in Silicon Valley, he stopped tracking the spending, and when he sat down to catch up with his finances he faced the prospect of categorizing hundreds of transactions. It occurred to him that there must be a better way to spend his time. Why couldn't a computer do this for him? Why couldn't he outsource this job? Wasn't this the kind of grunt work meant for silicon chips? The result of this was a company, Mint.com, so successful that within two years it was sold for $170 million to Intuit, the maker of Quicken software.

Mint's computers are now tracking the finances of nearly six million people, which makes it one of the largest exercises ever conducted into that second major step in self-control: monitoring behavior. It's also one of the more encouraging developments in the history of artificial intelligence. Like other companies offering to electronically monitor other aspects of your life—how much you weigh, how well you sleep, how much exercise you get—Mint.com is using computers for a profoundly humanistic endeavor. Ever since *Frankenstein,* science fiction writers have fretted about artificial intelligences that become aware of their own powers and turn against their human creators. Political writers worried about the consequences of widespread computer surveillance—Big Brother is watching! But now that computers are getting smarter, now that more and more of them are watching us, they're not becoming self-aware (at least not yet) and they're not seizing power from us. Instead, they're enhancing our powers by making *us* more self-aware.

Self-awareness is a most peculiar trait among animals. Dogs will bark angrily at a mirror because they don't realize they're looking at themselves, and most other animals are similarly clueless when they're subjected to a formal procedure called the mirror test. First the animal is dabbed with a spot of odorless dye, then it's put in front of a mirror to contemplate this strange-colored spot. The test is to see whether the animal touches the spot or indicates in some other way that it realizes the spot is on its own body (such as turning the body to get a better view of the spot). Chimpanzees and the other apes can pass the test, and so can dolphins, elephants, and a few more, but most animals flunk. If they want to touch the spot, they reach for the mirror instead of their own body. Human infants also flunk this test, but by their second birthday most of them can pass it. Even if these two-year-olds didn't notice the spot being applied, as soon as they see the mirror image they reach up to touch their own forehead, often with a startled reaction. And that's just the beginning stage of self-awareness. Before long this trait will turn into the curse of adolescence. Somehow the carefree confidence of childhood is smothered by embarrassment and shame as teenagers become exquisitely sensitive to their own imperfections. They look in the mirror and ask the same question that psychologists have been studying for decades: Why? What's the point of self-awareness if it makes you feel miserable?

I'm Self-aware, Therefore I . . . ?

In the 1970s, social psychologists studying subjects in self-conscious situations began to understand why self-awareness developed in humans. The researchers who pioneered these procedures, Robert Wicklund and Shelley Duval, were initially mocked by colleagues who thought these studies quaint and not necessarily scientific. But the eventual results were too intriguing to ignore. When people were placed in front of a mirror, or told that their actions were being filmed, they consistently changed their behavior. These self-conscious people worked harder at laboratory tasks. They gave more valid answers to questionnaires (meaning that their answers jibed more closely with their actual behavior). They were more consistent in their actions, and their actions were also more consistent with their values.

One pattern in particular stood out. A person might notice a table and think nothing more than, *Oh, there's a table.* But the self was rarely noticed in such a neutral way. Whenever people focused on themselves, they seemed to compare what they saw with some sort of idea of what they should be like. A person who looked in the mirror usually didn't stop at, *Oh, that's me.* Rather, the person was more likely to think, *My hair is a mess,* or *This shirt looks good on me,* or *I should remember to stand up straight,* or, inevitably, *Have I gained weight?* Self-awareness always seemed to involve comparing the self to these ideas of what one might, or should, or could, be.

The two psychologists came up with a word for these ideas: *standards.* Self-awareness involves a process of comparing yourself to standards. Initially the assumption was that the standards were usually ideals—notions of what would constitute perfection. This led to the conclusion that self-awareness would nearly always be unpleasant, because the self is never perfect. Wicklund and Duval maintained that view for several years, arguing that self-awareness is inherently unpleasant. It sounded plausible in some ways—particularly if you were trying to understand teenagers' angst—but it seemed odd from an evolutionary standpoint. Why would our ancestors have kept holding themselves to impossible standards? What was the evolutionary advantage of feeling bad? Moreover, the notion that self-awareness is inherently unpleasant didn't jibe with the enjoyment derived by so many nonadolescents when thinking about themselves or looking in the mirror. Further research showed that people can make themselves feel good by comparing themselves to the "average person"—who we all like to think is inferior to ourselves. We also can often get pleasure by comparing our current selves to our past selves, because we generally think we're improving with age (even if our bodies may be the worse for wear).

Still, even if people mostly compare themselves to easy standards that make them feel good, that doesn't explain the evolution of human self-awareness. Nature doesn't really care whether you feel good. It selects for traits that improve survival and reproduction. What good is self-awareness for that? The best answer came from the psychologists Charles Carver and Michael Scheier, who arrived at a vital insight: *Self-awareness evolved because it helps self-regulation.* They had conducted their own experiments observing people sitting at a desk where there happened to be a mirror. The mirror seemed a minor accessory—not even important enough to mention to the people—yet it caused profound differences in all kinds of behavior. If the people could see themselves in the mirror, they were more likely to follow their own inner values instead of following someone else's orders. When instructed to deliver shocks to another person, the mirror made people more restrained and less aggressive than a control group that wasn't facing a mirror. A mirror prompted them to keep working harder at a task. When someone tried to bully them into changing their opinion about something, they were more likely to resist the bullying and stick to their opinion.

In an experiment one Halloween, some of the trick-or-treaters who visited the home of a psychologist were asked their names, directed to a side room, and told to take one—and only one—piece of candy. The room had a table with several bowls of attractive candies, and the children could easily violate the instructions without any consequences—which many of them did when the mirror in the room was turned backward against the wall. But if the mirror was facing frontward and they could see themselves, they were much more likely to resist the temptation. Even when they were looking at themselves disguised by a Halloween costume, they felt self-conscious enough to do the right thing.

The link between self-awareness and self-control was also demonstrated in experiments involving adults and alcohol. Researchers found that one of the chief effects of drinking was to reduce people's ability to monitor their own behavior. As drinkers' self-awareness declines, they lose self-control, so they get into more fights, smoke more, eat more, make more sexual blunders, and wake up the next day with many more regrets. One of the hardest parts of a hangover is the return of self-awareness, because that's when we resume that crucial task for a social animal: comparing our behavior with the standards set by ourselves and our neighbors.

Keeping track is more than just knowing where things are. It means knowing where things are in relation to where they should be. Our ancestors lived in groups that rewarded members for living up to the common values, norms, and ideals. Therefore, people who could adjust their actions to meet those standards fared better than the ones who were oblivious to their own social faux pas. Changing personal behavior to meet standards requires willpower, but willpower without self-awareness is as useless as a cannon commanded by a blind man. That's why self-awareness evolved as an innate trait among our early ancestors on the savanna—and why it has kept developing recently in more treacherous social environs.

The Quantified Self

Anthony Trollope believed it unnecessary—and inadvisable—to write for more than three hours a day. He became one of the greatest and most prolific novelists in history while holding a full-time job with the British Post Office. He would rise at five-thirty, fortify himself with coffee, and spend a half hour reading the previous day's work to get himself in the right voice. Then he would write for two and a half hours, monitoring the time with a watch placed on the table. He forced himself to produce one page of 250 words every quarter hour. Just to be sure, he counted the words. "I have found that the 250 words have been forthcoming as regularly as my watch went," he reported. At this rate he could produce 2,500 words by breakfast. He didn't expect to do so every single day—sometimes there were business obligations or fox hunts—but he made sure each week to meet a goal. For each of his novels, he would draw up a working schedule, typically planning for 10,000 words a week, and then keep a diary.

"In this I have entered, day by day, the number of pages I have written, so that if at any time I have slipped into idleness for a day or two, the record of that idleness has been there, staring me in the face, and demanding of me increased labour, so that the deficiency might be supplied," he explained. "There has been the record before me, and a week passed with an insufficient number of pages has been a blister to my eye, and a month so disgraced would have been a sorrow to my heart."

A blister to my eye. You won't find anything in the psychological literature summarizing so vividly the impact of monitoring. Trollope was a social scientist ahead of his time. But this revelation about his working technique, which was published posthumously in his autobiography, ruined his literary reputation for a good while. Critics and fellow writers — particularly the ones who couldn't meet deadlines — were appalled at his system. How could an artist work by the clock? How could inspiration be precisely scheduled and monitored? But Trollope had anticipated their criticisms in his autobiography.

"I have been told that such appliances are beneath the notice of a man of genius," he wrote. "I have never fancied myself to be a man of genius, but had I been so I think I might well have subjected myself to these trammels. Nothing surely is so potent as a law that may not be disobeyed. It has the force of the water drop that hollows the stone. A small daily task, if it be really daily, will beat the labours of a spasmodic Hercules." Trollope was an anomaly — few people can turn out 1,000 good words an hour — and he himself could have been benefited from slowing down occasionally (and cutting some of those 250 word digressions). But he managed to produce masterpieces like *Barchester Towers* and *The Way We Live Now* while living a very good life. While other novelists were worrying about money and struggling to turn in chapters overdue at their publishers, Trollope was prospering and remaining ahead of schedule. While one of his novels was being serialized, he usually had at least one other completed novel, often two or three, awaiting publication.

"I have not once, through all my literary career, felt myself even in danger of being late with my task," he wrote. "I have known no anxiety as to 'copy.' The needed pages far ahead — very far ahead — have almost always been in the drawer beside me. And that little diary, with its dates and ruled spaces, its record that must be seen, its daily, weekly demand upon my industry, has done all that for me."

Trollope's watch and diary were state-of-the-art tools for the nineteenth century, and they were effective enough for his purposes. But suppose, instead of putting pen to paper, he had worked on a computer. Suppose that on a typical day he had to use sixteen different programs in addition to his word-processing program, and that over the course of the day he visited forty different Web sites. And suppose that throughout the day he was interrupted every 5.2 minutes by an instant message. How much good would his watch do him? How could his diary keep track of all his work?

He would need a new tool, something like RescueTime, a program that follows customers' every second of computer usage. Users get reports that track exactly how they spent their time—often a depressing discovery. The computer-use statistics provided in the paragraph above were compiled by RescueTime by averaging the behavior of its hundreds of thousands of users. The founder of RescueTime, Tony Wright, was surprised to see that nearly a third of his day was spent on what he calls "the long tail of information porn"—visits to Web sites unrelated to his chief work. The typical visit was only a couple of minutes, but together they consumed two and a half hours a day.

This sort of tracking sounds Orwellian to some people, but it's part of one of the fastest-growing industries in Silicon Valley. The popularity of smartphones and other devices means that people are spending more and more time connected, and increasingly they're using connectivity to track their behavior: what they eat, how far they walk, how long they run, how many calories they burn, how their pulses vary, how efficiently they sleep, how quickly their brains operate, how their moods change, how often they have sex, what affects their spending, how often they call their parents, how long they procrastinate.

In 2008, Kevin Kelly and Gary Wolf created a Web site called Quantified Self, or QS, catering to users of self-regulation technology. The QS movement is still small and heavily geeky, but already it has spread far from Silicon Valley, and devotees in cities around the world are convening—in person—to talk gadgets, share data, and encourage one another.

Esther Dyson, the famously prescient Internet guru and investor, sees the Quantified Self movement as both a smart financial investment and virtuous public policy: a revolutionary new industry that will flourish by selling what's good for you. Instead of paying doctors and hospitals to repair your body, you can monitor yourself to avoid illness. Instead of heeding marketers' offerings of fast foods and instant pleasures, you can set up your life so that you're bombarded with messages promoting health and conscientiousness. "So far, marketers have been really effective at selling goods and other things that undermine our willpower," Dyson says. "We need to apply those techniques to strengthen it."

Dyson has always been disciplined herself—she's been swimming an hour every day for decades—but she finds it even easier now that she's monitoring herself with new electronic sensors like the Fitbit clip, the BodyMedia armband, and the Zeo "sleep coach" headband. By measuring her movements, her skin temperature and moisture, and her brain waves, these sensors tell her exactly how much energy she expends during the day and how many hours of good sleep she gets at night.

"Self-quantification changes my behavior on the margins," she says. "I walk up more stairs and take fewer escalators because I know I get more points for the extra steps. If I'm at a party in the evening, I'll tell myself that if I leave now, I could go to bed at nine-thirty instead of ten-thirty, and I'd get more sleep, and my sleep number would look better in the morning. In many ways, it frees me to do the right thing because I can blame my behavior on the numbers."

Thanks to companies like Mint.com, it's easier than ever for people to follow Charles Darwin's advice about tracking finances, but these new tools are doing more than just the grunt work of monitoring behavior. Keeping track is the first step, but it's not necessarily enough. Thomas Jefferson was astonishingly compulsive about noting every penny he earned and spent—even on July 4, 1776, when his revolutionary declaration of human rights was being finalized and adopted, he made sure to record in his memorandum book what he spent for a thermometer and some gloves. As president, he tracked the White House's bills for butter and eggs at the same time that he was making the Louisiana Purchase. Yet he didn't put the details in perspective until it was too late. When he eventually stepped back to balance his assets and liabilities, he was shocked to discover that he was disastrously in debt. Recording the data had given him a false sense of being in control of his finances, but it wasn't enough. He needed the sort of analysis offered by Mint's computers.

Once you let Mint look at your banking and credit card transactions, it categorizes them to show where your money is going—and whether you're spending more than you make. Mint can't force you to change your habits (the computers can only read your records, not touch your money), but it can make you think twice. It can e-mail a weekly financial summary and send a text message when your account balance is low. It will nudge you with an e-mail reporting "Unusual Spending on Restaurants" and alert you when you exceed your budget for clothing or groceries. Besides generating some guilty sensations in the spendthrift brain, Mint offers rewards for virtue. You can establish a variety of short-term and long-term goals—taking a vacation, buying a home, saving up for retirement—and then get progress reports.

"Mint will help you set a goal and a timetable and then watch your spending," Patzer says. "It'll say, If you cut back one hundred dollars a month on restaurants, you can retire 1.3 years sooner or buy your BMW twelve days sooner. You don't think about these goals on a day-to-day basis. You want that iPad. You want that coffee. You want to go out with your friends. This quantifies how your short-term behavior affects the long-term goals so you have a chance of actually budgeting in a way that makes a difference."

No one knows exactly how well this works yet, because Mint is a commercial operation, not a controlled experiment. But there are already some encouraging signs, as we found when we asked the Mint research staff to look for broad trends in people's spending habits before and after they joined Mint. It wasn't easy to isolate Mint's effects against the larger background trend taking place between 2008 and 2010: a general increase in spending by everyone as the economy slowly improved after the panic of 2008. Still, the data—culled from two billion transactions of three billion anonymous users—showed some clear benefits of monitoring. For the great majority (80 percent) of people, the upward trajectory of their spending was tempered after they joined Mint and began monitoring their transactions. And most people's spending was further tempered if they used the information to set up budgets and goals on Mint. The biggest effects were observed in people's spending on groceries, restaurants, and credit card finance charges—some very sensible categories for cutting back.

Some people are so horrified to see their spending totals that they vow to take drastic actions right away, but Mint's founder advises a gradual approach. "If you cut too hard and too fast, you'll never stick with it and you'll hate yourself," Patzer says. "If you're spending $500 a month on restaurants and you try to set a new budget of $200, you'll end up saying, *'Forget that!'* It's too hard. But if you reduce to $450 or $400, you can make that without radically changing your lifestyle. Then the next month you can go another $50 or $100. Keep the monthly changes to 20 percent until you get things under control."

Not-So-Invidious Comparisons

Once you've taken the first two steps in self-control—setting a goal and monitoring your behavior—you're confronted with a perennial question: Should you focus on how far you've come or how much remains to be done? There's no simple, universal answer, but it does make a difference, as demonstrated in experiments by Ayelet Fishbach of the University of Chicago. She and a Korean colleague, Minjung Koo, asked employees at a Korean advertising agency to describe their current role at the agency and their current projects. Then, by random assignment, half were told to reflect on what they had achieved thus far in their current role, dating back to when they had joined the agency. The rest were instructed to reflect on what they planned to achieve but had not yet accomplished. The ones who wrote about what they had already achieved had higher satisfaction with their current tasks and projects, as compared with the ones who reflected on what they had not yet achieved. But the latter were more motivated to reach their goals and then move on to more challenging new projects. Those who focused on what they had already done did not seem eager to move on to more difficult and challenging tasks. They were reasonably content with where they were and what they were currently doing. For contentment, apparently, it pays to look at how far you've come. To stoke motivation and ambition, focus instead on the road ahead.

Either way, you can gain additional benefits by comparing yourself with others, and that's never been easier to do, thanks to the abundance of networked data. Mint will tell you how your rent and restaurant bills and clothing purchases compare with your neighbors' or with the national average. RescueTime will tell give you a percentile ranking of your productivity—or your aimless Web surfing—in relation to the average user. Flotrack and Nikeplus and other sites let runners share their mileage and times with friends and teammates.

You can get gadgets and smartphone apps to compare your energy usage with your neighbors'—and the comparisons make a difference, as demonstrated in a study of utility customers in California. When people got bills comparing their monthly electricity usage with the neighborhood average, the people in the above-average homes promptly cut back on their use of electricity.

These sorts of comparisons become even more powerful when you start openly sharing your data with others. As we researched this book, we heard plenty of stories about people who benefited from monitoring themselves, like using pedometers to keep track of their daily steps. But the most enthusiastic walkers were the ones who shared each day's tally with a few friends. They were applying a sound psychological principle that was demonstrated in some of Baumeister's earliest experiments, long before he got involved in studying self-control: *Public information has more impact than private information.* People care more about what other people know about them than about what they know about themselves. A failure, a slipup, a lapse in self-control can be swept under the carpet pretty easily if you're the only one who knows about it. You can rationalize it or just plain ignore it. But if other people know about it, it's harder to dismiss. After all, the other person might not buy the excuses that you make, even though you find them quite satisfying. And you'll have even more trouble selling that excuse when you expand from one person to a whole social network.

By going public, you're not just exposing yourself to potential shame. You're also outsourcing the job of monitoring, which can ease the burden on yourself. An outsider can often encourage you by pointing out signs of progress that you've taken for granted. And when things are going badly, sometimes the best solution is to look elsewhere for help. One popular QS application, Moodscope, was developed by an entrepreneur battling depression who wanted help monitoring his condition. He devised an application that lets him take a quick daily test to gauge his mood. Besides using it to record his own emotional ups and down so that he can look for patterns and causes, he created an option for the results to be automatically e-mailed to his friends. That way, when his mood darkens, his friends see the data and get in touch with him.

"The digital tools and the data are just catalysts for people to motivate themselves and one another," Dyson says. "You find the model that works best for you. Maybe you compare numbers with your friends because you don't want to be ashamed in front of them. Or you don't want to let down the team. Different people are motivated in different ways."

If you're a spendthrift, you can try to control yourself by letting a tightwad friend be alerted when you start a spending binge. And if you both study your patterns of spending, you can start to understand what causes the binges. Do you make impulsive purchases when you're in a good mood and your willpower is low? Or are you one of the compulsive shoppers who buy when they're feeling depressed or insecure. If so, you're suffering from what psychologists call misregulation, the mistaken belief that buying something will regulate your mood for the better, when in fact you'll just feel worse afterward.

Even if you're not a spendthrift, you could still benefit from tracking your spending and comparing it with what your neighbors are doing. You might discover that you're an extreme tightwad—not the worst problem to have, but still a problem, and one that's surprisingly common. Behavioral economists have found that neurotic penny-pinching may be even more prevalent than neurotic overspending, affecting some one in five people. Brain scans have similarly pinpointed the culprit: an insula that reacts with hyperactive horror at the prospect of parting with cash.

The result is a condition that researchers call hyperopia (the opposite of myopia), in which you focus too much on the future at the expense of the present. Such penny-pinching can waste time, alienate friends, drive your family crazy, and make you miserable. The studies show that tightwads aren't any happier than spendthrifts, and that they suffer a case of saver's remorse when they look back on all the opportunities they passed up. When the time comes for the final monitoring, when you're adding up not just your assets but your life, you don't want to rediscover that old proverb about there being no pockets in shrouds. The Quantified Self consists of much more than dollars.

6.

CAN WILLPOWER BE
STRENGTHENED?

(Preferably Without Feeling
David Blaine's Pain)

The more the body suffers, the more the spirit flowers.

—David Blaine's philosophy, borrowed from St. Simeon
Stylites, a fifth-century ascetic who lived for decades
atop a pillar in the Syrian desert

We wish to consider a scientific explanation for David Blaine.
We don't mean an explanation for *why* Blaine does what
he does. That's impossible, at least for psychologists, and probably
for psychiatrists, too. When he is not doing his famous magic tricks,
Blaine works as a self-described endurance artist, performing feats involving willpower instead of illusion. He stood for thirty-five hours
more than eighty feet above New York's Bryant Park, without a
safety harness, atop a round pillar just twenty-two inches wide. He
spent sixty-three sleepless hours in Times Square encased in a giant

block of ice. He was entombed in a coffin with six inches of head-room for a week, during which he consumed nothing except water. He later went on to conduct another water-only fast, whose results were published in the *New England Journal of Medicine:* a loss of fifty-four pounds in forty-four days. He spent those forty-four days without food suspended above the Thames River in a sealed transparent box, inside which the temperatures ranged from subfreezing to 114 degrees Fahrenheit.

"Breaking the comfort zone seems to be the place where I always grow," says Blaine, echoing St. Simeon's notion that suffering makes the spirit flower. We won't attempt to analyze that rationale. The *why* is beyond our ken.

We're interested in the *how* of Blaine's feats. How he endures is a mystery that matters to people who aren't endurance artists. Whatever one thinks of his ordeals (or his psyche), it would be useful to figure out what keeps him going. If we could isolate his secret for fasting forty-four days, maybe the rest of us could use it to last until dinner. If we knew how he endured a week of being buried alive, we might learn how to sit through a two-hour budget meeting. Exactly what does he do to build and sustain his willpower? How, for instance, did Blaine not immediately give up when everything went wrong during his attempt to break the world record for breath holding? He'd spent more than a year preparing for this feat by learning to fill his lungs with pure oxygen and then remain immobile under water, conserving oxygen by expending as little energy as possible. Blaine could relax so completely, both mentally and physically, that his heart rate would drop to below fifty beats per minute, sometimes below twenty. During a practice session at a swimming pool at Grand Cayman Island, his pulse dropped by 50 percent as soon as he began the breath-hold, and he kept his head under water for sixteen minutes with little apparent stress. He emerged just shy of the world record of 16:32, looking serene and reporting that he hadn't felt any pain, and had barely been aware of his body or surroundings.

But several weeks later, when he went on *Oprah* to try to break the world record in front of judges from Guinness, there were a couple of complications in addition to the pressure of performing for a television audience. Instead of floating facedown in a pool, he had to face the studio audience from the inside of a giant glass sphere. To remain vertical and not float to the surface, he had to keep his feet wedged into straps at the bottom of the sphere. As he filled his lungs with oxygen, he worried that the muscular effort to keep his feet in place would eat up too much oxygen. His pulse was higher than usual, and when he started holding his breath, it stayed above 100 instead of plummeting. To make matters worse, he could hear his racing pulse on a heart-rate monitor that had inadvertently been placed too close to the sphere, continually distracting—and distressing—him with its rapid *beep-beep-beep.* By the second minute, his pulse was 130 and he realized he wasn't going to be able to control it. It remained above 100 as the minutes ticked by and his body used up its oxygen. Instead of being lost in a state of meditative bliss, he was acutely aware of his racing pulse and the excruciating buildup of carbon dioxide inside his body.

By the eighth minute, he was barely halfway to the record and convinced he wouldn't make it. By the tenth minute, his fingers were tingling as his body shunted blood from the extremities to preserve vital organs. By the twelfth minute, his legs were throbbing and his ears were ringing. By the thirteenth minute, he feared that the numbness in his arm and the pain in his chest were precursors to a heart attack. A minute later he felt contractions in his chest and was nearly overwhelmed with the impulse to breathe. By the fifteenth minute his heart was skipping beats and his pulse was erratic, jumping to 150, down to 40, back over 100. Now convinced that a heart attack was coming, he released his feet from the straps so that the emergency team could pull him out of the sphere when he blacked out. He floated upward, forcing himself to remain just below the surface, still expecting to black out any second, when he heard the audience cheer and realized that he'd broken the old record of 16:32. He looked at the clock and held on until the next minute, emerging from the water with a new Guinness record of 17:04.

"This was a whole other level of pain," he said shortly afterward. "I still feel as if somebody hit me in the stomach with the hardest punch they could."

So how did he will his way through it?

"That's where the training comes in," he said. "It gives you the confidence to pull through a situation that isn't so easy."

By training, he didn't mean simply his recent exercises in breath holding, although there had been plenty of them during the previous year. Each morning he'd do a series of ordinary breath-holds (starting with regular air instead of pure oxygen) separated by short intervals, gradually increasing the duration and the pain. Over the course of an hour, he'd end up holding his breath for forty-eight minutes, and then he'd have a pounding headache for the rest of the day. Those daily breathing drills got his body used to the pain of carbon dioxide buildup. But just as important were the other kinds of exercises he'd been conducting for more than three decades, since the age of five. He had long been a believer in the notion that willpower is a muscle that can be strengthened. He picked up this idea partly through reading about the Victorian training of his childhood hero, Houdini, and partly by trial and error.

Growing up in Brooklyn, Blaine forced himself to practice card tricks hour after hour, day after day. He learned to win swimming races by not coming up for air the entire length of the pool—and then, with practice, eventually won five hundred dollars in bets by swimming five lengths under water. In the winter, he eschewed a coat, wearing only a T-shirt even when walking for miles on bitterly cold days. He regularly took cold baths and conducted the occasional barefoot run in the snow. He slept on the wooden floor of his bedroom, and once spent two straight days in a closet (his tolerant mother brought him food). He got in the habit of continually setting goals that had to be met, like running so far every day, or jumping to grab a leaf from the branch of a certain tree every time he walked under it. At age eleven, after reading about fasting in the novel *Siddhartha* by Hermann Hesse, he tried it himself and soon got up to four days on just water. By age eighteen he managed a ten-day fast with just water and wine. Once he became a professional endurance artist, he reverted to the same techniques before a stunt, including little rituals that had nothing directly to do with the stunt.

"Some sort of OCD [obsessive-compulsive disorder] kicks in whenever I'm about to do a long-term challenge," he told us. "I make tons of weird goals for myself. Like, when I'm jogging in the park in the bike lane, whenever I go over a drawing of a biker, I have to step on it. And not just step on it—I have to hit the head of the biker perfectly with my foot, so that it fits right under my sneaker. Little things like that annoy anyone running with me, but I believe if I don't do them, I won't succeed."

But why believe that? Why would stepping on the drawing of a biker help you hold your breath longer?

"Getting your brain wired into little goals and achieving them, that helps you achieve the bigger things you shouldn't be able to do," he said. "It's not just practicing the specific thing. It's always making things more difficult than they should be, and never falling short, so that you have that extra reserve, that tank, so you know you can always go further than your goal. For me that's what discipline is. It's repetition and practice."

These exercises certainly appear to work for Blaine, but his endurance feats hardly constitute scientific evidence—or a model for anyone else. David Blaine is about as far as you can get from a random sample. A child who voluntarily takes cold baths and goes on four-day fasts is not representative of any known population. Maybe Blaine's feats are mainly due not to his training but to the willpower that he was born with. Perhaps all the training was simply evidence of how unusually disciplined he always was. He, like the Victorians, thought that training strengthened his willpower like a muscle, but maybe he just happened to start off with a very strong muscle. To see if these training techniques really worked, or could make a difference for anyone else, you would need to test them with people who were not endurance artists—the sort of people who would never regard a saint living on a pillar as a role model.

Willpower Workouts

To social scientists, the idea of strengthening willpower didn't seem very promising at first glance. After all, the ego-depletion experiments in Baumeister's lab showed that exertions of willpower left people with less self control. Choosing radishes over chocolate chip cookies caused an immediate depletion of willpower, and there was no reason to assume the same sort of exercise could eventually lead to more strength in the long term.

Still, if there was any possibility of strengthening willpower, the payoff could be enormous. Once the first ego-depletion research findings were published, the research group huddled to discuss ways of increasing willpower. Mark Muraven, the graduate student who had designed and carried out the first experiments to show ego depletion, discussed strength-building exercises with his advisers, Baumeister and Dianne Tice. Because no one had any idea what might work, they decided on a scattershot approach. They would assign different participants different exercises, and see if any new strength developed. One obvious problem was that some people would start out with more self-control than others, just as some athletes would start out with bigger muscles and more stamina. To control for that, the researchers would have to do the equivalent of measuring individual changes in muscle power and stamina. They would first bring college students into the lab for an initial baseline test of self-control, followed by a quick depleting task to see how much it declined. Then everyone would be sent home to perform some kind of exercise on their own for a couple of weeks, followed by another round of tests in the lab. Different exercises were chosen to test various notions of what was involved in "character building"—or, more precisely, which mental resources had to be fortified. Did acts of self-control deplete you because of the energy needed to override one response in favor of another? Or was it the energy required to monitor your behavior? Or the energy to alter your state of mind?

One group of students was sent home with instructions to work on their posture for the next two weeks. Whenever they thought of it, they were to try to stand up straight or sit up straight. Since most of these (or any) college students were used to casually slouching, the exercises would force them to expend energy overriding their habitual response. A second group was used to test the notion that willpower was exhausting because of the energy required for self-monitoring. These students were told to record whatever they ate for the next two weeks. They didn't have to make any changes to their diet, though it was possible that some of them might have been shamed into a few adjustments. (*Hmm. Monday, pizza and beer. Tuesday, pizza and wine. Wednesday, hot dogs and Coke. Maybe it would look better if I ate a salad or an apple now and then.*) A third group was used to check the effects of altering one's state of mind. They were instructed to strive for positive moods and emotions during the two weeks. Whenever they found themselves feeling bad, these students should strive to cheer themselves up. Sensing a potential winner, the researchers elected to make this group twice as large as the other groups, so as to get the most statistically reliable results.

But the researchers' hunch was dead wrong. Their favorite strategy turned out to do no good at all. The large group that practiced controlling emotions for two weeks showed no improvement when the students returned to the lab and repeated the self-control tests. In retrospect, this failure seems less surprising than it did back then. Emotion regulation does not rely on willpower. People cannot simply will themselves to be in love, or to feel intense joy, or to stop feeling guilty. Emotional control typically relies on various subtle tricks, such as changing how one thinks about the problem at hand, or distracting oneself. Hence, practicing emotional control does not strengthen your willpower.

But other exercises do help, as demonstrated by the groups in the experiment that worked on their posture and recorded everything they ate. When they returned to the lab after two weeks, their scores on the self-control tests went up, and the improvement was significantly higher by comparison with a control group (which did no exercises of any kind during the two weeks). This was a striking result, and with careful analyses of the data, the conclusions became clearer and stronger. Unexpectedly, the best results came from the group working on posture. That tiresome old advice—"Sit up straight!"—was more useful than anyone had imagined. By overriding their habit of slouching, the students strengthened their willpower and did better at tasks that had nothing to do with posture. The improvement was most pronounced among the students who had followed the advice most diligently (as measured by the daily logs the students kept of how often they'd forced themselves to sit up or stand up straight).

The experiment also revealed an important distinction in self-control between two kinds of strength: power and stamina. At the first lab session, participants began by squeezing a spring-loaded handgrip for as long as they could (which had been shown in other experiments to be a good measure of willpower, not just physical strength). Then, after expending mental energy through the classic try-not-to-think-of-a-white-bear task, they did a second handgrip task to assess how they fared when willpower was depleted. Two weeks later, when they returned to the lab after working on their posture, their scores on the initial handgrip tests didn't show much improvement, meaning that the willpower muscle hadn't gotten more powerful. But they had much more stamina, as evidenced by their improved performance on the subsequent handgrip test administered after the researchers tried to fatigue them. Thanks to the students' posture exercises, their willpower didn't get depleted as quickly as before, so they had more stamina for other tasks.

You could try the two-week posture experiment to improve your own willpower, or you could try other exercises. There's nothing magical about sitting up straight, as researchers subsequently discovered when they tested other regimens and found similar benefits. You can pick and choose from the techniques they studied, or extrapolate to create your own system. The key is to concentrate on changing a habitual behavior.

One simple way to start is by using a different hand for routine tasks. Many habits are linked to your dominant hand. Right-handed people, in particular, tend to use their right hands for all sorts of things without giving the matter the slightest thought. Making yourself switch to your left hand is thus an exercise in self-control. You can resolve to use your left hand instead of your habitual right hand for brushing your teeth, using a computer mouse, opening doors, or lifting a cup to your lips. If it seems too onerous to do this all day, try it for a set period. Some research studies have assigned people to switch hands between eight A.M. and eight P.M. This lets people revert to their familiar habits in the evening, when they are already physically tired and mentally depleted from the day's activities. (Note to lefties: This strategy may not be as effective for you, because many left-handed people are actually fairly ambidextrous and have had more practice using their right hands in a world oriented for right-handed people. So using your right hand may not do as much for your willpower: No strain, no gain.)

Another training strategy is to change your speech habits, which are also deeply ingrained and therefore require effort to modify. You could, for instance, try speaking only in complete sentences. Break the adolescent habit of peppering your discourse with "like" and "you know" constantly. Avoid abbreviations, so that you always call everything by its full name. Say "yes" and "no" instead of "yeah" or "yup," "nah" or "nope." You could also try avoiding those tradition- ally taboo words: curses. Today this taboo strikes many people as outdated, maybe even nonsensical: Why should society produce a set of words that everybody knows but nobody is allowed to say out loud? But the value of having forbidden words may lie precisely in the exercise of resisting the impulse to say them.

Any of these techniques should improve your willpower and could be a good warm-up for tackling a bigger challenge, like quitting smoking or sticking to a budget. But you may find it tough to keep up these techniques for very long. Sticking to arcane exercises that don't offer an obvious reward can be a daunting challenge, as re- searchers discovered when they followed up on the first willpower- strengthening experiments. The initial results caused great excitement among psychologists, because self-control was one of only two traits known to produce a wide spectrum of benefits, and the other trait, intelligence, had turned out to be quite difficult to improve. Pro- grams like Head Start boosted intellectual performance while the students were enrolled, but the gains seemed to fade pretty quickly once they left. By and large, there didn't seem to be much you could do to increase the intelligence you were born with. That made self- control seem especially precious, and social scientists set out testing systematic programs for improving it. The result, over the course of a decade, was a mix of successes and flops as researchers discovered the difficulty in getting people to do the assigned exercises. It wasn't enough to find a workout that could theoretically build willpower. It had to be a workout that worked.

From Strength to More Strength

Some of the most successful strategies were developed by two Aus- tralian psychologists, Meg Oaten and Ken Cheng. They generally recruited people who wanted to improve one specific aspect of their lives and could be given direct help in that area. Half got the help immediately, and the others served as a control group and received the help later. This procedure, called the waiting-list control group, was a good way of making sure that the test group and the control group had similar goals and desires. Everyone was offered the same service, but some waited for it, and during that time they took the same tests and measures as the ones who were given exercises to strengthen their willpower. And those exercises were directly related to the people's goals, so that they would be encouraged by seeing the benefits of complying.

One of the experiments involved people who all wanted to improve their physical fitness but hadn't been regular exercisers. Some immediately received a membership in a gym and met with one of the experimenters to form a plan for regular workouts. They kept a log in which they recorded every workout and exercise session. Another experiment involved students who wanted to improve their study habits. The ones who got the immediate help met with an experimenter to set long-term goals and assignments, and to break down the tasks into smaller steps. Their study plan was coordinated with other obligations (like a side job), and the students kept a study log and diary to monitor progress. Yet another experiment gave people a chance to improve their money management by meeting with an experimenter to draw up a budget and plan ways to save more money. Besides keeping track of how much they spent and earned, they also kept a log recording their feelings and their struggles not to spend money—how they forced themselves to stay home to avoid the temptations in store windows, or sacrificed vacations to save money, or postponed purchases they would ordinarily have made.

In all the experiments, participants came to the lab from time to time for an exercise that seemed irrelevant to their self-improvement programs. The experimental subjects had to watch a computer screen with six black squares. Three of the squares would flash briefly, and then all the squares would start sliding around the screen, randomly switching positions. After five seconds, each participant had to use a computer mouse to indicate which of the squares were the ones that had flashed initially. Thus, to do well, you had to make a mental note of which squares to watch and then follow them as they moved around. What made it extra hard was that during this exercise, a nearby television was showing Eddie Murphy doing a stand-up comedy routine in front of an audience that was howling at his material. If you turned to watch him or even just focused too much on his jokes, you'd lose track of the squares. To score well, you had to ignore the jokes and the laughter, focusing instead on the boring squares, a feat that definitely required self-control. The research participants took this test twice at each session. The first time was soon after they arrived at the lab and were fresh. The second came a bit later, after their willpower had been depleted.

The pattern of results was largely the same in all these experiments. As the weeks went by, the people who regularly exercised self-control in doing physical workouts, studying, or money management got progressively better at ignoring Eddie Murphy's comedy routine and tracking the moving squares. In particular, the main improvements were found in resisting the effects of depletion (that is, on the last self-control test administered at each lab session). Thus, exercise increased people's stamina, allowing them to hold out against temptations even when their mental resources had been depleted.

Not surprisingly, they also advanced toward their goals. Those in the fitness program got fitter; those working on study discipline got more schoolwork done; the people in the money-management program saved more money. But—and here was a truly pleasant surprise—they also got better at other things. The students who did the study-discipline program reported doing physical workouts a bit more often and cutting down on impulsive spending. Those in the fitness and money-management programs said they studied more diligently.

Exercising self-control in one area seemed to improve all areas of life. They smoked fewer cigarettes and drank less alcohol. They kept their homes cleaner. They washed dishes instead of leaving them stacked in the sink, and did their laundry more often. They procrastinated less. They did their work and chores instead of watching television or hanging out with friends first. They ate less junk food, replacing their bad eating habits with healthier ones. You might think that people who start doing physical workouts would naturally start eating better, but in fact the reverse has often been observed in other studies: Once you start exercising, you feel virtuous and therefore entitled to reward yourself with high-calorie treats. (That's an example of the "licensing effect," when you act as if one good deed gives you license to sin.) But in this experiment, the group of exercisers didn't yield to that temptation. Nor did the group of budget-conscious people yield to the predictable temptation to cut down on their grocery bills by passing up the more expensive fresh foods and other healthy fare in favor of cheaper food. If anything, they began spending *more* money on healthy food, apparently because of an overall increase in self-control.

Some of the people even reported improvements in controlling their tempers, an intriguing finding that was tested in a subsequent study of domestic violence by Oaten together with Eli Finkel of Northwestern University and other psychologists. The researchers asked people about their likelihood to become physically aggressive toward their relationship partners, such as slapping or punching them or attacking them with a weapon, in various situations, such as being "disrespected" by the partner or walking in on the partner having sex with someone else. Then the researchers had the participants in the study perform willpower exercises for two weeks, except for a control group. After the two weeks, the ones who did the exercises reported fewer tendencies to behave violently when provoked by a loved one, both in comparison with their own pre-exercise baseline and in comparison with the controls who did not exercise. (For ethical and practical reasons, researchers have to be content with having people report their inclinations to behave violently, as opposed to trying to measure how often people actually hit, assault, or otherwise harm their loved ones.) Improved self-control predicted less domestic violence.

All in all, these findings point toward the remarkable benefits of exercising willpower. Without realizing it, people gained a wide array of benefits in areas of their lives that had nothing to do with the specific exercises they were performing. And the lab tests provided an explanation: Their willpower gradually got stronger, so it was less readily depleted. Focusing on one specific form of self-control could yield much larger benefits, just as self-experimenters from Ben Franklin to David Blaine had maintained. The experiments showed that you didn't have to start off with the exceptional self-control of a Franklin or a Blaine to benefit: As long as you were motivated to do some kind of exercise, your overall willpower could improve, at least over the course of the experiment.

But what about afterward? As remarkable as the results were, the experiments had lasted only a few weeks or months. How hard would it be to keep up the self-discipline indefinitely?

Here, once again, the case of David Blaine is instructive.

The Toughest Stunt of All

Before we told David Blaine about the scientific research into willpower, we asked him which of his feats had been the most difficult. This was not a simple choice for him, understandably. So many ordeals, so many varieties of agony. The seventeen-minute breath-hold on *Oprah* was awful but brief. For sustained terror, there was the last part of his thirty-five-hour stint standing on the pillar, when he was fighting hallucinations and the urge to nod off (and fall eight stories to his death). For prolonged pain, there were the forty-four days without food in the Plexiglas box above the Thames. Not only did he have to watch people below eating merrily away, but he also had to look at a giant advertisement for batteries with the slogan "When Willpower Isn't Enough." He tried to appreciate the humor of the ad, but that got progressively difficult. "By the thirty-eighth day, my mouth was tasting like sulfur because my body was eating its own organs," he recalled. "I ached all over. When your body starts eating its muscles, it feels like a knife being stabbed into your arm."

But the toughest of his stunts, Blaine told us, was the sixty-three hours encased in ice. When they sealed him in six tons of glacial ice in Times Square, the ice was barely half an inch from his face. He was overcome with an uncharacteristic surge of claustrophobia, and he started shivering from the cold immediately. The ice kept him miserably cold for the next three days even though the outside weather turned unseasonably warm, which created a new problem: melting ice that caused a steady Chinese-water-torture drip of glacial water onto the exposed skin of his neck and back. Meanwhile, he couldn't nod off because leaning against the ice would cause frostbite, and the sleep deprivation became the biggest problem on the last day, when he was supposed to wait to be freed on a prime-time network television special.

"I started to feel I wasn't right," Blaine said. "I've been through organ failure, but there's nothing worse than mental illness. I looked through the ice at a guy standing in front of me and asked him what time it was. He says, 'Two o'clock.' I say to myself, *Oh, man, I'm not done with this until ten P.M. That's eight more hours!* I tell myself it won't be so bad once there's only six hours left, so I just have to get through the next two hours. That's the kind of time-shift technique I use to change perspective so I get through these stunts. I waited for at least two hours, just patiently waited, and it was difficult. I was hearing voices. I was seeing people's bodies carved into the ice. And I don't realize that these are all hallucinations from sleep deprivation. You don't know what's going on—you think it's real because you're awake. So I waited two hours, and I looked at a guy through the ice and asked, 'What time is it?'"

Gazing through the ice, Blaine still had enough mental resources to realize that this guy looked much like the guy at two o'clock. Then he discovered that it *was* the same guy.

"He goes, 'Two-oh-five,'" Blaine recalled. "That's when things got really bad."

Somehow he stayed in the ice until the prime-time removal, but he was so dazed, incoherent, and weak that he had to be rushed off immediately in an ambulance. "At the end I started to think I was in purgatory. I genuinely believed that I was being judged, and that this was a place I was waiting to go to heaven or hell. Those last eight hours were the worst state I've ever been in. To go through something that horrific and not quit—that took something that was beyond me."

Yes, that did indeed sound like the toughest feat of them all. But then something else occurred to Blaine once he heard about the experiments by Baumeister and other scientists. After learning of the wide-ranging benefits of the willpower-strengthening exercises, Blaine nodded and said, "That makes perfect sense. You're building discipline. Now that I think about it, when I'm training for a stunt and I have a goal, I change everything. I have self-control in every aspect of my life. I read all the time. I eat perfectly. I do good things—I visit kids in hospitals and do as much of that as I can. I have a whole different energy. Complete self-control. I eat food based on nutrition. I don't overindulge. I don't drink. I don't waste time, basically. But as soon as I'm done with that, I go to the opposite extreme, where I have no self-control, and it seems to spread through everything. It seems like when I stop eating right, then I'm not able to sit down and read for the same amount of time. I can't focus the same way. I don't use my time the same way. I waste a lot of time. I'll drink. I'll do silly things. After a stunt I'll go from 180 pounds to 230 pounds in three months."

At this point, as he chatted in his apartment in Greenwich Village, Blaine was in his between-stunts mode. He'd completed a brief stunt—brief for him, anyway—that involved a few days of hanging out with sharks, completely unprotected in the open ocean, for four hours a day, and he was starting to work on plans for drifting across the Atlantic Ocean in a glass bottle, but that project was still indefinite. So he'd been relaxing and putting on pounds. "You're catching me at a time when I'm the opposite of disciplined," he said. "I'll eat perfectly for five days and then eat horrifically for ten days. I'll eat perfectly for ten days and then eat like a maniac for twenty. And then, when I'm ready to train again, when I get really serious, I'll drop about three pounds a week, and that stays consistent, so I'll drop twelve pounds a month. So in five months, I'm completely transformed and my discipline levels are really high. It's amazing. I have self-discipline in work, but I have none in my life sometimes."

Hanging out with sharks, holding his breath for seventeen minutes, freezing for sixty-three hours and ending up in purgatory—all that he could handle, but the mundane daily stuff could still frustrate him. His ordeal in the ice set a world endurance record, but the feat didn't make it into the Guinness book because he never got around to filling out the paperwork. He had the papers, but he kept procrastinating. He had fasted for forty-four hours in London, but nowadays he didn't have the willpower to avoid the food in his refrigerator. One reason, of course, was the ready availability. "I don't think I could have succeeded on a forty-four-day-straight fast if I was in this apartment," he said. "At the box in London, there was no way for me to be tempted because I was in that space. Which was part of my reason to make it public, because I knew that I would have to do it." But even if he couldn't do a seven-week fast at home, why couldn't he simply cut back a little on the daily meals? Why did keeping up a modicum of discipline—in eating and reading and working efficiently—seem so difficult at the moment?

Because he didn't have the motivation. He had nothing to prove to the public or to himself. He and everyone else knew that he could control himself when he wanted to, and nobody was going to fault him for giving himself a break between stunts. For all his amazing willpower, he faced the same problem as the rest of us when dealing with the biggest self-control challenge of all: maintaining the discipline not just for days or weeks but for years and years. For that you need techniques from a different kind of endurance artist.

7.

OUTSMARTING YOURSELF IN THE HEART OF DARKNESS

Self-control is more indispensable than gunpowder.

—Henry Morton Stanley

In 1887, Henry Morton Stanley went up the Congo River and inadvertently started a disastrous experiment. This was long after his first journey deep into Africa, as a journalist in 1871, when he'd become famous by finding a Scottish missionary and reporting the first words of their encounter: "Dr. Livingstone, I presume." Now, at age forty-six, Stanley was a veteran explorer leading his third African expedition. As he headed into an uncharted expanse of rain forest, he left part of the expedition behind in a riverside camp to await further supplies. The leaders of this Rear Column, who came from some of the most prominent families in Britain, proceeded to become an international disgrace.

Those men, along with a British soldier and doctor who were left in charge of a fort along the route, lost control once Stanley was no longer there to command them. They refused medical treatment to sick natives and allowed Africans under their command to perish needlessly from disease and poisonous food. They kidnapped and bought young African women to keep as sex slaves. When one of the very young concubines cried to be returned to her mother and father, she was ignored; when another escaped, she was retrieved and trussed to prevent another escape. The British commander of the fort savagely beat and maimed Africans, sometimes stabbing them with a sharp steel cane, sometimes ordering men to be shot or flogged almost to death for trivial offenses. Most of his officers raised no objection. When some Pygmies living near the British fort—a mother and several children—were caught stealing food, parts of their ears were cut off. Other thieves were shot and decapitated so that their skulls could be displayed as warnings outside the fort. One of the officers in the Rear Column, a naturalist who was an heir to the Jameson whiskey fortune, paid for an eleven-year-old girl to be killed and eaten by cannibals—while he made sketches of the ritual.

At this point, Joseph Conrad was just about to embark on his own journey up the Congo, and it would be another decade before he created Kurtz, the savage imperialist in *Heart of Darkness* who "lacked restraint in the gratification of his various lusts" because he was "hollow at the core" and "the wilderness found him out." But the perils of the African wilderness already seemed quite clear to many Europeans once they read the nonfiction stories from Stanley's Rear Column. Critics called for an end to such expeditions, and it was the last of its kind, much to Stanley's dismay. He joined in the condemnation of his men's behavior, and he certainly appreciated the dangers of the wilderness, but he didn't regard them as insuperable.

For while the Rear Column was going berserk, Stanley was maintaining discipline in a much wilder setting. He and the forward portion of the expedition spent months struggling to find a way through the dense Ituri rain forest. They suffered through torrential rains and waist-deep mud while fending off incessant swarms of stinging flies and biting ants. They were weakened by continual hunger, crippled by festering sores and ulcers, incapacitated by malaria and dysentery. They were maimed and killed, and sometimes eaten, by natives who attacked them with poisoned arrows and spears. At one point, several people were dying daily of disease and starvation. Of those who started with Stanley on this trek into "darkest Africa," as he called that sunless expanse of jungle, fewer than one in three emerged with him.

You would be hard-pressed to name any explorer in history who endured such sustained misery and terror so deep in the wilderness. Perhaps the only expedition as grueling was the previous transcontinental journey by Stanley that established the sources of the Nile and the Congo rivers. Yet Stanley persevered through all the travails, year after year, expedition after expedition. His European companions marveled at his "strength of will." Africans called him Bula Matari: Breaker of Rocks. The African aides and porters who survived his expeditions went on to enlist again and again with him, admiring him not just for his hard work and resolve but also for his kindness and equanimity under hellish conditions. While others blamed the wilderness for turning men into savages, Stanley said he benefited from it: "For myself, I lay no claim to any exceptional fineness of nature; but I say, beginning life as a rough, ill-educated, impatient man, I have found my schooling in these very African experiences which are now said by some to be in themselves detrimental to European character."

What did that schooling teach him? Why didn't the wilderness ever find him out? In his day, Stanley's feats enthralled the public and awed artists and intellectuals. Mark Twain predicted that Stanley would be almost the only one of his contemporaries to remain famous a century later. "When I contrast what I have achieved in my measurably brief life with what Stanley has achieved in his possibly briefer one," Twain observed, "the effect is to sweep utterly away the ten-storey edifice of my own self-appreciation and to leave nothing behind but the cellar." Anton Chekhov declared that one Stanley was worth a dozen schools and a hundred good books. The Russian writer saw Stanley's "stubborn invincible striving towards a certain goal, no matter what the privations, dangers and temptations for personal happiness," as "personifying the highest moral strength."

But the establishment in Britain and much of Europe was always leery of this brash newspaperman from America, and there were jealous rivals eager to fault his exploration tactics, particularly after the scandal of the Rear Column. In the ensuing century, his reputation plummeted as biographers and historians criticized his expeditions and his association in the early 1880s with King Leopold II, the profiteering Belgian monarch whose ivory traders would later provide the direct inspiration for *Heart of Darkness.* As colonialism declined and Victorian character building lost favor, Stanley came to seem less like a paragon of self-control and more like a selfish control freak. He was depicted as a brutal exploiter, a ruthless imperialist who hacked and shot his way across Africa. This cruel conquistador was often contrasted with the saintly Dr. Livingstone, the solitary traveler who crossed the continent selflessly looking for souls to save.

But recently yet another Stanley has emerged, a much more intriguing one for modern audiences than either the dauntless hero or the ruthless control freak. This explorer prevailed in the wilderness not by selfishness, not because his will was indomitable, but because he appreciated its limitations and used long-term strategies that psychologists are now beginning to understand.

This new version of Stanley was found, appropriately enough, by Dr. Livingstone's biographer, Tim Jeal, a British novelist and expert on Victorian obsessives. From researching David Livingstone's life, Jeal was suspicious of the conventional Livingstone-Stanley dichotomy. When thousands of Stanley's letters and papers were unsealed in the past decade, Jeal drew on them to produce a revisionist tour de force, *Stanley: The Impossible Life of Africa's Greatest Explorer.* The acclaimed biography depicts a deeply flawed character who seems all the more brave and humane for his mixture of ambition and insecurity, virtue and fraud. His self-control in the wilderness becomes even more remarkable considering the secrets he was hiding at his core.

The Empathy Gap

If self-control is partly a hereditary trait—which seems likely—then Stanley began life with the genetic odds against him. He was born in Wales to an unmarried eighteen-year-old woman who went on to have four other illegitimate children by at least two other men. He never knew his father. His mother promptly abandoned him to her father, who cared for him until he died when the boy was six. Another family took him in briefly, but then one of the boy's new guardians took him on a journey. Told he was going to his aunt's home, the confused boy instead ended up inside a large stone building. It was a workhouse, and the adult Stanley would never forget how, in the moment his deceitful guardian fled and the door slammed shut, he "experienced for the first time the awful feeling of utter desolateness."

The boy, who was then named John Rowlands, would go through life trying to hide the shame of the workhouse and the stigma of his illegitimate birth. After leaving the workhouse at age fifteen and traveling to New Orleans, he began denying his Welsh roots and pretending to be an American, complete with the accent. He called himself Henry Morton Stanley and told of taking the name from his adoptive father, a wonderfully kind and hardworking cotton trader in New Orleans. In the tales he concocted about his adoptive family, Stanley claimed to be raised by parents who taught self-control. The dying words he ascribed to his fantasy mother were "Be a good boy."

"Moral resistance was a favourite subject with him," Stanley wrote of his fantasy father. "He said the practice of it gave vigour to the will, which required it as much as the muscles. The will required to be strengthened to resist unholy desires and low passions, and was one of the best allies that conscience could have." Not surprisingly, this advice from an imaginary parent happened to jibe precisely with Stanley's own regimen for avoiding the vices of his real parents. At age eleven, despite living in what could hardly be called luxurious conditions at the workhouse in Wales, he was already "experimenting on Will" by imposing extra hardships on himself:

> I rose at midnight to wrestle in secret with my wicked self, and, while my schoolfellows sweetly reposed, I was on my knees, laying my heart bare before Him who knows all things. . . . I would promise to abstain from wishing for more food, and, to show how I despised the stomach and its pains, I would divide one meal out of the three among my neighbours; half my suet pudding should be given to Ffoulkes, who was afflicted with greed, and, if ever I possessed anything that excited the envy of another, I would at once surrender it.

Virtue, he discovered, took time. "Often it appeared as though it were wholly useless to struggle against evil, yet there was an infinitesimal improvement in each stage. The character was becoming more and more developed." By his twenties he was a successful war correspondent and preacher of self-discipline to his friends. When one of them suggested he take a vacation, he dismissed the idea with a wonderful bit of verbiage (and self-importance): "It is only by railway celerity that I can live." He wouldn't even be able to enjoy a vacation, he wrote to his friend, because his conscience would torment him for wasting time. Nothing could interfere with his goal: "I mean by attention to my business, by self-denial, by indefatigable energy, to become, by this very business, my own master."

But once he reached Africa, Stanley also came to recognize the limits of anyone's willpower. Although he credited his experiences there with ultimately strengthening him, he also saw the toll that

Africa took on men unaccustomed to its rigors and temptations. "It is difficult for anyone who has not undergone experiences similar to ours to understand the amount of self-control each had to exercise, for fifteen hours every day, amid such surroundings as ours," he wrote about their passage through the dark Ituri Forest. When Stanley first learned of some of the Rear Column's cruelties and depredations, he noted in his journal that most people would erroneously conclude that the men were "originally wicked." People back in civilization, Stanley realized, couldn't imagine the changes undergone by the men since leaving England:

> At home these men had no cause to show their natural savagery . . . they were suddenly transplanted to Africa & its miseries. They were deprived of butcher's meat & bread & wine, books, newspapers, the society & influence of their friends. Fever seized them, wrecked minds and bodies. Good nature was banished by anxiety. Pleasantness was eliminated by toil. Cheerfulness yielded to internal anguish . . . until they became but shadows, morally & physically of what they had been in English society.

Stanley was describing what the economist George Loewenstein calls the "hot-cold empathy gap": the inability, during a cool, rational, peaceful moment, to appreciate how we'll behave during the heat of passion and temptation. At home in England, the men may have coolly intended to behave in a virtuous manner, but they couldn't imagine how different their feelings would be in the jungle. The hot-cold empathy gap is still one of the most common challenges to self-control, albeit in less extreme versions. We deal with gaps more like the one observed by a friend of ours who grew up on a commune in Canada. She was the only child on the commune, mostly consisting of idealistic hippies. Among their ideals was to consume only the healthiest and most natural forms of food. Her mother, however, thought that a child ought to have cookies from the supermarket every now and then. For buying them, the mother had to endure lots of jokes and lectures about the evils of sugar, the perils of fattening junk food, the immorality of supporting international food corporations. The mother kept buying them anyway but then faced another problem. The cookies kept disappearing. Late in the evening, after partaking of natural substances like wine and cannabis, the commune dwellers' willpower was depleted, and their disapproval of corporate junk food was no match for their cravings for Oreos. Some parents have to hide cookies from their children; this mother found that her child was the *only* person to whom the location could be revealed. The cookies had to be hidden because the grown-ups suffered from the hot-cold empathy gap. They denounced junk food by day without realizing how much they'd want those evil cookies once they were tired and stoned.

In setting rules for how to behave in the future, you're often in a calm, cool state, so you make unrealistic commitments. "It's really easy to agree to diet when you're not hungry," says Loewenstein, a professor at Carnegie Mellon University. And it's really easy to be sexually abstemious when you're not sexually aroused, as Loewenstein and Dan Ariely found by asking young heterosexual adult men some personal questions. If, say, they were attracted to a woman and she proposed a threesome with a man, would they do it? Could they imagine having sex with a woman who was forty years older? Could they ever be attracted to a twelve-year-old girl? To get a woman to have sex, would they falsely tell her they loved her? Would they keep trying after she said no? Would they try to get her drunk, or give her a drug to lower her resistance?

When the men answered these questions sitting by a computer in a laboratory—an eminently cold state—they honestly thought they would be quite unlikely ever to do any of those things. In another part of the experiment, however, the men were instructed to answer the questions while they were masturbating and in a state of high sexual arousal. In that hot state, they gave higher ratings to all those possibilities. What had seemed highly unlikely began to seem more within the realm of possibility. It was just an experiment, but it showed how the wilderness might find them out, too. Turn up the heat, and the unthinkable becomes surprisingly thinkable.

We've said that willpower is humans' greatest strength, but the best strategy is not to rely on it in all situations. Save it for emergencies. As Stanley discovered, there are mental tricks that enable you to conserve willpower for those moments when it's indispensable. Paradoxically, these techniques require willpower to implement, but in the long run they leave you less depleted for those moments when it takes a strong core to survive.

The Ties That Bind

Stanley first encountered the miseries of the African interior at the age of thirty, when the *New York Herald* sent him to find Livingstone somewhere in the mysterious continent. He spent the first part of the journey slogging through a swamp and struggling with malaria, which left him delirious for a week with what he called "its insane visions, its frenetic brain-throbs & dire sickness." Then the entire expedition narrowly escaped being massacred during a local civil war. After six months of travel, so many men had died or deserted that, even after acquiring replacements, Stanley was down to thirty-four men, barely a quarter the size of the original expedition, and a dangerously small number for traveling through the hostile territory ahead. Stanley was beset by new bouts of fever and depressed by warnings from veteran Arab travelers that he would die if he continued. But one evening, during a break between fevers, he wrote a note to himself by candlelight:

> I have taken a solemn, enduring oath, an oath to be kept while the least hope of life remains in me, not to be tempted to break the

resolution I have formed, never to give up the search, until I find Livingstone alive, or find his dead body. . . . No living man, or living men, shall stop me, only death can prevent me. But death—not even this; I shall not die, I will not die, I cannot die!

Even allowing for the fevers and insane visions, it's hard to imagine that Stanley really believed he or his note had any sway over death. But the act of writing it was part of a strategy to conserve willpower that he used over and over with great success: precommitment. The essence of this strategy is to lock yourself into a virtuous path. You recognize that you'll face terrible temptations to stray from the path, and that your willpower will weaken. So you make it impossible—or somehow unthinkably disgraceful or sinful—to leave the path. Precommitment is what Odysseus and his men used to get past the deadly songs of the Sirens. He had himself lashed to the mast with orders not to be untied no matter how much he pleaded to be freed to go to the Sirens. His men used a different form of precommitment by plugging their ears so they couldn't hear the Sirens' songs. They prevented themselves from being tempted at all, which is generally the safer of the two approaches. If you want to be sure you don't gamble at a casino, you're better off staying out of it rather than strolling past the tables and counting on your friends to stop you from placing a bet. Better yet is to put your name on the list of people (maintained by casinos in some states) who are not allowed to collect any money if they place winning bets.

No one, of course, can anticipate all temptations, especially today. No matter what you do to avoid physical casinos, you're never far from virtual casinos, not to mention all the other enticements perpetually available on the Web. But the technology that creates new sins also enables new precommitment strategies. A modern Odysseus can try lashing himself to his browser with software that prevents him from hearing or seeing certain Web sites. A modern Stanley can use the Web in the same way that the explorer used the social media of his day. In Stanley's private letters, newspaper dispatches, and public declarations, he repeatedly promised to reach his goals and to behave honorably—and he knew, once he became famous, that any failure would make headlines. Having piously lectured his men about the perils of drunkenness and the need to shun sexual temptations in Africa, he knew how conspicuous his own lapses would be. By creating the public persona of himself as Bula Matari, the unyielding Breaker of Rocks, he forced himself to live up to it. As a result of his oaths and his image, Jeal said, "Stanley made it impossible in advance to fail through weakness of will."

Today you don't need to be famous to worry about ruining your image with a lapse in willpower. You can precommit yourself to virtue by using social-networking tools that will expose your sins, like the "Public Humiliation Diet" followed by a writer named Drew Magary. He vowed to weigh himself every day and promptly reveal the results on Twitter—which he did, and lost sixty pounds in five months. If you'd rather put someone else in charge of the humiliation, you could install software from Covenant Eyes that will track your Web browsing and then e-mail a list of the sites you visit to anyone you designate in advance—like, say, your boss or your spouse. Or you could sign a "Commitment Contract" with stickK.com, a company founded by two Yale economists, Ian Ayres and Dean Karlan, and a graduate student, Jordan Goldberg. It allows you to pick any goal you want—lose weight, stop biting your nails, use fewer fossil fuels, stop calling an ex—along with a penalty that will be imposed automatically if you don't reach it. You can monitor yourself or pick a referee to report on your success or failure. The penalty might simply be a round of e-mails from stickK.com to your designated list of supporters—friends and relatives, generally, although you could choose some enemies, too. But you can also make it financially costly by setting up an automatic payment from your credit card to charity. For an extra incentive, you can assign the payment to an "anticharity," which is a group you'd hate to support—like, say, the presidential library of either Bill Clinton or George W. Bush. Not surprisingly, stickK.com's users seem to be motivated by financial stakes (just as Stanley was—he knew he had to come up with stories to sell newspapers and books) and by the presence of a referee. People who draw up a contract without a financial penalty or a referee succeed only 35 percent of the time, whereas the ones with a penalty and a ref succeed nearly 80 percent of the time, and the ones who risk more than one hundred dollars do better than those who risk less than twenty dollars—at least according to what is reported to stickK .com, which doesn't independently verify the results. The true success rate is presumably lower because some referees are reluctant to report failures that would hurt their friends financially. And whatever the success rate, this is obviously a self-selected sample of people already motivated to change, so it's hard to know exactly how much difference the stickK.com contracts make. But the efficacy of contracts with monitors and penalties has been independently demonstrated in a more rigorous offline experiment, conducted by Karlan and other economists, among more than two thousand smokers in the Philippines who said they wanted to quit.

The economists randomly offered some of these Philippine smokers a commitment contract with a bank, which would give them a weekly opportunity to make a deposit into an account paying no interest. It was suggested that the smokers deposit the amount of money ordinarily spent on cigarettes, but the level was strictly voluntary— each week they could deposit as much as they wanted, or nothing at all (and many of the smokers ended up depositing nothing). At the end of six months, the people would submit to a urine test. If the test found any nicotine in their body, they'd forfeit all the money in the account (which the bank would donate to charity). From a strictly financial standpoint, it was hardly an ideal investment strategy for the smokers who accepted the contract. They could have guaranteed themselves a better return simply by putting the money into a regular interest-paying savings account. They not only gave up the chance for interest but also put themselves at risk of losing it all—and indeed, at the six-month mark, more than half of them did end up flunking the test. The urge to smoke was so strong that a majority of them yielded to it even though they knew they'd lose their money.

The good news, though, was that this incentive did help some of the smokers to quit, and they stayed off cigarettes even after passing the six-month test and collecting the money in their account. At that point, the program officially ended, and the subjects didn't expect to be monitored any further. But the researchers wanted to see how lasting the effects were, so they waited another six months, until the one-year mark, and then surprised all the subjects by asking them to take another urine test. Even though the people no longer had any financial incentive to stay off nicotine, the effects of the program were still evident. Compared with a control group that was offered a different stop-smoking program, the smokers offered a commitment contract were nearly 40 percent more likely to be nicotine-free after a year. Given an incentive to temporarily restrain their smoking, they were more likely to make a lasting change in their lives. What began as a precommitment turned into something permanent and more valuable: a habit.

The Brain on Autopilot

Imagine, for a moment, that you are Henry Stanley awaking on a particularly inauspicious morning. You emerge from your tent in the Ituri rain forest. It's dark, of course. It's been dark for four months. Your stomach, long since ruined on previous African expeditions by parasites, recurrent diseases, and massive doses of quinine and other medicines, is in even worse shape than usual. You and your men have been reduced to eating berries, roots, fungi, grubs, caterpillars, ants, and slugs—when you're lucky enough to find them. The closest thing to a good meal recently was your donkey, which you shot in order to feed the group. The ravenous men ate every part of it, even fight-ing over the hooves and desperately licking blood on the ground before it seeped into the soil.

Dozens of people were so crippled—from hunger, disease, inju-ries, and festering sores—that they had to be left behind at a spot in the forest that is grimly being referred to as Starvation Camp. You've taken the healthier ones ahead to look for food, but they've been dropping dead along the way, and there's still no food to be found. You fear you've just gone from one starvation camp to another, and you have begun imagining, in morbid detail, how you and the other men will collapse and die on the forest floor. You envision the reac-tion of the forest's insects to each man's death: "Before he is cold, a 'scout' will come, then two, then a score, and, finally, myriads of fierce yellowbodied scavengers, their heads clad in shining horn-mail; and, in a few days, there will only remain a flat layer of rags, at one end of which will be a glistening, white skull."

But as of this morning, you're not dead yet. There's no food in camp, but at least you're alive. Now that you've arisen and taken care of nature's first call of the morning, what's the next thing to do?

For Stanley, this was an easy decision: shave. As one of his ser-vants in England would later recall: "He had often told me that, on his various expeditions, he had made it a rule, always to shave care-fully. In the Great Forest, in 'Starvation Camp,' on the mornings of battle, he had never neglected this custom, however great the diffi-culty; he told me he had often shaved with cold water, or with blunt razors." Why would somebody starving to death insist on shaving? When we asked Stanley's biographer about this extreme punctilious-ness in the jungle, Jeal said it was a typical manifestation of the man's orderliness.

"Stanley always tried to keep a neat appearance—with clothes, too—and set great store by the clarity of his handwriting, by the con-dition of his journals and books, and by the organization of his boxes," Jeal said. "He praised the similar neatness of Livingstone's arrangements. The creation of order can only have been an antidote to the destructive capacities of nature all around him." Stanley himself offered a similar explanation for his need to shave in the jungle: "I always presented as decent an appearance as possible, both for self-discipline and for self-respect."

Now, you might think the energy spent shaving in the jungle would be better devoted to looking for food. Wouldn't that exercise of self-control leave you more depleted and less able to exert willpower for something vital? But orderly habits like that can actually improve self-control in the long run by triggering automatic mental processes that don't require much energy. Stanley's belief in the link between external order and inner self-discipline has been confirmed recently in some remarkable studies. In one experiment, a group of participants answered questions sitting in a nice neat laboratory room, while others sat in the kind of place that inspires parents to shout, "Clean up your room!" The people in the messy room scored lower in self-control on many measures, such as being unwilling to wait a week for a larger sum of money as opposed to taking a smaller sum right away. When offered snacks and drinks, people in the neat lab room chose apples and milk instead of the candy and sugary colas preferred by their peers in the pigsty.

In a similar experiment conducted online, some participants answered questions on a clean, well-designed Web site on which everything was correctly positioned and properly spelled. Others were asked the same questions on a sloppy Web site with spelling errors and other problems. On the messy site, people were more likely to say that they would gamble rather than take a sure thing, that they would curse and swear, and that they would take an immediate but small reward rather than waiting for a larger but delayed reward. The messy Web site also elicited lower donations to charity. Charity and generosity have been linked to self-control, partly because self-control is needed to overcome our natural animal selfishness, and partly because, as we'll see later, thinking about others can increase our own self-discipline. The orderly Web sites, like the neat lab rooms, provided subtle cues guiding people unconsciously toward self-disciplined decisions and actions helping others.

By shaving every day, Stanley could benefit from this same sort of orderly cue without having to expend much mental energy. He didn't have to make a conscious decision every morning to shave. Once he had expended the willpower to make it his custom, it became a relatively automatic mental process requiring little or no further willpower. His dutiful behavior at Starvation Camp was extreme, but it fits a pattern recently observed by Baumeister working together with Denise de Ridder and Catrin Finkenauer, two Dutch researchers who led an analysis of a large set of published and unpublished studies on people who scored high in self-control as measured in a personality test. These studies reported experiments involving a variety of behaviors, which the researchers divided into a couple of broad categories: mainly automatic or mainly controlled. The researchers assumed, logically enough, that people with high self-control would tend to exercise it most noticeably in the behavior they controlled the most. Yet when the results were totaled up in a meta-analysis, just the opposite pattern appeared. The people with high self-control were distinguished by their behaviors that took place more or less automatically.

At first the researchers were baffled. Their results suggested that we don't use self-control on controllable behaviors. How could that be? They checked and rechecked their codings and calculations, but that was indeed the finding. Only when they went back to the original studies did they begin to understand what this result meant. And it meant a serious change in how to think about self-control.

The behaviors they had coded as automatic tended to be linked to habits, whereas the more controlled sorts of behaviors tended to be unusual or one-time-only actions. Self-control turned out to be most effective when people used it to establish good habits and break bad ones. People with self-control were more likely to regularly use condoms, and to avoid habits like smoking, frequent snacking, and heavy drinking. It took willpower to establish patterns of healthy behavior—which was why the people with more willpower were better able to do it—but once the habits were established, life could proceed smoothly, particularly some aspects of life.

Another unexpected finding from the meta-analysis was that self-control was particularly helpful for performance in work and school, while the weakest effects were involved with eating and dieting. Although people with relatively high self-control did a little better at controlling their weight, the effect was much weaker than in other aspects of their lives. (We'll discuss the reason for that disconnect—and the case against dieting—in a later chapter.) Their self-control yielded moderate benefits in helping them to be well adjusted emotionally (being happy, having healthy self-esteem, avoiding depression) and to get along with their close friends, lovers, and relatives. But the greatest benefits of their self-control showed up in school and in the workplace, confirming other evidence that successful students and workers tend to rely on good habits. Valedictorians are generally not the sort who stay up studying all night just before the big exam—instead, they keep up with the work all semester long. Workers who produce steadily over a long period of time tend to be most successful in the long run.

Among university professors, for example, getting tenure is a major hurdle and milestone, and at most universities tenure depends heavily on having published some high-quality, original work. One researcher, Bob Boice, looked into the writing habits of young professors just starting out and tracked them to see how they fared. Not surprisingly, in a job where there is no real boss and no one sets schedules or tells you what to do, these young professors took a variety of approaches. Some would collect information until they were ready and then write a manuscript in a burst of intense energy, over perhaps a week or two, possibly including some long days and very late nights. Others plodded along at a steadier pace, trying to write a page or two every day. Others were in between. When Boice followed up on the group some years later, he found that their paths had diverged sharply. The page-a-day folks had done well and generally gotten tenure. The so-called "binge writers" fared far less well, and many had had their careers cut short. The clear implication was that the best advice for young writers and aspiring professors is: Write every day. Use your self-control to form a daily habit, and you'll produce more with less effort in the long run.

We often think of willpower in heroic terms, as a single act at a crucial moment in life—sprinting at the end of the marathon, getting through the pain of childbirth, enduring an injury, dealing with a crisis, resisting the seemingly irresistible temptation, beating the impossible deadline. Those are the feats that remain in memory and make the best stories. Even the most critical biographers of Stanley hailed his bursts of literary productivity on deadline. After finishing that awful trek through the Ituri Forest and returning to civilization, he quickly produced an international bestseller, *In Darkest Africa.* By working from six in the morning until eleven at night, he wrote the two-volume, nine-hundred-page work in just fifty days—binge writing at its most extreme. But he could never have chronicled the expedition so quickly without the copious notes and orderly records he routinely kept along the way. By making his diary a habit, like his shaving, he kept writing day after day while conserving his willpower for the next nasty surprise in the jungle.

But Enough About Me

At age thirty-three, not long after finding Livingstone, Stanley found love. He had always considered himself hopeless with women, but his new celebrity increased his social opportunities when he returned to London, and there he met a visiting American named Alice Pike. She was just seventeen, half his age, and he noted in his diary that she

was "very ignorant of African geography, & I fear of everything else."
But he was smitten, and within a month they were engaged. They
agreed to marry once Stanley returned from his next African expedition. He set off from the east coast of Africa carrying her photograph,
wrapped in oilskin, next to his heart, while his men lugged the pieces
of a twenty-four-foot boat named the *Lady Alice*, which Stanley used
to make the first recorded circumnavigations of the great lakes in the
heart of Africa. Then, having traveled thirty-five hundred miles,
Stanley continued westward for the most dangerous part of the trip.
He planned to take the *Lady Alice* down the Lualaba River to wher-
ever it led—maybe the Nile (Livingstone's theory), maybe the Niger,
maybe the Congo (Stanley's hunch, which would prove correct). No
one knew, because even the fearsome Arab slave traders had been
intimidated by tales of bellicose cannibals downstream.

Before heading down that river, Stanley wrote to his fiancée,
telling her that he weighed just 118 pounds, having lost 60 pounds
since seeing her. His many ailments included another bout of malaria,
which had him shivering on a day when the temperature in the sun
hit 138 degrees Fahrenheit. He expected worse hardships ahead, but
he didn't focus on them in the last letter he would be able to dispatch
until reaching the other side of Africa. "My love towards you is un-
changed, you are my dream, my stay, my hope, and my beacon," he
wrote to her. "I shall cherish you in this light until I meet you, or
death meets me."

Stanley clung to that hope for another thirty-five hundred miles,
taking the *Lady Alice* down the Congo River, surviving attacks from
cannibals chanting a war cry of "Niama! Niama!"—Meat! Meat! Only
half of his companions completed the journey to the Atlantic coast,
which took nearly three years and claimed the life of every European
except Stanley. Upon reaching civilization, Stanley eagerly sought
love letters from his fiancée, but instead he got a note from his pub-
lisher with some awkward news (and dubious use of the exclamation
point): "I now come to a delicate subject which I have long debated

with myself whether I should write about or wait for your arrival. I think however I may as well tell you at once that your friend Alice Pike is married!" Stanley was distraught to hear that his dream woman had abandoned him (for the son of a railroad-car manufacturer in Ohio), and he was hardly mollified by a note from her congratulating him for the expedition while breezily mentioning her marriage and acknowledging that the *Lady Alice* had "proved a truer friend than the Alice she was named after." To Stanley, the engagement was further proof of his romantic ineptitude. He had obviously crossed Africa with the wrong woman's photograph next to his heart.

But however badly it turned out, Stanley did get something out of the relationship and that photograph: a distraction from his own wretchedness. He may have fooled himself about her loyalty, but he was smart during his journey to fixate on a "stay" and a "beacon" far removed from his grim surroundings. It was a more elaborate version of the successful strategy used by the children in the classic marshmallow experiment. Those who kept looking at the marshmallow quickly depleted their willpower and gave in to the temptation to eat it right away; those who distracted themselves by looking around the room (or sometimes just covering their eyes) managed to hold out. Similarly, paramedics distract patients from their pain by talking to them about anything except their condition, and midwives try to keep women in labor from closing their eyes (which would enable them to focus on the pain). They recognize the benefits of what Stanley called "self-forgetfulness." He blamed the breakdown of the Rear Column on their leader's decision to stay put in camp so long, waiting and waiting for additional porters, instead of setting out sooner into the jungle on their own journey. "The cure of their misgivings & doubts would have been found in action," he wrote, rather than "enduring deadly monotony." As horrible as it was for Stanley going through the forest with sick, famished, and dying men, their journey's "endless occupations were too absorbing and interesting to allow room for baser thoughts." Stanley saw the work as a mental escape:

> For my protection against despair and madness, I had to resort to
> self-forgetfulness; to the interest which my task brought. . . . I had
> my reward in knowing that my comrades were all the time con-
> scious that I did my best, and that I was bound to them by a
> common sympathy and aims. This encouraged me to give myself
> up to all neighbourly offices, and was morally fortifying.

This talk of "common sympathy" and "neighbourly offices" may
sound suspiciously self-serving coming from someone with Stanley's
reputation for aloofness and severity. After all, this was the man renowned for the coldest greeting in history: "Dr. Livingstone, I presume?" Even Victorians found it ridiculously stiff for two Englishmen
meeting in the middle of Africa. But what's most revealing about the
famous line, according to Jeal, is that Stanley never uttered it. The
first record of it occurs in Stanley's dispatch to the *New York Herald,*
written well after the meeting. It's not in the diaries of either man.
Stanley tore out the crucial page of his diary, cutting off his account
of the encounter just as they were about to greet each other. Stanley,
chronically insecure about his workhouse roots, apparently invented
the line afterward to make himself sound dignified. He'd always admired the stiff-upper-lip credo of British gentleman explorers, and he
sometimes tried to mimic their sanqfroid by affecting a dispassion-
ate air toward his adventures. But he lacked their flair—and their
discretion. While they omitted or downplayed the violent encounters
and disciplinary tactics on their African expeditions, Stanley vastly
exaggerated those aspects, partly to sound tougher, partly to sell
newspapers and books.

As a result, Stanley ended up with a reputation as the harshest
and most violent explorer of his age, when in fact he was unusually
humane toward Africans, even by comparison with the gentle Livingstone, as Jeal demonstrates. For his time, Stanley was remarkably
free of racial prejudice. He spoke Swahili fluently and established
lifelong bonds with his African companions. He severely disciplined

white officers who mistreated blacks under their command, and he continually restrained his men from violence and other crimes against local villagers. While he did sometimes get in fights when negotiations and gifts failed, the image of Stanley shooting his way across Africa was a myth. The secret to his success lay not in the battles he described so vividly but in two principles that Stanley summarized after his last expedition:

> I have learnt by actual stress of imminent danger, in the first place, that self-control is more indispensable than gunpowder, and, in the second place, that persistent self-control under the provocation of African travel is impossible without real, heartfelt sympathy for the natives with whom one has to deal.

As Stanley realized, self-control is not selfish. Willpower enables us to get along with others and override impulses that are based on personal short-term interests. It's the same lesson that Navy SEAL commandos learn during a modern version of Stanley's ordeals: the famous Hell Week test of continual running, swimming, crawling, and shivering that they must endure on less than five hours' sleep. At least three-quarters of the men in each SEAL class typically fail to complete training, and the survivors aren't necessarily the ones with the most muscles, according to Eric Greitens, a SEAL officer. In recalling the fellow survivors of his Hell Week, he points out their one common quality: "They had the ability to step outside of their own pain, put aside their own fear, and ask: How can I help the guy next to me? They had more than the 'fist' of courage and physical strength. They also had a heart large enough to think about others."

Throughout history, the most common way to redirect people away from selfish behavior has been through religious teachings and commandments, and these remain an effective strategy for self-control, as demonstrated by research that we'll discuss later. But what if, like Stanley, you're not a believer? After losing his faith in God and religion at an early age (a loss he attributed to the slaughter he witnessed in the American Civil War), he faced a question that vexed other Victorians: How can people remain moral without the traditional restraints of religion? Many prominent nonbelievers, like Stanley, responded by paying lip service in public to religion while also looking for secular ways to inculcate a sense of "duty." During the awful trek through the Ituri jungle, he exhorted the men by quoting one of his favorite couplets, from Tennyson's "Ode on the Death of the Duke of Wellington":

> Not once or twice in our fair island-story,
> The path of duty was the way to glory.

Stanley's men didn't always appreciate his efforts—the Tennyson lines got very old for some of them—but his approach embodied a correct principle of self-control: Focus on lofty thoughts. The effects of this strategy were recently tested by a team of researchers headed by Kentaro Fujita, of New York University, and his thesis adviser, Yaacov Trope. They used a series of methods to move people's mental processes to either high or low levels. High levels were defined by abstraction and long-term goals. Low levels were the opposite. For instance, people were asked to reflect either on why they did something or on how they did something. "Why" questions push the mind up to higher levels of thinking and a focus on the future. "How" questions bring the mind down to low levels of thinking and a focus on the present. Another procedure that produced similar results was to have people move up or down from a given concept, like the word *singer*. To induce a high-level mind-set, people were asked, "A singer is an example of what?" In contrast, to induce a low-level mind-set, they were asked, "What is an example of a singer?" Thus the answer pushed them to think either more globally or more specifically.

These manipulations of mental state had no inherent relation to self-control. Yet self-control improved among people who were encouraged to think in high-level terms, and got worse among those who thought in low-level terms. Different measures were used in assorted experiments, but the results were consistent. After engaging in high-level thinking, people were more likely to pass up a quick reward for something better in the future. When asked to squeeze a handgrip, they could hold on longer. The results showed that a narrow, concrete, here-and-now focus works against self-control, whereas a broad, abstract, long-term focus supports it. That's one reason why religious people score relatively high in measures of self-control, and why nonreligious people like Stanley can benefit by other kinds of transcendent thoughts and enduring ideals. Stanley always combined his ambitions for personal glory with a desire to be "good," as he'd imagined his dying mother telling him. He found his calling along with Livingstone when he saw firsthand the devastation being wrought by the expanding network of Arab and East-African slave traders. From then on, he considered it his life's mission to end the slave trade.

Ultimately, what sustained Stanley through the jungle, and through the rejections from his family and his fiancée and the British establishment, was his stated belief that he was engaged in a "sacred task." By modern standards, he can seem bombastically pious, but he was sincere. "I was not sent into the world to be happy," he wrote. "I was sent for special work." During his descent of the Congo, he would earnestly write himself exhortations like, "I hate evil and love good." At the worst point along the river, when he was despondent over the drowning of two of his closest companions, when he was close to dying himself from starvation and there seemed no prospect of finding food, he consoled himself with the loftiest thought he could summon:

> This poor body of mine has suffered terribly . . . it has been degraded, pained, wearied & sickened, and has well nigh sunk under the task imposed on it; but this was but a small portion of myself.

For my real self lay darkly encased, & was ever too haughty & soaring for such miserable environments as the body that encumbered it daily.

Was Stanley, in his moment of despair, succumbing to religion and imagining himself with a soul? Maybe. But given his lifelong struggles, given all his stratagems to conserve his powers in the wilderness, it seems likely that he had something more secular in mind. His "real self," as Bula Matari saw it, was his will.

8.

DID A HIGHER POWER HELP ERIC CLAPTON AND MARY KARR STOP DRINKING?

Holy Mother, hear my cry,
I've cursed your name a thousand times.
I've felt the anger running through my soul;
Holy Mother, can't keep control.

—Eric Clapton, in his song "Holy Mother"

If you'd told me even a year before . . . that I'd wind up whispering my sins in the confessional or on my knees saying the rosary, I would've laughed myself cock-eyed. More likely pastime? Pole dancer. International spy. Drug mule. Assassin.

—Mary Karr, in her memoir *Lit*

During Eric Clapton's many suicidal moments, when wealth and fame and his music were no longer enough, he was sustained by one thought: If he killed himself, he would no longer be able to drink. Alcohol was his great enduring love, supplemented by serious affairs with cocaine, heroin, and just about any kind of drug he could get his hands on. When he first checked himself into the Hazelden clinic in his late thirties, he suffered a seizure during detox because he didn't warn the medical team that he'd been taking Valium—which he'd considered a "lady's drug" so minor it wasn't worth mentioning.

Clapton remained sober for several years after that stint in rehab, but then one summer evening, near his home in England, he drove past a crowded pub and had a thought. "My selective memory," as he puts it, "told me that standing at the bar in a pub on a summer's evening with a long, tall glass of lager and lime was heaven, and I chose not to remember the nights on which I had sat with a bottle of vodka, a gram of coke, and a shotgun, contemplating suicide."

He ordered the beer, and before long he was back to binges and suicidal feelings. On one particularly low night, he started work on "Holy Mother," a song pleading for divine help. He hurt his career and wrecked his marriage, but he couldn't stop drinking even after being seriously hurt in a drunk-driving accident. The birth of his son inspired him to return to Hazelden, but toward the end of his rehab he still felt powerless to resist the bottle.

"Drinking was in my thoughts all the time," he writes in his autobiography, *Clapton*. "I was absolutely terrified, in complete despair." As he was panicking one night alone in his room at the clinic, he found himself sinking to his knees and begging for help.

"I had no notion who I thought I was talking to, I just knew that I had come to the end of my tether," he recalls. "I had nothing left to fight with. Then I remembered what I had heard about surrender, something I thought I could never do, my pride just wouldn't allow it, but I knew that on my own I wasn't going to make it, so I asked for help, and, getting down on my knees, I surrendered." Since that moment, he says, he has never seriously considered taking another drink, not even on the horrifying day in New York when he had to identify the body of his son, Conor, who had fallen fifty-three stories to his death.

That night at Hazelden, Clapton was suddenly blessed with

self-control, but how he got it is more difficult to explain than how he'd lost it. His problems with alcohol could be described in precise physiological terms. Contrary to popular stereotype, alcohol doesn't increase your impulse to do stupid or destructive things; instead, it simply removes restraints. It lessens self-control in two ways: by lowering blood glucose and by reducing self-awareness. Therefore, it mainly affects behaviors marked by inner conflict, as when part of you wants to do something and part of you does not, like having sex with the wrong person, spending too much money, getting into a fight—or ordering another drink, and then another. This is the sort of inner conflict that cartoonists used to illustrate with the good angel on one shoulder and the bad angel on the other, but it's not much of a contest after a few drinks. The good angel is out of commission. You need to intervene earlier, to stop the binge before it begins, which is no problem when there's a staff at a place like Hazelden to do the job for you. But what would suddenly give you the strength to do it on your own? Why did Clapton's decision to "surrender" leave him with *more* self-control?

"An atheist would probably say it was just a change of attitude," he says, "and to a certain extent that's true, but there was much more to it than that." Ever since then, he has prayed for help every morning and night, kneeling down because he feels the need to humble himself. Why kneel and pray? "Because it works, as simple as that," Clapton says, repeating a discovery that reformed hedonists have been reporting for thousands of years. Sometimes it happens instantly, as with Clapton or St. Augustine, who reported receiving a direct command from God to stop drinking, whereupon "all the darkness of doubt vanished away."

And sometimes it takes a while, as with a supremely cynical agnostic like Mary Karr, the author of *The Liars' Club,* her bestselling memoir of growing up in an oil-refinery town in East Texas. Her mother, who married seven times, was an alcoholic who once set her daughter's toys on fire and tried to stab her to death, according to the memoir. Karr grew up to become a successful poet and to struggle with her own alcoholism. After one binge that ended with her car spinning out of control across a highway, Karr resolved to remain sober and dutifully followed the Alcoholics Anonymous advice to seek a higher power. She put a cushion on the floor and knelt for the first time in her life to say a prayer—or at least her version of a prayer. The best she could come up with was: *Higher power, where the fuck have you been?* She still didn't believe in any kind of deity, but she did decide to keep offering thanks every evening for remaining sober. About a week later, as she writes in her memoir *Lit,* she expanded her nightly prayer by listing other things for which she was grateful, and then mentioning some things she wanted, like money.

"It takes me a full five minutes to shut up begging," she recalls, "and it sounds crazy to say it, but for the first time in about a week, I don't want a drink at all." She went on being skeptical about a higher power, and when members of her AA group urged her to "surrender," she protested: "But what if I don't believe in God? It's like they've sat me in front of a mannequin and said, Fall in love with him. You can't will feeling." Religion was so irrational, and yet, when she found herself desperately craving a drink at a cocktail party for the New York literati at the Morgan Library, she retreated to the ladies' room, went into a stall, and irrationally sank to her knees to pray: *Please keep me away from a drink. I know I haven't been really asking, but I really need it. Please, please, please.* Just as with Clapton, it worked for her: "The primal chattering in my skull has dissipated as if some wizard conjured it away."

That wizardry can be especially hard to understand for agnostics, a group that includes us. (We're both lapsed Christians who don't spend much time on our knees praying to any higher power, either at home or in church.) But after looking at the data, we have no trouble believing there's some kind of power working at 12-step meetings and religious services. Although many scientists are skeptical of institutions that promote spirituality—and psychologists, for some reason, have been particularly skeptical of religion—self-control researchers have developed a grudging respect for the practical results. Even when social scientists can't accept supernatural beliefs, they recognize that religion is a profoundly influential human phenomenon that has been evolving effective self-control mechanisms for thousands of years. Alcoholics Anonymous couldn't have attracted millions of people like Eric Clapton and Mary Karr without doing something right. Does a belief in a higher power really give you more control over yourself? Or is something else going on—something that even nonbelievers could believe in?

The Mystery of AA

With the exception of organized religion, Alcoholics Anonymous probably represents the largest program ever conducted to improve self-control. It attracts more problem drinkers than do all professional and clinical programs combined, and many professional therapists routinely send their clients to AA meetings. Yet social scientists still aren't exactly sure what AA accomplishes. It's hard to study a decentralized organization without systematic records: AA's chapters operate autonomously and, of course, insist on members remaining anonymous. The local chapters follow the same general 12-step program, but these steps weren't systematically devised—the number of steps was initially chosen to match the number of Christ's apostles. A researcher would want at the very least to test the twelve steps one at a time, to see which ones (if any) have an effect.

AA members are fond of comparing alcoholism to diseases like diabetes, hypertension, depression, or Alzheimer's, but the analogy is problematic. Sure, there are physiological aspects of alcoholism— some people seem genetically predisposed to it—but going to AA is nothing like going to the hospital. Diabetics and hypertensives don't treat their conditions by sitting around offering one another encouragement. As various skeptics have observed, clinicians do not think that depressed people would benefit from spending time attending meetings with other depressed people. The progression of most diseases does not directly depend on people repeatedly taking voluntary self-destructive actions: No one can suddenly make a firm decision to abstain from heart disease or Alzheimer's. Alcoholism is more complicated, and these complexities have left researchers puzzling over the contradictory results from studies of AA. Some say the lack of consistent evidence casts doubt on AA's efficacy; others say researchers just haven't figured out how to factor out all the confounding variables.

AA's defenders note that alcoholics who frequently attend AA meetings tend to drink less than ones who attend infrequently, but the critics wonder about cause and effect. Does frequent attendance make people more likely to abstain, or does abstinence make people more likely to keep attending? Perhaps the ones who fall off the wagon are too ashamed to keep showing up. Or perhaps they simply started off with less motivation and more psychological problems.

Despite these uncertainties, researchers have found some evidence that AA works. When two things go together and researchers want to know which one causes the other, they sometimes try to track them over time and see which comes first—assuming that causation moves forward across time, so the cause precedes the effect. After tracking more than two thousand men with drinking problems for two years, a team led by John McKellar of Stanford University concluded that attendance at AA meetings led to fewer future problems with drinking (and not the reverse—they found no evidence that the presence or absence of drinking problems affected attendance at meetings later on). Moreover, the benefits of AA remained even after taking into account the men's initial level of motivation and psychological problems. Other researchers have likewise concluded that AA is at least more effective than nothing. The failure rate among members is high—it's normal for them to relapse periodically—but they usually resume abstinence. In fact, AA seems to be at least as effective as professional treatments for alcoholism.

Project MATCH, a large-scale research project in the 1990s, tested the theory that all treatments work, but not equally well for everyone. Presumably, some people should do better in AA, while others should benefit from professional treatment. Some alcoholics in the project were assigned to take part in AA, while others underwent one of two clinical programs administered by experts: cognitive-behavioral therapy or motivational-enhancement therapy. Some alcoholics were randomly assigned, while others were matched to the treatment type that was deemed best for them. Several years and millions of dollars later, it turned out that all the treatments were about equally effective, and that there was very little benefit from trying to match people to the optimal treatment. (In fact, it wasn't even clear that any of the treatments were better than nothing, because the project didn't include a control group receiving no treatment, so there was no way to tell if the people would have done just as well on their own.)

All in all, then, AA seems to be at least as good as, if not better than, professional treatments costing much more. Even if researchers haven't figured out exactly what it does, we can point to some familiar ways in which AA appears to help. We know that self-control starts with setting standards or goals, and we can see that AA helps people set a clear and attainable goal: Do not have a drink today. (AA's mantra is "One day at a time.") Self-control depends on monitoring, and AA offers help there, too. Members get chips for remaining sober for certain numbers of consecutive days, and when they get up to speak, they often start by saying how many days they have been sober. Members also choose a sponsor, with whom they are supposed to remain in regular, even daily, contact—and that, too, is a powerful boost for monitoring.

There are also a couple of other explanations for the correlation between attending AA meetings and drinking less. The less-inspiring

explanation is "warehousing," to borrow a term used by some skeptical sociologists to explain what high school does. They see school
as a kind of warehouse that stores kids during the day, keeping them
out of trouble, so that its benefits come less from what happens in
the classroom than from what doesn't happen elsewhere. By a similar logic, evenings spent attending AA meetings are spent not drinking. We think it unlikely that warehousing accounts for the entire
benefit of AA, or even the majority, but it undoubtedly contributes
something.

The other, more uplifting, explanation is that the meetings offer
social support. Like everyone else, alcoholics and drug addicts are
capable of remarkable feats of self-control in order to gain social acceptance. In fact, that desire for peer approval is often what got them
in trouble initially. Most people don't enjoy their first taste of alcohol
or tobacco. Most people are scared to put unfamiliar drugs into their
bodies. It takes real self-discipline to inject yourself with heroin the
first time. Teenagers will disregard everything—their own fears, their
parents' warnings, physical pain, the possibility of going to jail or
dying—because they're convinced that social acceptance requires
them not only to take risks but to do so in a cool, seemingly uncon-
cerned manner. They exert self-control to overcome their inhibitions
and more self-control to hide their negative feelings. When the young
Eric Clapton went with friends to a jazz festival in rural England, he
drank enough at a pub to start dancing on tables—and that was his
last memory until he woke up the next morning by himself in the
middle of nowhere.

"I had no money, I had shit myself, I had pissed myself, I had
puked all over myself, and I had no idea where I was," he recalls.
"But the really insane thing was, I couldn't wait to do it all again. I
thought there was something otherworldly about the whole culture
of drinking, that being drunk made me a member of some strange,
mysterious club."

That's the negative side of peer pressure. The positive side comes from craving acceptance and support from people with different desires, like the members of the AA groups who helped Clapton and Karr stay sober. The people at those meetings may ultimately matter far more than the twelve steps or the belief in a higher power. They may even *be* the higher power.

Heaven (like Hell) Is Other People

One of the newest and most ambitious alcoholism studies involves a group of men in the Baltimore area who were in therapy for alcohol abuse. Many had been ordered by a court to choose between receiving professional treatment or going to prison, so they were hardly the ideal population of people trying to quit. They may have only been going through the motions as an alternative to prison. The researchers, led by Carlo DiClemente of the University of Maryland, measured a large assortment of psychological variables and then tracked the men intensively for several months to test a variety of hypotheses, many of which didn't work out. But the researchers did isolate an important external factor that predicted whether the men would remain sober and how serious their lapses would be—whether they'd go on a binge, or stop at a drink or two and then get back on the wagon. The drinkers were asked if they contacted other people for help and social support for their efforts to avoid drinking. The ones who were better at getting support from other people ended up abstaining more frequently and doing less overall drinking.

Social support is a peculiar force and can operate in two different ways. Plenty of research suggests that being alone in the world is stressful. Loners and lonely people tend to have more of just about every kind of mental and physical illness than people who live in rich social networks. Some of that is because people with mental and physical problems make fewer friends, and indeed, some potential friends may shy away from someone who seems maladjusted. But simply being alone or lonely leads to problems also. A lack of friends tends to contribute to alcohol and drug abuse.

Still, all social support is not the same. Having friends may be great for your mental and physical health. But if your friends are all drinkers and drug users, they may not be much help in restraining your own impulses. They may directly or indirectly pressure you to drink as an integral part of socializing. In nineteenth-century America, for example, there was a social convention called the "barbecue law," which meant that all the men who gathered for a barbecue were expected to drink until they were soused. To refuse a drink entailed a serious insult to the host and the rest of the party. More recently, many studies have found that people drink more when they're encouraged by their friends. People struggling with an alcohol or drug problem need social support for *not* drinking, and that's where a group like AA can be vitally helpful. Alcoholics have spent so much of their lives surrounded by drinkers that they can't imagine the benefits of a different kind of peer pressure. It wasn't until Clapton was stuck inside Hazelden that he began looking for help from other people trying to stop drinking. Karr dutifully took herself to some AA meetings at a church during her first attempts to remain sober, but at first she was put off by the motley crowd and the earnest stories.

She kept her distance until, after one particularly bad binge, she followed the AA advice and chose one member of the group, a fellow academic in Boston, as her sponsor—her personal counselor. She had no patience for the sponsor's talk about a higher power, but the daily conversations still made a difference: "With her ministrations, I do not—for two months—drink: a white-knuckled, tooth-grinding effort that impresses no one outside the church basement I go to a few nights per week." When the two women met for coffee to celebrate the two months of sobriety, Karr complained about the losers and loons in their AA group and their "spiritual crap." Then, as Karr recalls, her sponsor suggested another way to think of a higher power, and of the group in the church basement:

"Here, she says, are a bunch of people. They outnumber you, outearn you, outweigh you. They are, ergo—in some simplistic calculation—a power greater than you. They certainly know more about staying sober than you. . . . If you have a problem, bring it to the group."

Part of the group's power comes from the passive act of sitting there and listening. To novices, AA meetings can seem pointless because most of the speakers just take turns telling their own stories instead of responding to one another and offering advice. But the act of telling a story forces you to organize your thoughts, monitor your behavior, and discuss goals for the future. A personal goal can seem more real once you speak it out loud, particularly if you know the audience will be monitoring you. A recent study of people undergoing cognitive therapy found that resolutions were more likely to be kept if they were made in the presence of other people, especially a romantic partner. Apparently, promising your therapist that you will cut down on drinking is not a powerful boost to self-control, but promising your spouse makes a big difference. Your spouse, after all, is the one who's going to smell your breath.

To quantify the power of peer-group pressure, economists studied a group of Chilean street vendors, seamstresses, and other low-income "microentrepreneurs" who had received loans from a nonprofit group. These people, mostly women, met in groups every week or two to receive training and to monitor the repayment of their loans. The economists Felipe Kast, Stephan Meier, and Dina Pomeranz randomly assigned these people to different savings programs. Some were simply given a no-fee savings account; others received the account plus the opportunity at their regular meetings to announce their savings goals and then have their progress discussed. The women subject to peer scrutiny saved nearly twice as much money as the others. The result seemed to confirm the power of the group, but where did the power come from? Could these effects be achieved with a "virtual peer group"? In a follow-up experiment, instead of discussing their savings out loud at a meeting, the Chilean women regularly received text messages noting their weekly progress (or lack thereof) along with information on how the rest of the savers in their group were doing. Surprisingly, these text messages seemed to be about as effective as the meetings, apparently because the messages provided the women with a virtual version of the same key benefits: regular monitoring and the chance to compare themselves with their peers.

Smoking cigarettes has long been regarded as a personal physical compulsion due to overwhelming impulses in the smoker's brain and body. Hence there was considerable surprise in 2008 when the *New England Journal of Medicine* published a study showing that quitting smoking seems to spread through social networks. The researchers, Nicholas Christakis and James Fowler, found that kicking the habit seemed to be contagious. If a member of a married couple quit smoking, the odds of the other spouse quitting would increase dramatically. The odds also got better if a brother, sister, or friend quit. Even coworkers had a substantial effect, as long as the people worked together in a fairly small firm.

Smoking researchers have been especially intrigued by places where very few people smoke, because the assumption was that these remaining few must be seriously addicted. Indeed, one popular theory was that more or less everybody who can easily quit smoking has already done so, leaving behind a hard core of heavily addicted smokers who could not kick the habit for love or money. But wave after wave of evidence has contradicted this theory. While some people will go on puffing all by themselves, smokers who live mainly among nonsmokers tend to have high rates of quitting, indicating again the power of social influence and social support for quitting. Studies of obesity have detected similar patterns of social influence, as we'll discuss later.

Sacred Self-control

If you're in a religious congregation and ask God for longer life, you are likely to get it. It doesn't even seem to matter which god you ask. Any sort of religious activity increases your longevity, according to the psychologist Michael McCullough (who isn't religiously devout himself). He looked at more than three dozen studies that had asked people about their religious devotion and then kept track of them over time. It turned out that the nonreligious people died off sooner, and that at any given point, a religiously active person was 25 percent more likely than a nonreligious person to remain alive. That's a pretty hefty difference, especially when the measure is being alive versus dead, and that result (published in 2000) has since been confirmed by other researchers. Some of those long-lived people no doubt liked to think that God was directly answering their prayers. But divine intervention was not the kind of hypothesis that appealed to social scientists, if only because it was so tough to test in the lab. They have found more earthly causes.

Religious people are less likely than others to develop unhealthy habits, like getting drunk, engaging in risky sex, taking illicit drugs, and smoking cigarettes. They're more likely to wear seat belts, visit a dentist, and take vitamins. They have better social support, and their faith helps them cope psychologically with misfortunes. And they have better self-control, as McCullough and his colleague at the University of Miami, Brian Willoughby, recently concluded after analyzing hundreds of studies of religion and self-control over eight decades. Their analysis was published in 2009 in the *Psychological Bulletin*, one of the most prestigious and rigorous journals in the field. Some of the effects of religion were unsurprising: Religion promotes family values and social harmony, in part because some values gain in importance by being supposedly linked to God's will or other religious values. Less obvious benefits included the finding that religion reduces people's inner conflicts among different goals and values. As we noted earlier, conflicting goals impede self-regulation, so it appears that religion reduces such problems by providing believers with clearer priorities.

More important, religion affects two central mechanisms for self-control: building willpower and improving monitoring. As early as the 1920s, researchers reported that students who spent more time in Sunday school scored higher on laboratory tests of self-discipline. Religiously devout children were rated relatively low in impulsiveness by both parents and teachers. We don't know of any researchers who have specifically tested the self-control consequences of regular prayers or other religious practices, but these rituals presumably build willpower in the same way as the other exercises that have been studied, like forcing yourself to sit up straight or speak more precisely.

Religious meditations often involve explicit and effortful regulation of attention. The beginner's exercise in Zen meditation is to count one's breaths up to ten and then do it again, over and over. The mind wanders quite naturally, so bringing it back to focus narrowly on one's breathing builds mental discipline. So does saying the rosary, chanting Hebrew psalms, repeating Hindu mantras. When neuroscientists observe people praying or meditating, they see strong activity in two parts of the brain that are also important for self-regulation and control of attention. Psychologists see an effect when they expose people to religious words subliminally, meaning that the words are flashed on a screen so quickly that the people aren't consciously aware of what they've seen. People who are subliminally exposed to religious words like *God* or *Bible* become slower to recognize words associated with temptations like *drugs* or *premarital sex*. "It looks as if people come to associate religion with tamping down these temptations," says McCullough, who suggests that prayers and meditation rituals are "a kind of anaerobic workout for self-control."

Religious believers build self-control by regularly forcing them-selves to interrupt their daily routines in order to pray. Some reli-gions, like Islam, require prayers at fixed times every day. Many religions prescribe periods of fasting, like the day of Yom Kippur, the month of Ramadan, and the forty days of Lent. Religions man-date specific patterns of eating, like kosher food or vegetarianism. Some services and meditations require the believer to adopt and hold specific poses (like kneeling, or sitting cross-legged in the lotus posi-tion) so long that they become uncomfortable and require discipline to maintain them.

Religion also improves the monitoring of behavior, another of the central steps to self-control. Religious people tend to feel that someone important is watching them. That monitor might be God, a supernatural being who pays attention to what you do and think, often even knowing your innermost thoughts and reasons, and can't be easily fooled if you do something apparently good for the wrong reason. In a notable study by Mark Baldwin and his colleagues, fe-male undergraduates read a sexually explicit passage on a computer screen. Then some of the women were subliminally shown a photo-graph of the pope. Afterward, when asked to rate themselves, the Catholic women (that is, the ones who accepted the pope's religious authority and associated him with God's commandments) rated them-selves more negatively, presumably because their unconscious had registered the image of the pope and left them with a sense of disap-proval for having read and possibly enjoyed the erotic reading.

Regardless of whether religious people believe in an omniscient deity, they are generally quite conscious of being monitored by human eyes: the other members of their religious community. If they attend a house of worship regularly, they feel pressured to control their behavior according to the community's rules and norms. Even out-side of church, religious people often spend time with one another and may feel that their misbehaviors will be noticed with disapproval. Religions also encourage monitoring through rituals, such as the

Catholic sacrament of confession and the Jewish holiday of Yom Kippur, that require people to reflect on their moral failures and other shortcomings.

Of course, it takes some discipline to even start practicing a religion, because you have to attend services, memorize prayers, and follow rules. One reason for the higher levels of self-control found among religious people is that the congregations are biased samples of people who started out with higher self-control than average. But even after taking that factor into account, researchers still see evidence that self-control improves with religion, and many people instinctively reach the same conclusion—that's why they take up religion when they want more control. Other people in times of personal troubles rediscover the faith they'd learned in their childhood but then abandoned. Their religious reawakening may involve a vague regret that if they'd lived the proper way, they wouldn't be having their current problems (with alcohol or drugs or debt), but underlying that regret is most likely the recognition that the discipline of religion will help them get back on track.

Mary Karr, the lifelong agnostic, ended up surrendering so completely that she was baptized a Catholic and even went through the Spiritual Exercises of St. Ignatius, an advanced series of rigorous, time-consuming prayers and meditations. Her path, clearly, is not for everyone. Even if you were willing to adopt Catholicism or another religion just to improve your self-control, you probably couldn't gain most of the benefits without genuine belief. Psychologists have found that people who attend religious services for extrinsic reasons, like wanting to impress others or make social connections, don't have the same high level of self-control as the true believers. McCullough concludes that the believers' self-control comes not merely from a fear of God's wrath but from the system of values they've absorbed, which gives their personal goals an aura of sacredness.

He advises agnostics to look for their own set of hallowed values. That might be a devout commitment to helping others, the way that

Henry Stanley made it his "sacred task" in Africa to end the slave trade. It might be a commitment to improve others' health, or spread humane values, or preserve the environment for future generations. It's probably no coincidence that environmentalism is especially strong in rich countries where traditional religion has waned. The devotion to God seems to give way to a reverence for nature's beauty and transcendence. Environmentalists' exhortations to reduce consumption and waste are teaching children some of the same self-control lessons offered in religious sermons and Victorian primers. Secular greens seem to be instinctively replacing one form of self-discipline with another, and one kind of rules with another: organic instead of kosher, sustainability instead of salvation.

Nor is it just a coincidence that people who have set aside the Bible end up buying so many books with new sets of rules for living. They replace the Ten Commandments with the 12 Steps or the Eightfold Path or the 7 Habits. Even if they don't believe in the God of Moses, they like the idea of codes on sacred tablets. These sorts of rules and dogmas may leave you cold—and make you nervous—but don't dismiss them all as useless superstition. There's another way to regard these rules, and it comes with enough statistical charts, mathematical game theory, and economic jargon to please the most secular scientists.

Bright Lines

When Eric Clapton relapsed on that summer evening, when he drove by the pub and couldn't resist stopping in for a drink, he was undone by what's called "hyperbolic discounting." The most precise way to explain that concept is with graphs and hyperbolas, but we'll try a visual metaphor (mixed with an old allegory).

Think of Eric Clapton on that Saturday evening as a repentant sinner who is literally on the road to salvation, like the hero of *Pil-*

grim's Progress, the seventeenth-century allegory. Suppose that he, too, is journeying toward a Celestial City. While traveling through the open countryside, he can see the city's far-off golden spires and keeps heading in their direction. This evening he looks ahead and notices a pub, strategically situated at a bend in the road so that it's directly in front of travelers. From this distance it looks like a small building, and he still keeps his eyes fixed on the grander spires of the Celestial City in the background. But as Eric the Pilgrim approaches the pub, it looms larger, and when he arrives, the building completely blocks his view. He can no longer see the golden spires in the distance. Suddenly the Celestial City seems much less important than this one little building. And thus, verily, our pilgrim's progress endeth with him passed out on the pub's floor.

That's the result of hyperbolic discounting: We can ignore temptations when they're not immediately available, but once they're right in front of us we lose perspective and forget our distant goals. George Ainslie, a renowned psychiatrist and behavioral economist with the Department of Veterans Affairs, worked out the mathematics of this foible by using some clever variations of the familiar experiments testing long-term and short-term rewards. For instance, if you won a lottery with a choice of prizes, would you prefer $100 to be paid six years from today, or $200 to be paid nine years from today? Most people will choose the $200. But what if the choice were between $100 today and $200 three years from today? A rational discounter would apply the same logic and conclude once again that the extra money is worth the wait, but most people will instead demand the quick $100. Our judgment is so distorted by the temptation of immediate cash that we irrationally devalue the future prize. Ainslie found that as we approach a short-term temptation, our tendency to discount the future follows the steep curve of a hyperbola, which is why this tendency is called hyperbolic discounting. As you devalue the future (like those heroin addicts in Vermont who couldn't think beyond the next hour), you lose your concern about a hangover tomorrow, and you're not focused on your vow to go through the rest of your life sober. Those future benefits now seem trivial in relation to the immediate pleasure at the pub. What's the harm in stopping by for one drink?

For many people, of course, there is no harm in stopping for a drink, just as some people (not many) can enjoy one cigarette at a party and not smoke again for months. But if you're someone who can't control your drinking or your smoking, you can't look on that drink or cigarette as an isolated event. You can't have one glass of champagne because you're toasting your best friend's wedding. You need to see the one lapse as a precedent that will establish a long-term pattern. For our pilgrim, that means recognizing that if he pops into the village pub for one drink, he's going to have another and another, and may never make it to the Celestial City. So, before the road takes him too close to the pub and warps his judgment, he needs to prepare himself.

The simplest policy might be to just avoid pubs. Before getting close to one, he could leave the main road and take a detour around it. But how could he be sure he'd follow that policy consistently? Suppose, as he prepares to take the detour around the pub, he remembers that farther down the road, in the next city, is a tavern that's unavoidable. It sits right next to the only bridge spanning the river he must cross. He fears that when he reaches that city tavern tomorrow evening, he'll yield to temptation. Suspecting that his dream of a long sober walk to the Celestial City might be doomed, Eric the Pilgrim starts bargaining with himself: *If I'm going to get drunk anyway tomorrow evening, what difference does it make if I stop for a drink now? Carpe diem! Bottoms up!* For him to resist a drink tonight, he needs to be confident that he won't yield to temptation tomorrow.

He needs the help of "bright lines," a term that Ainslie borrows from lawyers. These are clear, simple, unambiguous rules. You can't help but notice when you cross a bright line. If you promise yourself to drink or smoke "moderately," that's not a bright line. It's a fuzzy boundary with no obvious point at which you go from moderation to excess. Because the transition is so gradual and your mind is so adept at overlooking your own peccadilloes, you may fail to notice when you've gone too far. So you can't be sure you're always going to follow the rule to drink moderately. In contrast, zero tolerance is a bright line: total abstinence with no exceptions anytime. It's not practical for all self-control problems—a dieter cannot stop eating all food—but it works well in many situations. Once you're committed to following a bright-line rule, your present self can feel confident that your future self will observe it, too. And if you believe that the rule is sacred—a commandment from God, the unquestionable law of a higher power—then it becomes an especially bright line. You have more reason to expect your future self to respect it, and therefore your belief becomes a form of self-control: a self-fulfilling mandate. I think I won't, therefore I don't.

Eric Clapton discovered that bright line in one moment at Hazelden, and he appreciated its power once again when he chaired an AA meeting not long after the death of his son. He spoke about the third of the twelve steps—handing your will over to the care of a higher power—and told the group how his compulsion to drink had vanished the instant he got down on his knees at Hazelden and asked for God's help. From then on, he told them, he never doubted he would have the will to remain sober, not even on the day his son died. After the meeting, a woman came up to him.

"You've just taken away my last excuse to have a drink," she told him. "I've always had this little corner of my mind which held the excuse that, if anything were to happen to my kids, then I'd be justified in getting drunk. You've shown me that's not true." Upon hearing her, Clapton realized that he had found the best way to honor the memory of his son. Whatever you call his gift to that woman—social support, faith in God, trust in a higher power, a bright line—it left her with the will to save herself.

9.

RAISING STRONG CHILDREN: SELF-ESTEEM VERSUS SELF-CONTROL

You're a superstar no matter who you are or where you come from—and you were born that way!

—Lady Gaga

Brats are not born. They're made.

—Deborah Carroll, a.k.a. Nanny Deb

Thanks to the wonders of reality TV, middle-class parents across the United States have experienced a privilege once limited to the wealthy: outsourcing their jobs to a British nanny. Their stories vary, as you would expect from unhappy families, but the basic narrative arc is the same for each episode of this genre, whether it's *Nanny 911* or *Supernanny.* It begins in a home with children running wild—crying, screaming, spitting, pulling hair, flinging sippy cups, scrawling crayon graffiti on sheets, smashing toys, punching parents, strangling siblings. They're literally climbing the walls of a ranch house in suburban St. Louis at the start of a classic *Nanny 911* episode titled "The Little House of Horrors." Then, and none too soon, a British nanny arrives at the home dressed in full Victorian regalia—black skirt, pin-striped black vest, black stockings, burgundy cloche and matching cape with gold buttons and chain—as the narrator makes a solemn announcement: "Parents of America, help is on the way!"

How did it come to this?

You might think the programs are hyping the children's misbehavior, but the producers will tell you that the restrictions of prime-time television prevented them from showing some of the worst moments, like when a four-year-old on Long Island looked up at the woman who'd given him life and said, "Fuck off, Mom!" What's gone wrong? The immediate impulse is to fault the parents, and we'll get to the ones in that St. Louis home shortly. But it's not fair to put all the blame on them or any of the other parents seeking foreign aid. America's parents couldn't have produced these brats all by themselves. They had lots of help from the nation's leading educators, journalists, and, above all, psychologists.

The theory of self-esteem was a well-intentioned attempt to use psychology for the public good, and it did indeed seem promising at first. Baumeister spent much of his early career on the self-esteem bandwagon. He was impressed by research showing that students with high self-esteem had high grades, while students with low-self esteem tended to struggle in school. Other studies revealed that unwed mothers, drug addicts, and criminals had low self-esteem. The correlations weren't large, but they were statistically significant, and the results inspired a movement led by psychotherapists like Nathaniel Branden. "I cannot think of a single psychological problem—from anxiety and depression, to fear of intimacy, to spouse battery or child molestation—that is not traceable to the problem of low self-esteem," Branden wrote. Andrew Mecca, the drug-treatment expert who became chairman of California's task force on self-esteem, explained that "virtually every social problem can be traced to people's lack of self-love." All this enthusiasm led to a new approach to child rearing imparted by psychologists, teachers, journalists, and artists like Whitney Houston. She summed up this philosophy in her 1980s hit song "The Greatest Love of All," which was revealed to be none other than . . . oneself. The key to success was self-esteem. For children to succeed, she explained, they simply need to be shown "all the beauty they possess inside."

It was a novel but irresistible idea to the millions who began trying to improve children's academic skills by encouraging them to think, *I'm really good at things.* At home, parents practiced dispensing extra praise. Coaches made sure everyone got a trophy, not just the winners. The Girl Scouts adopted a program called "uniquely ME!" In school, children made collages of their favorite traits and discussed what they liked best about one another. "Mutual admiration society" used to be a disparaging phrase, but today's young adults grew up with it as the social norm. Whitney Houston's message was carried to the next generation by Lady Gaga, who reassured her fans at a concert, "You're a superstar no matter who you are or where you come from—and you were born that way!" The fans cheered her right back, naturally, and then Lady Gaga reciprocated by lifting a bright torch and sweeping its light across the audience. "Hey, kids!" she shouted. "When you leave tonight, you don't leave loving me more. You leave loving *yourself* more!"

All these mutual affirmation exercises were pleasant enough, and they were supposed to do even more long-term good than conventional lessons. When the state of California asked researchers to evaluate the evidence on self-esteem, the news seemed promising. Neil Smelser, the distinguished sociologist at Berkeley who edited the report, declared on the first page that "many, if not most, of the major problems plaguing society have roots in the low self-esteem of many of the people who make up society."

He also noted, in a later passage that wasn't nearly as newsworthy, that it was "disappointing" to see the lack of really solid scientific evidence "to date." But better results were expected once more work was done, and there was plenty of money available for self-esteem research. The studies continued, and eventually another institution commissioned another report. This time it was not a political unit, like the state of California, but a scientific body, the Association for Psychological Science. The conclusions did not inspire any performances from Whitney Houston or Lady Gaga.

From Self-esteem to Narcissism

The psychologists on the review panel, which included Baumeister, sifted through thousands of studies looking for the ones that met high standards of research quality. The panel found several hundred, like the one that tracked high school students for several years in order to understand the correlation between self-esteem and good grades. Yes, students with higher self-esteem did have higher grades. But which came first? Did students' self-esteem lead to good grades, or did good grades lead to self-esteem? It turned out that grades in tenth grade predicted self-esteem in twelfth grade, but self-esteem in tenth grade failed to predict grades in twelfth grade. Thus, it seemed, the grades came first, and the self-esteem came afterward.

In another carefully controlled study, Donald Forsyth tried boosting the self-esteem of some of the students in his psychology class at Virginia Commonwealth University. He randomly assigned some students who got a C grade or worse on the midterm to receive a weekly message boosting their self-esteem, and some students with similar grades to get a neutral weekly message. The weekly pep talks presumably helped the students feel better about themselves, but it didn't help their grades—quite to the contrary. When they took the final exam, not only did they do worse than the control group but their grades were even lower than what they'd gotten on the midterm. Their average score dropped from 59 to 39—from borderline passing down to hopeless.

Other evidence showed that, across the country, students' self-esteem went up while their performance declined. They just felt better about doing worse. In his own research, Baumeister puzzled over the observation that some people doing truly awful things—like professional hit men and serial rapists—had remarkably high levels of self-esteem.

After reviewing the scientific literature, the panel of psychologists concluded that there is no modern epidemic of low self-esteem, at least not in the United States, Canada, or western Europe. (There's not much known about trends of how people regard themselves in, say, Myanmar.) Most people already feel pretty good about themselves. Children in particular tend to start off with very positive views of themselves. The consensus of the scientific literature happens to jibe with anecdotal evidence from the Baumeister household, where there have been conversations like this:

> **Daughter** (4 years old): I know everything.
> **Mother:** No, honey, you don't know everything.
> **Daughter:** Yes, I do. I know everything.
> **Mother:** You don't know the square root of thirty-six.
> **Daughter** (without batting an eye): I'm keeping all the really big numbers a secret.
> **Mother:** It's not a really big number. It's only six.
> **Daughter:** I knew that.

And this was a child whose parents had *not* attempted to boost her self-esteem.

The review panel also concluded that high self-esteem generally does not make people more effective or easier to get along with. People with high self-esteem think they're more popular, charming, and socially skilled than other people, but objective studies find no difference. Their self-esteem generally does not lead to better performance at school or at work, and it does not help prevent cigarette smoking, alcohol and drug use, or early sexual behavior. While there may be a correlation between low self-esteem and problems like drug addiction and teenage pregnancy, that doesn't mean that low self-esteem causes these problems. It works the other way: Being a sixteen-year-old pregnant heroin addict can make you feel less than wonderful about yourself.

There seem to be only two clearly demonstrated benefits of high self-esteem, according to the review panel. First, it increases initiative, probably because it lends confidence. People with high self-esteem are more willing to act on their beliefs, to stand up for what they believe in, to approach others, to risk new undertakings. (This unfortunately includes being extra willing to do stupid or destructive things, even when everyone else advises against them.) Second, it feels good. High self-esteem seems to operate like a bank of positive emotions, which furnish a general sense of well-being and can be useful when you need an extra dose of confidence to cope with misfortune, ward off depression, or bounce back from failure. These benefits might be useful to people in some jobs, like sales, by enabling them to recover from frequent rejections, but this sort of persistence is a mixed blessing. It can also lead people to ignore sensible advice as they stubbornly keep wasting time and money on hopeless causes.

On the whole, benefits of high self-esteem accrue to the self while its costs are borne by others, who must deal with side effects like arrogance and conceit. At worst, self-esteem becomes narcissism, the self-absorbed conviction of personal superiority. Narcissists are legends in their own mind and addicted to their grandiose images. They have a deep craving to be admired by other people (but don't feel a special need to be liked—it's adulation they require). They expect to be treated as special beings and will turn nasty when criticized. They tend to make very good first impressions but don't wear well. When the psychologist Delroy Paulhus asked people in groups to rate one another, the narcissists seemed to be everyone's favorite person, but only during the first few meetings. After a few months, they usually slipped to the bottom of the rankings. God's gift to the world can be hard to live with.

By most measures in psychological studies, narcissism has increased sharply in recent decades, especially among young Americans. College professors often complain that students now feel entitled to high grades without having to study; employers report problems with young workers who expect a quick rise to the top without paying their dues. This trend toward narcissim is even apparent in song lyrics over the past three decades, as a team of researchers led by Nathan DeWall demonstrated in a clever study showing that words like "I" and "me" have become increasingly common in hit songs. Whitney Houston's "Greatest Love of All" has been taken to another level by musicians like Rivers Cuomo, the lead singer of Weezer, who wrote and performed a popular song in 2008 titled "The Greatest Man That Ever Lived." It was autobiographical.

This broad rise in narcissism is the problem child of the self-esteem movement, and it is not likely to change anytime soon, because the movement persists despite the evidence that it's not making children become more successful, honest, or otherwise better citizens. Too many students, parents, and educators are still seduced by the easy promises of self-esteem. Like the students in Forsyth's class in Virginia, when the going gets tough, people with high self-esteem often decide they shouldn't bother. If other people can't appreciate how terrific they are, then it's the other people's problem.

Exceptional Asians

There's one notable exception to the trend toward narcissism observed in psychological studies of young Americans. It doesn't appear among young Asian-Americans, probably because their parents have been influenced less by the self-esteem movement than by a cultural tradition of instilling discipline. Some Asian cultures put considerably more emphasis on promoting self-control, and from earlier ages, than is common in America and other Western societies. Chinese parents and preschools pressure children quite early in life to become toilet trained and acquire other basic forms of impulse control. By one estimate, two-year-old Chinese children are expected to have levels of control that correspond roughly to what American children reach at age three or four.

A clear difference between Chinese and American toddlers emerges when they're asked to override their natural impulses. In one test, for instance, the toddlers are shown a series of pictures and instructed to say "day" whenever they see the moon, and "night" whenever they see the sun. In other tests, the toddlers try to restrain themselves to a whisper when they're excited, and play a version of Simon Says in which they're supposed to obey one kind of command but ignore another kind. The Chinese four-year-olds generally perform better on these tests than Americans of the same age. The Chinese toddlers' superior self-control might be due in part to genes: There's evidence that the genetic factors associated with ADHD (attention deficit hyperactivity disorder) are much rarer in Chinese children than in American children. But the cultural traditions in China and other Asian countries undoubtedly play an important role in instilling self-discipline, and those traditions in Asian-American homes have contributed to the children's low levels of narcissism as well as their later successes. Asian-Americans make up only 4 percent of the U.S. population but account for a quarter of the student body at elite universities like Stanford, Columbia, and Cornell. They're more likely to get a college degree than any other ethnic group, and they go on to earn salaries that are 25 percent above the American norm.

Their success has led to the popular notion that Asians are more intelligent than Americans and Europeans, but that's not how James Flynn explains their achievements. After carefully reviewing IQ studies, Flynn concludes that the scores of Chinese-American and Japanese-American people are very similar to whites of European descent. If anything, the Asian-Americans' IQ is slightly lower, on average, although they do show up more at both the upper and lower extremes. The big difference is that they make better use of their intelligence. People working in what Flynn calls elite professions, like physicians, scientists, and accountants, generally have an IQ above a certain threshold. For white Americans, that threshold is an IQ of 110, but Chinese-Americans manage to get the same elite jobs with an IQ of only 103. Moreover, among the people above each threshold, Chinese-Americans have higher rates of actually getting into those jobs, meaning that a Chinese-American with an IQ above 103 is more likely to get an elite job than an American with an IQ above 110. The pattern is similar for Japanese-Americans. By virtue of self-control—hard work, diligence, steadiness, reliability—the children of immigrants from East Asia can do as well as Americans with higher IQs.

Delayed gratification has been a familiar theme in the homes of immigrants like Jae and Dae Kim, who were born in South Korea and raised two daughters in North Carolina. The sisters, Soo and Jane, became a surgeon and a lawyer, respectively, as well as the co-authors of *Top of the Class,* a book about Asian parents' techniques for fostering achievement. They tell how their parents started teaching them the alphabet before their second birthday, and how their mother was never one to reward a child whining for candy at the supermarket. When they reached the checkout counter, before the girls had a chance to beg, Mrs. Kim would preempt them by announcing that if they each read a book the following week, she would buy them a candy bar on the *next* shopping trip. Later, when Soo went off to college and asked her parents for a cheap used car to get around, they refused but offered to buy her a brand-new car if she was admitted to medical school. Thus, these parents did provide good things for their daughters—but each treat was meted out as a reward for some valued achievement.

The many Asian-American success stories have forced developmental psychologists to revise their theories about proper parenting. They used to warn against the "authoritarian" style, in which parents set rigid goals and enforced strict rules without much overt concern for the child's feelings. Parents were advised to adopt a different style, called "authoritative," in which they still set limits but gave more autonomy and paid more attention to the child's desires. This warmer, more nurturing style was supposed to produce well-adjusted, self-confident children who would do better academically and socially than those from authoritarian homes. But then, as Ruth Chao and other psychologists studied Asian-American families, they noticed that many of the parents set quite strict rules and goals. These immigrants, and often their children, too, considered their style of parenting to be a form of devotion, not oppression. Chinese-American parents were determined to instill self-control by following the Confucian concepts of *chiao shun*, which means "to train," and *guan*, which means both "to govern" and "to love." These parents might have seemed cold and rigid by American standards, but their children were flourishing both in and out of school.

The contrast with American notions showed up in a study of women in the Los Angeles area who were the mothers of toddlers. When asked how parents could contribute to children's academic success, the mothers who had emigrated from China most frequently mentioned setting high goals, enforcing tough standards, and requiring children to do extra homework. Meanwhile, the native-born mothers of European ancestry were determined *not* to put too much pressure on children. They most frequently mentioned the importance of not overemphasizing academic success, of stressing the child's social development, and of promoting the idea that "learning is fun" and "not something you work at." Another of their chief concerns was promoting the child's self-esteem—a concept of just about no interest to the Chinese mothers in the study, or to Amy Chua, who has become the most outspoken (and entertaining) advocate of what she calls "Chinese parenting" in her bestselling book, *The Battle Hymn of the Tiger Mother.*

Chua's version of parenting—no sleepovers, no playdates—is too extreme for our tastes, particularly the three-hour violin lessons. But we admire her insight into the problems with the self-esteem movement: "As I watched American parents slathering praise on their kids for the lowest of tasks—drawing a squiggle or waving a stick—I came to see that Chinese parents have two things over their Western counterparts: (1) higher dreams for their children, and (2) higher regard for their children in the sense of knowing how much they can take." Chua's basic strategies—set clear goals, enforce rules, punish failure, reward excellence—aren't all that different from the ones being imparted to American homes on *Nanny 911* by Deborah Carroll, the member of the "team of world-class nannies" who gets assigned to the truly hard cases, like the Paul family portrayed in that "Little House of Horrors" episode. In her dealings with American children, Carroll says, she's simply applying the lessons of her own youth in Wales.

"When I was in school," Carroll recalls, "it was such a big thing to get a gold or silver star. It was so important to have a sense that I worked really hard to achieve something. When I ironed my grandfather's shirts, he insisted on paying me because I did it so well—he told me I did it better than my grandmother, and I loved that feeling of accomplishment. That's where your self-esteem comes from, not from being told you're the greatest." Like Amy Chua and the Kims in North Carolina and so many other Asian immigrants, Nanny Deb independently arrived at the same educational conclusions as the Association for Psychological Science's review panel: Forget about self-esteem. Work on self-control.

Nanny Deb and the Triplets

When Carroll arrived at the Pauls' home near St. Louis, she wasn't particularly worried about the hellions she'd seen on video climbing the walls, spitting on the floor, and swinging from light fixtures. She knew that four-year-olds could be a handful, especially when there were three of them running wild. But she had had enough experience with other American houses of horrors to realize that there were bigger problems to deal with.

"In homes like this, the children are very, very easy," Carroll says. "They're looking for structure. They're looking to feel safe, for someone who can tell them: 'I'm in charge. Things are going to be fine.' It's much harder to get the parents to stay on track. They have to learn how to get control of themselves to control the children."

Carroll had been dealing with parents like this since becoming a full-time nanny at the age of eighteen. One of her first jobs in London was with an American mother, married to a Briton, who would watch helplessly as her child went berserk. "The toddler would be literally spinning on the coffee table in a tantrum," Carroll recalls, "and the mother would just say to her, 'You're in a really bad space, honey.' There's nothing wrong with a toddler having a tantrum. It's natural. It's our job to teach them other ways to deal with it."

The Pauls weren't as mellow as that mother, but they seemed just as helpless when it came to discipline. When the father, Tim, came home from the office to find the living room covered in toys, he'd take a hockey stick and sweep them all into the closet. The mother, Cyndi, a former flight attendant accustomed to badly behaved adults, was overwhelmed by the triplets and had given up trying to get them to clean up their toys or get dressed. When Nanny Deb told them to put on their own socks—hardly an impossible feat for toddlers approaching kindergarten—one of them, Lauren, refused and ran into the kitchen to bring the socks to her mother. Sobbing hysterically, she begged over and over for help while desperately clutching her mother.

"This is very heartbreaking," Mrs. Paul said. "She'll do this for half an hour. It will be very frustrating here for a while. When she has her meltdown, she just asks the same question over and over. That's when I just zone out and I can no longer focus and I'm ready to just scream at everybody and just send them straight to bed."

This time, as usual, the child won. Mrs. Paul put on the socks for her, much to the exasperation of Carroll. "For four and a half years, she's gotten upset and you've let her get away with it," Carroll said to Mrs. Paul. "What's going to happen to her in second grade when she's not doing her math because she doesn't want to?"

Watching scenes like this, it's hard to believe that parents traditionally considered it their duty to beat their children. "Spare the rod, spoil the child" really was standard advice, and spoiling the child was considered to be the essence of failed parenting. The Puritan Cotton Mather put it even more starkly: "Better whipt, than damned." We're not advocating a return to spanking, much less whipping, but we do think parents need to rediscover their roles as disciplinarians. That doesn't mean being abusive or getting angry or imposing Draconian penalties. But it does mean taking the time to watch your child's behavior and impose appropriate rewards or punishments.

Whether you're giving a time-out to a toddler or revoking a teenager's driving privileges, there are three basic facets of punishment: severity, speed, and consistency. Many people associate strict discipline with severe penalties, but that's actually the least important facet. Researchers have found that severity seems to matter remarkably little and can even be counterproductive: Instead of encouraging virtue, harsh punishments teach the child that life is cruel and that aggression is appropriate. The speed of the punishment is much more important, as researchers have found in working with children as well as with animals. For lab rats to learn from their mistakes, the punishment generally has to occur almost immediately, preferably within a second of the misbehavior. Punishment doesn't have to be that quick with children, but the longer the delay, the more chance that they'll have forgotten the infraction and the mental processes that led to it.

By far the most important facet of punishment—and the most difficult one for parents—is consistency. Ideally, a parent should quickly discipline the child every single time he or she misbehaves, but in a restrained, even mild manner. A stern word or two is often enough as long as it's done carefully and regularly. This approach can initially be more of a strain on the parents than on the child. They're tempted to overlook or forgive some misdeed, if only because they're tired or because it may spoil the pleasant time everyone else is having. Parents may rationalize that they want to be kind; they may even tell each other to be nice and let this one go. But the more vigilant they are early on, the less effort is required in the long run. Consistent discipline tends to produce well-behaved children.

While parents like Cyndi Paul find it heartbreaking to start imposing discipline, children react well when reprimands are delivered briefly, calmly, and consistently, according to Susan O'Leary, a psychologist who has spent long hours observing toddlers and parents. When parents are inconsistent, when they let an infraction slide, they sometimes try to compensate with an extra-strict punishment for the next one. This requires less self-control on the parents' part: They can be nice when they feel like it, and then punish severely if they're feeling angry or the misbehavior is egregious. But imagine how this looks from the child's point of view. Some days you make a smart remark and the grown-ups all laugh. Other days a similar remark brings a smack or the loss of treasured privileges. Seemingly tiny or even random differences in your own behavior or in the situation seem to spell the difference between no punishment at all and a highly upsetting one. Besides resenting the unfairness, you learn that the most important thing is not how you behave but whether or not you get caught, and whether your parents are in the mood to punish. You might learn, for instance, that table manners can be dispensed with at restaurants, because the grown-ups are too embarrassed to discipline you in public.

"Parents find it hard to administer discipline in public because they feel judged," Carroll says. "They're afraid people will think they're a bad mother. But you have to get that out of your head. I've had people stare at me when I take a child out of a restaurant for being rude, but you can't worry about that. You have to do what's right for the child, and it really is all about being consistent. They have to grow up knowing what's appropriate and inappropriate behavior."

When Carroll applied her consistent brand of discipline in the Paul household, the results seemed miraculous. By the end of her weeklong stay, the triplets were making their beds and picking up their toys; Lauren was proudly putting on her socks; the parents looked calm and happy. At least, that was how it was edited to appear on the program, in keeping with the usual arc of chaos to bliss. But could this discipline really make a lasting difference once Nanny Deb and the cameras departed? We checked up on the Pauls in 2010, which was six years after Carroll's visit, and Mrs. Paul declared the experiment a long-term success. "We don't have any real big issues anymore," she said, explaining that the four-year-old hellions of television fame had grown up into ten-year-olds who were flourishing academically and serving on the school's leadership council. At home, they were still doing their chores.

"Until Nanny Deb came, I never thought they could do those chores themselves," Mrs. Paul told us. "I thought it was too much to ask them, but they just didn't have the guidance or structure to know what they were supposed to do. It's easy for a parent to say, 'Go and clean up your room,' but that doesn't tell the child anything. You may as well tell them to stare at the wall. You need the discipline to go in there with them and model exactly what to do—show them how to fold a piece of clothing and put it in the closet or the right drawer."

Once Mrs. Paul did that a few times, the children took to doing it on their own, although it still occasionally required some parental supervision—and the resolve not to backslide and do the jobs for the children. "Sometimes," Mrs. Paul said, "I come into the kitchen and their cereal bowls are still sitting there, and I find myself wanting to grab the bowls and clean up. It's easier for me to do that than go find them. But no matter where they are, I have to remember to ask them to come back and clear their own plates. That's where I have to exercise self-control."

Which brings us back to the familiar question for parents: How do you acquire and maintain self-control? How do you calmly, consistently discipline the children when, as Mrs. Paul realized, it's so often easier to let things slide? The answer, as ever, starts with setting goals and standards.

Rules for Babies and Vampires

Long before children can read rules or do chores, they can start learning self-control. Ask any parent who has survived the ordeal of Ferberization, which is based on a technique found in a Victorian child-rearing manual. It requires the parents, against all instinct, to ignore their infants' cries when they're left alone at bedtime. Instead of rushing to the infant's side, the parents let the infant cry for a fixed interval of time, then go offer some comfort, then withdraw for another fixed interval. The process is repeated until the child learns to control the crying and go to sleep without any help from the parents. It requires great self-control by the parents to ignore the heart-rending screams, but the infants usually learn quickly to put themselves to sleep without any crying. Once an infant acquires this self-control, everyone wins: The infant is no longer anxious at bedtime or when he or she wakes up alone in the middle of the night, and the parents don't have to spend their nights hovering by the crib.

We've seen parents successfully use a variant of this approach when an infant cries to be fed. Instead of immediately feeding the crying child, the mother lets the child know that the signal has been received but then waits for her or him to quiet down before offering the breast or the bottle. Again, it's hard to ignore the cries at first, and we realize that to some parents it sounds too cruel to even try. But once a child learns to ask for food without going into a crying frenzy, both child and parent end up calmer and happier. The children are learning that they have some power over themselves, that certain kinds of behavior are expected, and that actions have consequences — lessons that will become more and more important as they get older.

Nearly all experts agree that children need and want clear rules, and that being held accountable for obeying the rules is a vital feature of healthy development. But rules are helpful only if children know them and understand them, so the brighter the line, the better. Nanny Debs likes to call a special meeting to go over her "house rules," and then she posts a chore list in each child's bedroom along with a wooden pole that's used for keeping score. When children make the bed or clean their rooms or wash the dishes, they get to put a colored ring around the pole. Each ring entitles them to fifteen minutes of watching television or playing a video game, up to a total of an hour per day. If they misbehave, they first get a warning, and if they persist, the parent removes one of the rings.

To keep the rules consistent, parents need to coordinate with each other and with caretakers so that everyone knows what's expected. When your children are still toddlers, establish a system of rewards and punishments in advance, and when you're giving either one to a child, explain exactly why. As they get older, it becomes more useful to ask them what goals they have for themselves. Once you hear their ambitions, you can help get there with the right incentives, like making allowance payments contingent on doing chores, or promising bonuses for doing extra work. But to make these financial inducements worthwhile, parents have to show some restraint themselves.

Remember the Kims, who gave their daughter Soo the car she wanted, but only after she got into medical school. A teal-blue Toyota Tercel may not sound to you like a dream car, but Soo treasured it, lovingly washing and waxing it for years and years. When it finally broke down and had to be towed away, Soo broke down, too, and started crying. It meant everything to her because she had worked so hard to earn it.

By age six, some children can start learning to save money, but it's a struggle, as the psychologist Annette Otto discovered by watching children play a game in which they could save money to buy a desirable toy but also could spend it along the way on other toys and sweets. Many of the six-year-olds spent their money early in the game only to gradually realize that they might not have enough for the toy (and then stopped trying to save at all). In contrast, some nine-year-olds and many twelve-year-olds succeeded by saving first until they reached the amount they wanted, and then began to spend any additional money on treats. To encourage this orientation toward the future, parents can help children open savings accounts, keep track of the bank statements, and set goals and rewards. Research has shown that children who open bank accounts are more likely than others to grow up to be savers. So are children who grow up discussing money with their parents.

Some parents like to offer cash for good grades; others balk at paying for what children are supposed to be doing anyway. The most compelling argument against these payments is based on what psychologists call the overjustification effect: Rewards turn play into work. More precisely, studies have shown that when people are paid to do things that they like to do, they start to regard the task as paid drudgery. By that logic, wouldn't paying for grades undermine children's intrinsic love of learning?

We're not convinced by that argument. In the first place, grades are already extrinsic rewards, so inserting money into the arrangement does not change any relevance of the overjustification effect to any intrinsic love of learning. Second, performing well for money is a fact of adult life, so getting money for grades is a reasonable preparation for it. That would apply even if it were true that children who get money for grades somehow lose a little of their personal passion for learning. (Frankly, as much as we've enjoyed the research in our own careers, we wonder if love of learning is overrated as a motivational tool.) Money symbolizes value, and using it to pay for grades conveys to children the high value that society, and the family, places on school, particularly if the money is reserved for outstanding achievement.

We'll grant that paying children just for routinely attending school might well reduce their desire to go to school without pay (as if that were a concern). But if you're paying them for working extra hard and excelling, what's the problem? The results from randomized experiments in paying for grades have been mixed: In some places they haven't done much to improve students' performance, but in other places the payments seem to be remarkably effective. We don't see the downside in trying this experiment at home—although of course you can always stick with noncash rewards if you prefer. Just remember that if you want to instill self-control, you need to be consistent in whatever rewards you give. Don't haphazardly give the child something from your wallet for a good report card. Instead, set the goals in advance: how much money for each A, how much for each B, which subjects count most, etc. For a young child, you may have to set the payment schedule, but older children can start negotiating bonuses and penalties, and perhaps even drawing up formal contracts for both sides to sign. The rules and the rewards will change as the child gets older, but it's important to keep a disciplined system in place, no matter how difficult that seems when the dreaded teenage years arrive.

The problem with adolescents—from the parents' point of view—is that they have a child's power of self-control presiding over an adult's wants and urges. Whatever harmony emerged by age nine or eleven is disrupted by biological growth that gives rise to new sexual and aggressive impulses, and new thrill-seeking inclinations. At some level, teenagers know they need help. That's one reason they buy millions of copies of the *Twilight* novels, in which Edward the vampire and Bella the teenager know that she will lose her humanity, and probably her life, if they consummate their love. Thus they struggle:

Edward: Try to sleep, Bella.
Bella: No, I want you to kiss me again.
Edward: You're overestimating my self-control.
Bella: Which is tempting you more, my blood or my body?
Edward: It's a tie.

Their struggle is the same blockbuster ingredient that sold nineteenth-century romantic novels with titles like *Self-Control* and *Discipline* (both written by Mary Brunton, whose books outsold those of her contemporary rival, Jane Austen). Nineteenth-century farmers fretted about their children being tempted by the new freedoms available in industrial cities, but those temptations are mild compared with what's available today in suburbia and on the Web. Today's teenagers, even ones in no danger of becoming vampires, understand what Edward is feeling when he tells Bella: "I can never, never afford to lose any kind of control when I'm with you."

Until adolescents' self-control catches up with their impulses, parents have the thankless task of somehow providing strict external control while at the same time starting to treat the child as something closer to a grown-up. Probably the best compromise is to give the teenager more say in the rule-making process, and to do it when everyone is in a calm, well-rested state—not when the teenager first comes home at two in the morning. If teenagers can help draw up the rules, they begin to see these as personal commitments instead of parental whims. If they negotiate a curfew, they're more likely to respect it, or at least to accept the consequences for breaking it. And the more involved they get in setting goals, the more likely they are to proceed to the next step of self-control: monitoring themselves.

Wandering Eyes

Before his famous marshmallow experiments with children near Stanford University, Walter Mischel made another discovery about self-control while working in Trinidad. He went there with the intention of studying ethnic stereotypes. The two main ethnic groups in rural Trinidad were of different descent, one African, the other Indian, and they held negative but different stereotypes of each other. The Indians regarded the Africans as lacking in future orientation and inclined to indulge rather than save, whereas the Africans regarded the Indians as joyless savers who lacked a zest for life. Mischel decided to test these stereotypes by asking children from each group to choose between two candy bars. One candy bar was bigger and cost ten times as much as the other, but a child who chose it would have to wait a week to get it. The smaller, cheaper one was available right away.

Mischel found some support for the ethnic stereotypes, but in the process he stumbled on a much bigger and more meaningful effect. Children who had a father in the home were far more willing than others to choose the delayed reward. Most of the racial and ethnic variation could be explained by this difference, because the Indian children generally lived with both parents, whereas a fair number of the African children lived with a single mother. The value of fatherhood was also evident when Mischel analyzed just the African homes: About half of the children living with fathers chose the delayed reward, but none of the children in fatherless homes were willing to wait. Similarly, none of the Indian children living without a father were willing to wait.

These findings, which were published in 1958, didn't attract much attention at the time or in the ensuing decades, when it was dangerous to one's career to suggest that there might be drawbacks to single-parent homes. (Daniel Patrick Moynihan was excoriated for making that suggestion.) Starting in the 1960s, changes in federal policies, social norms, and divorce rates led to a great expansion in the number of children raised by only one parent, usually the mother. No one wanted to sound critical of those mothers — and we certainly don't want to denigrate their hard work and dedication. But eventually there were so many results like Mischel's that the data could no longer be ignored. As a general rule — with lots and lots of exceptions, including Bill Clinton and Barack Obama — children raised by single parents tend not to do as well in life as children who grow up with two parents. Even after researchers control for socioeconomic factors and other variables, it turns out that children from two-parent homes get better grades in school. They're healthier and better-adjusted emotionally. They have more satisfying social lives and engage in less antisocial behavior. They're more likely to attend an elite university and less likely to go to prison.

One possible explanation is that children in one-parent homes start off with a genetic disadvantage in self-control. After all, if the father (or mother, for that matter) has run off and abandoned the family, he may have genes favoring impulsive behavior and under-mining self-control, and his children might have inherited those same genes. Some researchers have attempted to correct for this by looking at children who were raised by single parents because the father was absent for reasons other than having abandoned the family (like being stationed overseas for a long time, or dying at a young age). Predictably, the results were in between. These children showed some deficits, but their problems were not as large as those of the children whose fathers had voluntarily left the home. The evidence suggested that, as usual, children are shaped by a mixture of genetics and the environment.

Whatever role is played by genes, there's an obvious environmental factor affecting children in single-parent homes: They're being watched by fewer eyes. Monitoring is a crucial aspect of self-control, and two parents can generally do a better job of monitoring. Single parents are so busy with essential tasks—putting food on the table, keeping the child healthy, paying bills—that they have to put a lower priority on making and enforcing rules. Two parents can divide the work, leaving them both with more time and energy to spend building the child's character. More adult eyes make a difference—and quite a lasting difference, to judge from the results of a study that started more than six decades ago.

In an attempt to prevent juvenile delinquency during the early 1940s, counselors visited more than 250 boys in their homes twice a month. They recorded observations about the family, the home, and the life of the boys. On average, the boys were about ten when the study began, and about sixteen when it ended. Decades later, when the boys had grown up and were in their forties and fifties, the notes were studied by a researcher named Joan McCord, who compared the teenage experiences with subsequent adult behavior—in particular, criminal behavior. A lack of adult supervision during the teenage years turned out to be one of the strongest predictors of criminal behavior. The counselors had recorded whether the boys' activities outside of school were usually, sometimes, or rarely regulated by an adult. The more time the teenagers spent under adult supervision, the less likely they were to be later convicted of either personal or property crimes.

The passage of decades has not erased the value of parental monitoring. A recent compilation of studies on marijuana use, totaling more than thirty-five thousand participants, showed a robust link to parental supervision. When parents keep tabs on where their children are, what they do, and whom they associate with, the children are much less likely to use illegal drugs than when parents keep fewer close tabs. Similarly, recent studies of diabetic children have found multiple benefits of parental supervision. Adolescents have higher self-control to the extent that their parents generally know where their offspring are after school and at night, what they do with their free time, who their friends are, and how they spend money. Although type I diabetes comes on early in life and may be mainly a result of genes, the adolescents with high trait self-control and high parental supervision have lower blood sugar levels (thus, less severe diabetic problems) than others. In fact, having a mother or father who keeps track of the child's activities, friends, and spending habits can even compensate to some degree for lower levels of self-control, in terms of reducing the severity of diabetes.

The more that children are being monitored, the more opportunities they have to build their self-control. Parents can guide them through the kind of willpower-strengthening exercises we've discussed earlier, like taking care to sit up straight, to always speak grammatically, to avoid starting sentences with "I," and to never say "yeah" for "yes." Anything that forces children to exercise their self-control muscle can be helpful: taking music lessons, memorizing poems, saying prayers, minding their table manners, avoiding the use of profanity, writing thank-you notes.

As they strengthen their willpower, children also need to learn when not to rely on it. In Mischel's marshmallow experiments near Stanford, many children tried to resist temptation by staring right at the marshmallow and willing themselves to be strong. It didn't work. Staring at the forbidden marshmallow kept reminding them of its allure, and as soon as willpower slackened for a moment, they gave in and ate it. By contrast, the children who managed to hold out—who waited fifteen minutes in order to get two marshmallows—typically succeeded by distracting themselves. They covered their eyes, turned their backs, fiddled with their shoelaces. That marshmallow experiment caused some researchers to conclude that controlling attention is what matters, not building willpower, but we disagree.

Yes, controlling attention is important. But you need willpower to control attention.

Playing to Win

For more than half a century, television has distracted children from other pursuits, and for more than half a century it's been blamed for just about everything that's wrong with kids. We don't want to join the generalized TV bashing, because we've seen children learn lots of useful things from television. But one thing they don't learn is how to control their attention. Successful television shows know how to grab and hold attention without making the same mental demands as other pastimes. Web surfing isn't quite as passive, but it doesn't foster much discipline either, particularly if you're just flitting from one site to another, never pausing to read anything longer than a tweet or a short post.

So how can children learn to focus their attention on something longer than a text message and more challenging than a YouTube video? The usual advice is to get them reading books, and we're only too happy to endorse that. (What author isn't?) But they can also work on attention by playing the right kinds of games, starting well before they're old enough to read. Some of the most successful recent self-control programs have drawn on the classic experiments of the Russian psychologist Lev Vygotsky and his followers, who used play to improve children's skills at certain tasks. The children in the experiments generally couldn't stand still for a long time, but their endurance increased if they pretended to be guards on watch. Similarly, they had a much easier time memorizing a list of words if they pretended they were going to a store and had to remember a list of things to buy.

The results of those laboratory experiments have been applied in a preschool program called Tools of the Mind, which encourages children to play pretend games that are planned (to some degree) in advance and are sustained for more than a few minutes (and possibly for as long as several days). As we have seen, much of self-control is about integrating behavior over time—passing up immediate gratification for future benefits—so playing a game over several days helps toddlers to start thinking longer-range. Prolonged dramatic play with other children also requires them to exert control over attention and sustain make-believe roles. Even simple pretend games like playing house or soldiers obligate toddlers to stay in character and to follow the game's rules when interacting with other children. Independent research has shown that children who participated in Tools of the Mind ended up with significantly better self-control, by standard laboratory tests, when compared with children who attended more conventional sorts of preschools.

Older children can reap some of these same benefits from another modern target of critics' wrath: video games. We'll grant that some of these games are mindless, that the violence can be gratuitous, and that some children spend way too much of their days shooting digital nemeses. But most of the popular criticisms have as much scientific basis as the old warnings about the dastardly perils of comic books, according to Lawrence Kutner and Cheryl Olson. These Harvard researchers, after reviewing the literature and conducting their own study of middle school children, concluded that most children aren't being hurt by playing video games, and that they can derive some of the same benefits from the games as from practicing music, playing sports, or pursuing other passions that require discipline. To succeed at a complex computer game, you need to focus your attention, learn intricate rules, and follow precise steps to reach a goal. It takes much more discipline than watching television.

The self-esteem movement, fortunately, never took hold in the video game industry, probably because children would have been too bored by games that began by telling them what great players they were. Instead, children have preferred games in which they start out as lowly "noobs" (as in *newbies*) who must earn respect through their accomplishments. To acquire skills, they fail over and over. The typical teenager must have endured thousands of digital deaths and virtual fiascos, yet somehow he retains enough self-esteem to keep trying. While parents and educators have been promoting the everybody-gets-a-trophy philosophy, children have been seeking games with more demanding standards. Players need concentration to fight off Ork after Ork; they need patience to mine for virtual gold; they need thriftiness to save up for a new sword or helmet.

Instead of bemoaning the games' hold over children, we should be exploiting the techniques that game designers have developed. They've refined the basic steps of self-control: setting clear and attainable goals, giving instantaneous feedback, and offering enough encouragement for people to keep practicing and improving. After noticing how hard people work at games, some pioneers are pursuing the "gamification" of life by adapting these techniques (like establishing "quests" and allowing people to "level up") for schools and workplaces and digital collaborations. Video games give new glamour to old-fashioned virtues. Success is conditional—but it's within your reach as long as you have the discipline to try, try again.

10.

THE PERFECT STORM
OF DIETING

It is a hard matter, my fellow citizens, to argue with the belly, since it has no ears.

—Plutarch

How did I let this happen again?

—Oprah Winfrey

There is nothing so universally desired in rich countries as flat abs. The more money we make, and the more of it we give to the diet industry, the more impossible that ideal seems. Losing weight is the most popular New Year's resolution year after year, diet after forsaken diet. In the long run, the vast majority of dieters fail. Therefore, we are not going to guarantee you an eternally svelte body. But we can tell you which techniques are more likely to help you lose weight, and we'll start with the good news. If you're serious about controlling your weight, you need the discipline to follow these three rules:

1. Never go on a diet.
2. Never vow to give up chocolate or any other food.

3. Whether you're judging yourself or judging others, never equate being overweight with having weak willpower.

You may not have kept your resolution to lose ten pounds this year, but that doesn't mean you should take up a diet or swear off sweets. And you certainly shouldn't lose faith in your ability to accomplish other feats, because being overweight is not a telltale sign of weak willpower, even if most people think so. Ask a few modern Americans what they use self-control for, and dieting is likely to be the first answer. Most experts have made the same assumption for decades. At professional conferences and in scientific journal articles, when researchers have to give an example to illustrate some problem of self-control, they tend to pick dieting more often than any other sort of example.

Recently, though, researchers have found that the relationship between self-control and weight loss is much less direct than everyone thought. They've discovered something we'll call the Oprah Paradox, in honor of the world's most famous dieter. Early in her career, when she was working as a newscaster, Oprah Winfrey's weight rose from 125 to 140 pounds, so she went to a diet doctor and was put on a twelve-hundred-calories-per-day plan. She followed it, lost 7 pounds the first week, and within a month was back down to 125. But then she gradually put it back on. When she hit 212 pounds, she gave up solid food for four months, subsisting on liquid diet supplements, and got back down to 145 pounds. But within a few years she was heavier than ever, at 237 pounds, and her journal was filled with prayers to lose weight. When she was nominated for an Emmy Award, she prayed for her rival talk-show host Phil Donahue to win. That way, as she later recalled, "I wouldn't have to embarrass myself by rolling my fat butt out of my seat and walking down the aisle to the stage." She had just about lost hope when she met Bob Greene, a personal trainer, whereupon the two of them transformed each other's lives.

He became a bestselling author of training regimens and reci-pes he used with Winfrey, and began selling his own line of Best Life food. Guided by Greene and her personal chef (who wrote his own bestseller), and by the nutritionists and doctors and other experts on her show, Winfrey changed what she ate, how she exercised, how she lived. She established weekly calendars of all her meals, specifying precisely when she would eat tuna, when salmon, when salad. Her assistants built her schedule around the meals and the workouts. She received emotional counsel from friends like Marianne Williamson, the spiritual writer, who discussed with her the relationship between weight and love.

The result was displayed on the cover of Winfrey's magazine in 2005: a radiant, sleek woman weighing 160 pounds. (Note, though, that this triumph still put her 20 pounds above what she weighed at the *start* of her first diet.) Winfrey's success story was an inspiration both to her fans and to an anthropologist at Emory University, George Armelagos. He used it to illustrate a historic shift that he dubbed the King Henry VIII and Oprah Winfrey Effect. In Tudor England, it wasn't easy keeping anyone as fat as Henry VIII. His diet required resources and labor from hundreds of farmers, gardeners, fishermen, hunters, butchers, cooks, and other servants. But today even commoners can get as fat as King Henry VIII — in fact, poor people tend to be fatter than the ruling classes. Thinness has become a status symbol because it's so difficult for ordinary people to achieve unless they're genetically lucky. To remain thin, it takes the resources of Oprah Winfrey and a new array of vassals: personal trainer, chef, nutritionist, counselor, assorted assistants.

Yet even that kingdom is no guarantee, as viewers of *Oprah* started to notice, and as Winfrey herself acknowledged in a refresh-ingly frank article four years after the celebratory cover. This time her magazine's cover showed the old picture of herself, at 160 pounds, next to her current 200-pound self. "I'm mad at myself," Winfrey told readers. "I'm embarrassed. I can't believe that after all these years, all the things I know how to do, I'm still talking about my weight. I look at my thinner self and think, 'How did I let this happen again?'" She explained it as a combination of overwork and medical problems, both of which could have depleted her willpower, but even then, Oprah Winfrey was obviously someone with self-discipline. She couldn't have kept the rest of her life going so successfully without self-control. She had extraordinary personal willpower, access to the world's finest professional advice, a cadre of dedicated monitors, plus the external pressure of having to appear every day in front of millions of people watching for any sign of weight gain. Yet despite all her strength and motivation and resources, she couldn't keep the pounds off.

That's what we call the Oprah Paradox: Even people with excellent self-control can have a hard time consistently controlling their weight. They can use their willpower to thrive in many ways—at school and work, in personal relationships, in their inner emotional lives—but they're not that much more successful than other people at staying slim. When Baumeister and his colleagues in the Netherlands analyzed dozens of studies of people with high self-control, they found that these self-disciplined people did slightly better than average at controlling their weight, but the difference wasn't as marked as in other areas of their lives. This pattern showed up clearly among the overweight college students in a weight-loss program who were studied by Baumeister along with Joyce Ehrlinger, Will Crescioni, and colleagues at Florida State University. At the outset of the program, the students who scored higher on personality tests of self-control had a slight advantage—they started out weighing a little less and having better exercise habits than the people with lower self-control—and their advantage increased over the course of the twelve-week program because they were better at following the rules to restrict eating and increase exercising. But while their self-discipline helped them control their weight, it didn't seem to make a huge difference either before or during the study. High self-control was better than low self-control, but not by much.

And if the researchers had tracked the students after the weight-loss program ended, no doubt many of them would have put the pounds right back on, just as Oprah Winfrey and so many other dieters have done. Their self-control would have been useful in helping them keep up the exercise routine, but exercising isn't enough to guarantee weight loss. Even though it seems logical that burning more calories would get rid of pounds, researchers have found that the body responds by craving more food, so increased exercise doesn't necessarily lead to long-term weight loss. (But it's still worthwhile for lots of other reasons.) Whether or not you have good self-control, whether or not you exercise, if you go on a diet, the odds are that you won't permanently lose weight.

One reason is basic biology. When you use self-control to go through your in-box or write a report or go jogging, your body doesn't react viscerally. It's not physically threatened by your decision to pay bills instead of watch television. It doesn't care whether you're writing a report or surfing the Web. The body might send you pain signals when you exercise too strenuously, but it doesn't treat jogging as an existential threat. Dieting is different. As the young Oprah Winfrey discovered, the body will go along with a diet once or twice—but then it starts fighting back. When fat lab rats are put on a controlled diet for the first time, they'll lose weight. But if they're then allowed to eat freely again, they'll gradually fatten up, and if they're put on another diet it will take them longer to lose the weight this time. Then, when they once again go off the diet, they'll regain the weight more quickly than the last time. By the third or fourth time they go through this boom-and-bust cycle, the dieting ceases to work; the extra weight stays on even though they're consuming fewer calories.

Evolution favored people who could survive famines, so once a body has gone through the experience of not getting enough to eat, it reacts by fighting to keep all the pounds it has. When you diet, your body assumes there's a famine and hangs on to every fat cell it can. The ability to lose weight through a drastic change in diet ought to be conserved as a precious, one-time capability. Perhaps you'll need it late in life, when your health or your survival will depend on being able to lose weight.

Instead of going for a quick weight loss today, you're better off using your self-control to make gradual changes that will produce lasting effects, and you have to be especially careful in your strategies. You face peculiarly powerful challenges at every stage of the self-control process—from setting a goal to monitoring yourself to strengthening your willpower. When they wheel over the dessert cart, you're not facing an ordinary challenge. It's more like the perfect storm.

The first step in self-control is to establish realistic goals. To lose weight, you could look in the mirror, weigh yourself, and then draw up a sensible plan to end up with a trimmer body. You could do that, but few do. People's goals are so unrealistic that an English bookmaker, the William Hill agency, has a standing offer to bet against anyone who makes a plan to lose weight. The bookmaker, which offers odds of up to 50 to 1, lets the bettors set their own targets of how much weight to lose in how much time. It seems crazy for a bookie to let bettors not only set the terms of the wager but also control its outcome—it's like letting a runner bet on beating a target time he sets himself. Yet despite these advantages, despite the incentive to collect payoffs that have exceeded seven thousand dollars, the bettors lose 80 percent of the time.

Female bettors are especially likely to lose, which isn't surprising considering the unrealistic goals set by so many women. They look in the mirror and dream the impossible dream: a "curvaceously thin" body, as it's known to researchers who puzzle over these aspirations. The supposed ideal of a 36-24-36 figure translates to someone with size 4 hips, a size 2 waist, and a size 10 bust—someone, that is, with ample breasts but little body fat, who must be either a genetic anomaly or the product of plastic surgery.

With this as the ideal, it's no wonder that so many people set impossible goals. When you detest what you see in the mirror, you need self-control *not* to start a crash diet. You need to remind yourself that diets typically work at first but fail miserably in the long run. To understand why, let's start with a strange phenomenon observed after the consumption of milkshakes in a laboratory.

The What-the-Hell Effect

The people arrived at the lab in what researchers call a "food-deprived state," which is more commonly known as "hungry." They hadn't eaten for several hours. Some were given a small milkshake to take the edge off; others drank two giant milkshakes with enough calories to leave a normal person feeling stuffed. Then both groups, along with other subjects who hadn't been given any kind of milkshake, were asked to serve as food tasters.

That was a ruse. If research subjects know their food intake is being monitored by someone studying overeating, they suddenly lose their appetite and come across as pillars of virtuous restraint. So the researchers, pretending to be interested only in their opinions about the taste of different snacks, sat each one in a private cubicle with several bowls of crackers and cookies and a rating form. As the people recorded their ratings, they could eat as many from each bowl as they wanted—and if they finished them all, they could always tell themselves they were just trying to do a good, thorough job of rating the crackers and cookies. They didn't realize that the ratings didn't matter, and that the researchers were just interested in how many cookies and crackers they ate, how the milkshakes affected them, and how the dieters in the group compared with the people who weren't on a diet.

The nondieters reacted predictably enough. Those who had just drunk the two giant milkshakes nibbled at the crackers and quickly filled out their ratings. Those who had drunk the one modest milkshake ate more crackers. And those who were still hungry after not eating for hours went on to chomp through the better part of the cookies and crackers. All perfectly understandable.

But the dieters reacted in the opposite pattern. The ones who had downed the giant milkshakes actually ate *more* cookies and crackers than the ones who'd had nothing to eat for hours. The results stunned the researchers, who were led by Peter Herman. Incredulous, they conducted further experiments, with similar results, until they finally began to see why self-control in eating can fail even among people who are carefully regulating themselves.

The researchers gave it a formal scientific term, *counterregulatory eating,* but in their lab and among colleagues it was known simply as the what-the-hell effect. Dieters have a fixed target in mind for their maximum daily calories, and when they exceed it for some unexpected reason, such as being given a pair of large milkshakes in an experiment, they regard their diet as blown for the day. That day is therefore mentally classified as a failure, regardless of what else happens. Virtue cannot resume until tomorrow. So they think, *What the hell, I might as well enjoy myself today*—and the resulting binge often puts on far more weight than the original lapse. It's not rational, but dieters don't even seem to be aware of how much damage these binges do, as demonstrated in a follow-up experiment by Janet Polivy, Herman's longtime collaborator. Once again, hungry dieters and nondieters were brought into the lab, and some of the dieters were given food with enough calories to put them over their daily limit. Later, the entire group was served sandwiches cut into quarters. Afterward, and unexpectedly, everyone was asked how many sandwich quarters he or she had eaten.

Most of the people answered the question with no trouble—after all, they'd just finished eating, and they knew how many sandwiches they'd taken. But one group was notably clueless: the dieters who'd been given enough food to exceed their daily limit. Some of them overestimated, and some underestimated. As a result, they were much further off the mark than either the nondieters or the dieters who were still under their daily food limit. As long as the diet wasn't busted for the day, the dieters tracked what they were eating. But once they broke the diet and succumbed to the what-the-hell effect, they stopped counting and became even less aware than nondieters of what they were eating. As we know, monitoring is the next step in self-control after setting a goal, but how can dieters do that if they stop keeping track of what they eat? One possible alternative would be to heed the body's signals that it's had enough sustenance. But for dieters, that turns out to be yet another losing strategy.

The Dieter's Catch-22

Humans are born with an innate gift for eating just the right amount. When an infant's body needs food, it sends a signal through hunger pangs. When the body has had enough food, the infant doesn't want to eat any more. Unfortunately, children start to lose this ability by the time they enter school, and it continues to decline later in life for some people—often the ones who need it the most. Why this occurs has been puzzling scientists for decades, starting with some research in the 1960s that revolutionized the study of eating.

In one experiment, researchers rigged a clock on the wall of a room where people could munch on snacks during the afternoon as they filled out stacks of questionnaires. When the clock ran fast, the obese people ate more than others, because the clock signaled to them that it must be getting close to dinnertime and therefore they must be hungry. Instead of heeding their body's internal signals, they ate according to external cues from the clock. In another study, researchers varied the kinds of snacks that were offered, sometimes offering shelled peanuts and sometimes whole peanuts. It didn't seem to matter to the normal-weight people, who ate about the same number of nuts either way. But the obese people ate far more when they were offered the shelled nuts, which apparently sent a stronger come-and-get-it message. Once again, the obese people responded more strongly to external cues, and researchers initially hypothesized it was the cause of their problem: They became obese because they ignored their body's internal signals of being full.

It was a reasonable theory, but eventually researchers realized that they were confusing cause and effect. Yes, obese people ignored their inner cues, but that's not why they became obese. It worked the other way: Their obesity made them likely to go on diets, and their diets caused them to rely on external instead of internal cues. For what is a diet but a plan imposing external rules? Dieters learn to eat according to a plan, not to their inner feelings and cravings. Dieting means being hungry a lot of the time (even if the marketers of diets are always promising otherwise).

More precisely, dieting means learning not to eat when you are hungry, preferably by learning to ignore those feelings of hunger. You mainly try to tune out the start-eating signal, but the start and stop signals are intertwined, so you typically lose touch with the stop-eating signal, too, particularly if the diet tells you exactly how much to eat. You eat by the rules, which works fine as long as you stick to them. But once you deviate from the rules, as just about everyone does, you have nothing left to guide you. That's why, even after downing a couple of big milkshakes, dieters and obese people not only continue but increase their eating. The milkshakes filled them up, but they still don't feel full. They have only the one bright line, and once they have passed it, there are no more limits.

Now, you could argue that the real lesson of these experiments is that dieters shouldn't take part in experiments involving milk-shakes. If they didn't go into the lab and drink all those calories, then they wouldn't cross the bright line and break their daily diet. So if the dieters could just follow their own rules all the time, if they never exceeded the daily limit, then they'd never succumb to the what-the-hell effect. Sure, they'd feel hungry, but they'd never go on a binge as long as they had the willpower to observe the rules.

All of which makes a certain sense, but only until you actually begin testing those dieters' willpower with movies, ice cream, and M&M's, as Kathleen Vohs and Todd Heatherton did in a series of experiments. The psychologists recruited young women, all chronic dieters, and showed them a classic tearjerker, the scene in *Terms of Endearment* in which the young mother, who is dying of cancer, says good-bye to her two little sons, her husband, and her mother. Half the dieters were instructed to try to suppress their emotional re-sponses, both internally and externally. The other half were told to let their feelings and tears flow naturally. Afterward, all the dieters filled out questionnaires about their mood, and each was taken indi-vidually to a different room for what was ostensibly an unrelated task: rating various kinds of ice cream. The ice cream was presented to each dieter in several large and only partly full tubs, which created the impression that the experimenters would not know how much was in there and how much each woman ate.

But, of course, the tubs had been carefully weighed beforehand, and they were weighed again afterward. The researchers found that there was no connection between the women's moods and their eat-ing: The ones who were sadder after the movie didn't eat extra ice cream to drown their sorrows. What mattered was not their mood but rather their will. The dieters who had suppressed emotions dur-ing the movie had a much harder time suppressing their appetite.

Having depleted their willpower, they ate considerably more ice cream—more than half again as much—as the women who'd been free to cry during the film. This is, of course, just one more demonstration of ego depletion. Still, it bears repeating that eating and dieting can be affected by things that seemingly have no connection to them. Trying to hide your feelings while watching a movie drains your willpower, rendering you more likely to overeat later on in a separate, ostensibly unrelated context.

In another test of the wills of young female dieters, each one was tempted by a bowl brimming with M&M's that was placed in the screening room with her as she watched a nature documentary (a non-tearjerker about bighorn sheep). For some of the women, the bowl was placed nearby, within easy reach, so they had to continually resist the temptation. For other women, the candy bowl was placed on the other side of the room and hence was easier to resist. Later, in a separate room with no food in sight, the women were given impossible puzzles to solve, that standard lab test of self-control. The dieters who had sat within arm's reach of the M&M's gave up sooner on the puzzles, demonstrating that their willpower had been depleted by the effort of resisting temptation. Clearly, if you're a dieter who doesn't want to lose self-control, you shouldn't spend a lot of time sitting right next to a bowl of M&M's. Even if you resist those obvious temptations, you'll deplete your willpower and be prone to overeating other foods later.

But there's also another way to avoid this problem, as illustrated in a third experiment involving young women and food. This time Vohs and Heatherton tested nondieters in addition to dieters, and a clear distinction emerged. It turned out that the nondieters could sit next to an array of snacks—Doritos, Skittles, M&M's, salted peanuts—without using up willpower. Some ate the snacks and some didn't, but either way, they weren't struggling to restrain themselves, so they remained relatively fresh for other tasks. The dieters, meanwhile, gradually depleted their willpower as they fought the urge to break their diet. They went through the same struggle that you see played out at social events when dieters are confronted with fattening food. The dieters can resist for a while, but each act of resistance further lowers their willpower.

Then, as they're weakening, they face yet another of the peculiarly maddening challenges of controlling eating. To continue resisting temptation, they need to replenish the willpower they've lost. But to resupply that energy, they need to give the body glucose. They're trapped in a nutritional catch-22:

1. In order not to eat, a dieter needs willpower.
2. In order to have willpower, a dieter needs to eat.

Faced with this dilemma of whether to eat or not, a dieter might try telling herself that the best option is to slightly relax the diet. She might reason that it's best to consume a little food and try to salve her conscience: *Look, I had to break the diet in order to save it.* But once she strays from the diet, we know what she's liable to tell herself: *What the hell.* And then: *Let the binge begin.*

Sweet food becomes especially hard to resist because, as we've already seen, self-control depletes the glucose in the bloodstream. If you've ever been on a diet and found yourself unable to shake those intrusive cravings for chocolate or ice cream, this is more than a matter of repressed desires coming back to haunt you. There is a sound physiological basis. The body "knows" that it has depleted the glucose in its bloodstream by exerting self-control, and it also seems to know that sweet-tasting foods are typically the fastest way to get an infusion of energy-rich glucose. In recent lab studies, college students who performed self-control tasks that had nothing to do with food or dieting found themselves having higher desires for sweet foods. When allowed to snack during the next task, those who had previously exerted self-control ate more sweet snacks, but not other (salty) snacks.

If these yearnings seem overpowering, we can suggest a couple of defensive strategies. The first is to use the postponed-pleasure ploy: Tell yourself that you can have a small sweet dessert later if you still want it. (We'll discuss this ploy later, too.) Meanwhile, eat something else. Remember, your body is craving energy because it has used up some of its supply with self-control. The body feels a desire for sweet foods, but that is only because that is a familiar and effective way to restore energy. Healthy foods will also provide the energy it needs. It's not what's on your mind, but it should do the trick.

Remember, too, that the depleted state makes you feel everything more intensely than usual. Desires and cravings are exceptionally intense to the depleted person. Dieting is a frequent drain on your willpower, and so the dieter will frequently be in a depleted state. That will, in effect, turn up the volume on many good and bad things that happen throughout the day. It will also make longings—yes, unfortunately, even the longings for food, which are already there— seem especially intense. This may help explain why, eventually, many dieters seem to cultivate a numbness to their body's wants and feelings about food.

There is no magical solution to the dieter's catch-22. No matter how much willpower you start off with, if you're a dieter and spend enough time sitting near the dessert buffet telling yourself *no*, eventually *no* will probably change to *yes*. You need to avoid the dessert cart—or, better yet, avoid going on a diet in the first place. Instead of squandering your willpower on a strict diet, eat enough glucose to conserve willpower, and use your self-control for more promising long-term strategies.

Planning for Battle

When you're not starving, when you have glucose, you can prepare for the battle of the bulge with some of the classic self-control strategies, starting with precommitment. The ultimate surefire form of precommitment—the true equivalent of Odysseus tying himself to the mast—would be gastric bypass surgery, which would physically prevent you from eating, but there are lots of more modest forms. You can begin by simply keeping fattening food out of reach and out of sight. You'll conserve willpower (as the women in the experiment did when the M&M's were moved out of reach) at the same time that you're avoiding calories. In one experiment, office workers ate a third less candy when it was kept inside a drawer rather than on top of their desks. A simple commitment strategy for avoiding late-night snacking is to brush your teeth early in the evening, while you're still full from dinner and before the late-night-snacking temptation sets in. Although it won't physically prevent you from eating, brushing your teeth is such an ingrained pre-bedtime habit that it unconsciously cues you not to eat anymore. On a conscious level, moreover, it makes snacking seem less attractive: You have to balance your greedy impulse for sugar against your lazy impulse to avoid having to brush your teeth again.

You can consider more elaborate commitment devices, like placing a bet with a bookmaker, or by locking in a weight-loss agreement at Web sites like fatbet.net or stickK.com, which allow you to name your own goals along with penalties. A tough penalty, like committing yourself to donate hundreds or thousands of dollars to a cause you detest, can make a difference, but don't expect money to work miracles when you set an impossible goal. Losing 5 or 10 percent of your weight is a realistic goal, but beyond that it becomes difficult to overcome the body's natural propensities. The typical bettor at the William Hill agency sets a goal of losing nearly three pounds per week for a total of almost eighty pounds—no wonder so many of them fail. The people putting up their money at stickK.com have a much better track record thanks to the Web site's policy of forbidding anyone from setting a goal of losing more than two pounds per week, or 18.5 percent of their body weight. It's possible to lose a lot of weight quickly by drastically altering your eating, but what good will that do if the regimen is too strict to follow permanently? Better to make smaller changes that can be sustained over the long haul. Take your time reaching your goal, and then don't let up, because the hardest part is keeping the weight off. If you use a system of rewards and penalties to reach your weight-loss goal, keep using the same kinds of incentives to maintain your weight.

You can also try a strategy that psychologists call an "implementation intention," which is a way to reduce the amount of time and effort you spend controlling your thoughts. Instead of making general plans to reduce calories, you make highly specific plans for automatic behavior in certain situations, like what to do when you're tempted by fattening food at a party. An implementation intention takes the form of if-then: If x happens, I will do y. The more you use this technique to transfer the control of your behavior to automatic processes, the less effort you will expend. This was demonstrated in some experiments involving the classic Stroop test of mental effort that was described in chapter 1: identifying mislabeled colors. If you see the word *green* printed in green ink, you can quickly identify the color of the ink, but it takes longer if the green ink is being used to form the word *blue*. And it takes still longer if your willpower has been depleted beforehand, as English researchers did with the people in one experiment. But they found it was possible to compensate for this weaker willpower by training people to ease the strain on their minds. Before the ink-color-identifying task began, the people would form an implementation plan: *If I see a word, I will ignore its meaning and look only at the second letter and the color of the ink.* This specific if-then plan made their task more automatic, requiring less conscious mental effort, and therefore doable even when their willpower was already weakened.

So before you get tempted by the food at a party, you can prepare yourself with a plan like: *If they serve chips, I will refuse them all.* Or: *If there is a buffet, I will eat only vegetables and lean meat.* It's a simple but surprisingly effective way to gain self-control. By making the decision to pass up the chips an automatic process, you can do it fairly effortlessly even late in the day, when your supply of willpower is low. And because it's relatively effortless, you can pass up the chips and still have enough willpower to deal with the next temptation at the party.

For a more radical form of precommitment, you could skip the party altogether and seek out gatherings with lower-calorie offerings—and thinner people. We're not suggesting you dump your chubby friends, but there does seem to be a connection between what you weigh and whom you socialize with. Researchers who have analyzed social networks find that obese people tend to cluster together, as do thin people. Social distance seems to matter more than physical distance: Your chances of being obese increase more because your best friend gains weight than because your next-door neighbor gains weight. It's difficult to disentangle cause and effect—no doubt people are seeking out others who share their habits and tastes. But it's also true that people reinforce one another's behavior and standards. One reason why members of Weight Watchers shed pounds (at least for a while) is that they're spending more time with other people who care about losing weight. It's the same phenomenon we noted earlier with smokers, who are more likely to quit if their friends and relatives also quit.

Peer pressure helps explain why people in Europe weigh less than Americans: They follow different social norms, like eating only at mealtimes instead of snacking throughout the day. When European social scientists come to the United States to study eating habits in campus laboratories, they're surprised to discover that they can run experiments whenever they want to because American college students are happy to eat food any time of the morning or afternoon. In France or Italy, it can be hard to find a restaurant open except at mealtimes. Those social norms produce habits that conserve willpower through automatic mental processes. Instead of consciously trying to decide whether to snack, instead of struggling with tempta-tion, Europeans rely on the equivalent of an implementation plan: *If it's four* P.M., *then I won't eat anything.*

Let Me Count the Weighs (and the Calories)

If you're trying to lose weight, how often should you weigh your-self? The standard advice used to be to not get on the scale every day, because your weight naturally fluctuates and you'll get discouraged on days it goes up for no apparent reason. If you want to keep up your motivation, the weight-loss experts said, you should weigh yourself just once a week. That advice seemed odd to Baumeister and other self-control researchers, because their work on other problems consistently showed that frequent monitoring improved self-control. Eventually, a careful long-term study tracked people who'd lost weight and were trying not to regain it. Some of these people weighed themselves daily; others didn't. It turned out that the conventional wisdom was wrong.

The people who weighed themselves every day were much more successful at keeping their weight from creeping back up. They were less likely to go on eating binges, and they didn't show any signs of disillusion or other distress from their daily confrontation with the scale. For all the peculiar challenges to losing weight, one of the usual strategies is still effective: The more carefully and frequently you monitor yourself, the better you'll control yourself. If it seems like too much of a chore to write down your weight every day, you can outsource some of the drudgery by using a scale that keeps an elec-tronic record of your weight. Some models will transmit each day's reading to your computer or smartphone, which can then produce a chart for your monitoring pleasure (or displeasure).

Even a very simple form of monitoring can make a big difference, as researchers discovered when they investigated an odd little mystery: Why do prisoners put on weight? Clearly it's not because of the irresistible prison cuisine. No gourmet chef is ever hired to cook when the clientele consists of customers who are literally captive. Yet men consistently come out of prison fatter than when they went in. The reason, according to Cornell's Brian Wansink, is that prisoners don't wear belts or tight-fitting clothes. In their jumpsuits and loose pants, they don't get the little signals of weight gain that other people get when their pants feel tighter and their belts have to be loosened a notch.

Besides monitoring your body, you can monitor what food you put into it. If you conscientiously keep a record of all the food you eat, you'll probably consume fewer calories. In one study, those who kept a food diary lost twice as much weight as those who used other techniques. It also helps to record how many calories are in the food, although that's notoriously tricky to estimate. All of us, even professional dietitians, tend to underestimate how much food is on a plate, especially when confronted with large portions. We've been further confused by the warnings of nutritionists and the tricks of food companies, who will use a label like "low-fat" or "organic" to create what researchers call a "health halo." Tierney investigated this phenomenon in the nutritionally correct neighborhood of Park Slope, Brooklyn, with an experiment designed by two researchers, Pierre Chandon and Alexander Chernev. Some of the Park Slopers were shown pictures of an Applebee's meal consisting of chicken salad and a Pepsi; others were shown the identical meal plus some crackers prominently labeled "Trans Fat Free." The people were so entranced by the crackers' virtuous label that their estimate for the meal with crackers was *lower* than for the same meal without crackers. The label magically translated into "negative calories," both in the informal experiment in Park Slope and in a formal peer-reviewed study published later by Chernev. Other studies have shown that both laypeople and nutritional experts consistently underestimate the calories in food labeled "low-fat," and consequently take bigger helpings.

To overcome these problems, you can try paying more attention to the calorie count of food when it's available on a label or a menu, or when you've got a smartphone with an app that monitors calories. When the calorie count is not available, you can at least try to pay attention to the food in front of you, which few people do. The two most common activities that are combined with eating are socializing and watching television—and both are associated with increased calorie consumption. Researchers have repeatedly shown that eating in front of the television increases snacking, and that viewers will eat more when their attention is engaged—as in a well-executed comedy or horror film—than when they're watching something boring. In one study, female dieters tripled the amount of food they ate when they were absorbed in a film.

People tend to eat more at meals with friends and family, when they're paying more attention to the company and less to what they eat. Add wine or beer, and they'll pay still less attention, because alcohol reduces self-awareness and therefore impairs monitoring. Even when they're sober, diners can be so oblivious that they'll go on sipping soup from a bowl that is continuously (and surreptitiously) refilled, as Brian Wansink demonstrated in a famous experiment at Cornell using soup bowls attached to hidden tubes. The people just went on sipping from the bottomless bowl because they were so used to eating whatever was put in front of them. If you're guided by external cues instead of by your own appetite, you're vulnerable to gaining weight whenever you're served large portions, which can easily happen without your being aware of it. When food is served on large plates or when drinks are poured in wide glasses, you tend to underestimate how many extra calories are being added because you don't have a good intuitive sense of three-dimensional volume. If a movie theater simply changed one dimension of a popcorn bag by, say, tripling its height, you could see right away that it holds three times as much popcorn. But when the bag gets simultaneously wider, deeper, and taller, it can triple in volume without looking three times as big. So you order the large—and then eat the whole thing. You can't control what kind of packaging and plates are used in theaters and restaurants, but at home you can reduce your portions by using small plates and thin glasses.

You can also make it easier to monitor your eating by not clearing the table too quickly. In an experiment at a sports bar, people ate far fewer chicken wings when the waiters left the discarded bones on their plates. At other tables, where the waiters zealously cleared away the bones, people could fool themselves into forgetting how many wings they'd eaten, but that was impossible at the tables still holding the evidence. The bones did the monitoring for them.

Never Say Never

The results of dieting research tend to be depressing, but every now and then there's an exception, and we've saved our favorite cheery finding for last. It's from a dessert-cart experiment conducted by marketing researchers trying to figure out the central problem of self-control: Why is self-denial so difficult? As Mark Twain put it in *The Adventures of Tom Sawyer:* "To promise not to do a thing is the surest way in the world to make a body want to go and do that very thing." That's one of the more frustrating aspects of the human psyche, but the researchers, Nicole Mead and Vanessa Patrick, looked for relief by considering different kinds of self-denial.

They started with some mental experiments using pictures of tasty, appealing foods. The experimental subjects were told to imagine these delicacies being offered on a dessert cart in a restaurant. Some imagined choosing their favorite and eating it. The rest, however, imagined passing up dessert in one of two ways. By random assignment, some imagined that they had decided not to eat these desserts at all, and the others imagined that they had told themselves not to have any now, but that they would indulge at some later time. It was the difference between pleasure denied and pleasure postponed.

Afterward, the experimenters measured how often the people were troubled or distracted by yearnings for the desserts. These researchers knew that unfinished tasks tend to intrude on the mind (due to the Zeigarnik effect, which we discussed in chapter 3), so they expected the desserts to be especially distracting to the people who had postponed the pleasure. Surprisingly, though, the people who had told themselves *Not now, but later* were less troubled with visions of chocolate cake than the other two groups—both the ones who had imagined eating it and the ones who had flatly denied themselves the pleasure. The researchers had expected the outright denial to cause fewer yearnings because the mind would consider the case closed— no more debate! But the opposite happened. The postponed pleasures did not intrude as much as the foregone ones. When it came to dessert, the mind wouldn't take no for an answer, at least not in this mental experiment.

But what if real food was involved? To find out, the researchers brought people in one at a time to watch a short film while sitting next to a bowl of M&M's (a perpetual favorite in laboratories because they're so easy to work with—no muss, no fuss). Some people were told to imagine they had decided to eat as much as they wanted while watching the movie. Others were told to imagine they had decided not to eat any of the candy. A third group was told to imagine they had decided not to eat the M&M's now but would have them later on. In general, the instructions were effective: The ones told to assume they had decided to eat actually did eat considerably more than the ones told to deny or postpone the pleasure. The study proceeded through some questionnaires, after which the experimenter (falsely) said the experiment was now over. Each person was asked to remain and fill out one more questionnaire, which was ostensibly concerned with the quality of the laboratory setting.

Then, seemingly as an afterthought, the experimenter gave the bowl of M&M's back to the person and said, "You're the last subject we have today, and everyone else is gone, so these are left over. Help yourself." The experimenter exited, leaving the participant alone to fill out the questionnaire and eat his or her fill, apparently without anyone watching or caring. But, as usual, the researchers cared very much. They had weighed the bowl beforehand, and weighed it once again after the participant left.

Left alone in that room with the M&M's, the people who'd told themselves to postpone pleasure had a golden opportunity to indulge themselves. You'd expect them to scarf the M&M's, while the people who'd sworn off the candy would either remain strong or perhaps just nibble. But exactly the opposite occurred. Those in the postponement condition actually ate significantly less than those in the self-denial condition. The findings would have been impressive if people had merely eaten equal amounts in the postponement condition and the refusal condition. After all, the ones in the postponement condition were fully expecting to enjoy the treats later.

The fact that they ate less than the others is remarkable. The result suggests that telling yourself *I can have this later* operates in the mind a bit like having it now. It satisfies the craving to some degree—and can be even more effective at suppressing the appetite than actually eating the treat. During that final part of the experiment, when all the people were left alone with a bowl of M&M's, the ones who'd postponed pleasure ate even less than the people who had earlier allowed themselves to eat the candy at will. Moreover, the suppression effect seemed to last outside the laboratory. The day after the experiment, all the people were sent an e-mail with a question: "How much do you desire M&M candies at this very moment, if someone offered them to you?" Those who had postponed gratification reported less desire to eat the candy than either the people who had refused the pleasure outright or those who had eaten their fill.

It takes willpower to turn down dessert, but apparently it's less stressful on the mind to say *Later* rather than *Never.* In the long run, you end up wanting less and also consuming less. Plus, you may derive more pleasure because of another effect that was demonstrated in a different sort of experiment: asking people how much they'd be willing to pay to kiss their favorite movie star today, and how much they'd pay for a kiss three days from now. Ordinarily, people will pay more for an immediate pleasure, but in this case they were willing to spend extra money to postpone the kiss, because it would let them spend three days savoring the prospect. Similarly, delaying the gratification of crème brûlée or molten chocolate cake gives time to enjoy the anticipation. As a result of that advance pleasure, when you ultimately do indulge, you may find less of a need to binge and more of an inclination to eat moderately. In contrast, when you swear off something altogether and then finally give in, you say, *What the hell,* and gorge yourself.

So when it comes to food, never say never. When the dessert cart arrives, don't gaze longingly at forbidden treats. Vow that you will eat all of them sooner or later, but just not tonight. In the spirit of Scarlett O'Hara, tell yourself: *Tomorrow is another taste.*

CONCLUSION:
THE FUTURE OF WILLPOWER—
MORE GAIN, LESS STRAIN

(As Long as You Don't Procrastinate)

Give me chastity and continence, but not yet.

—Prayer of St. Augustine during his pre-saintly youth

Like the young Augustine, everyone appreciates the benefits of self-control—someday. But when, if ever, is that day ever going to arrive for the nonsaints among us? If willpower is finite and temptations keep proliferating, how can there be a lasting revival of this virtue?

We don't minimize the obstacles, but we're still bullish on the future of self-control, at both the personal and the social level. Yes, temptations are getting more sophisticated, but so are the tools for resisting them. The benefits of willpower are appreciated more clearly than ever. You could sum up a large new body of research literature with a simple rule: *The best way to reduce stress in your life is to stop screwing up.* That means setting up your life so that you have a realistic chance to succeed. Successful people don't use their willpower as a last-ditch defense to stop themselves from di-

saster, at least not as a regular strategy, as Baumeister and his colleagues have observed recently on both sides of the Atlantic. When
they monitored Germans throughout the day (in the beeper study
we mentioned earlier), the researchers were surprised to find that
people with strong self-control spent *less* time resisting desires than
other people did.

At first Baumeister and his German collaborators were puzzled.
Self-control is supposedly for resisting desires, so why are the people
who have more self-control not using it more often? But then an
explanation emerged: These people have less need to use willpower
because they're beset by fewer temptations and inner conflicts.
They're better at arranging their lives so that they avoid problem
situations. This explanation jibed with the conclusion of another
study, by Dutch researchers working with Baumeister, showing that
people with good self-control mainly use it not for rescue in emergencies but rather to develop effective habits and routines in school
and at work. The results of these habits and routines were demonstrated in yet another recent set of studies, in the United States, showing that people with high self-control consistently report less stress
in their lives. They use their self-control not to get through crises but
to avoid them. They give themselves enough time to finish a project;
they take the car to the shop before it breaks down; they stay away
from all-you-can-eat buffets. They play offense instead of defense.

In this closing chapter we'll review the strategy for going on
offense, starting with one of the most obvious yet widely ignored
rules: Don't keep putting it off. Procrastination is an almost universal
vice. Cicero called procrastinators "hateful"; Jonathan Edwards
preached an entire sermon against the "sin and folly of depending on
future time." In modern surveys, 95 percent of people admit to doing
it at least sometimes (we have no idea who those other 5 percent
are—or whom they're trying to kid), and the problem seems to get
worse as societies modernize and temptations multiply. The psychologist Piers Steel, who has analyzed data from around the world over

the past four decades, reports that there's been a sharp increase in the ranks of dedicated ditherers—those who consider procrastination to be a defining personal characteristic. That category today includes more than 20 percent of the people surveyed internationally. In some American surveys, more than half the people consider themselves chronic procrastinators, and workers themselves estimate that they waste a quarter of their hours on the job—two hours per workday. At the typical wage, that means that each employee is being paid about $10,000 annually for time spent slacking off.

This vice has often been blamed, by psychologists as well as ditherers, on people's compulsion to do things perfectly. Supposedly these perfectionists are flooded with worry and anxiety whenever they try to start a project because they see it's not living up to their ideals, so they get bogged down or just stop working. This makes sense in theory, and doubtless it's true in some cases, but researchers have repeatedly failed to find a reliable link between procrastination and perfectionism. One reason psychologists were initially fooled into seeing a link might have been selection bias: A procrastinator with high standards would be likelier than a less ambitious ditherer to seek help for the problem, so perfectionists would show up more often in the offices of psychologists treating procrastinators. But there are plenty of other people with high standards who don't procrastinate and do perfectly good work without pulling all-nighters.

The trait that does seem to matter is impulsiveness, which shows up over and over in studies of procrastinators. This connection helps explain recent evidence that procrastination is more of a problem for men than it is for women, and especially for young men: Men have more hard-to-control impulses. When procrastinators are feeling anxious about a difficult job, or just bored by a mundane chore, they give in to the urge to improve their mood by doing something else. They go for the immediate reward, playing a video game instead of cleaning the kitchen or writing a term paper, and they try to ignore the long-term consequences. When thoughts of future deadlines intrude, they may even try telling themselves that it's smart to wait until the last minute: *I work best under deadline pressure!* But mostly they're kidding themselves, as Baumeister and Dianne Tice discovered.

The Deadline Test

The procrastination experiment took place in a wonderfully target-rich environment: a university campus. College students typically admit to spending a third of their waking hours procrastinating, and who knows how much more time is actually being wasted. Tice, who taught a course in health psychology at Case Western University, identified the procrastinators in her class through a couple of means. First, at the start of the term, she had the students fill out a questionnaire about their work habits. Then she assigned a paper due on a Friday late in the term. Tice also announced that students who missed the deadline could turn in a paper in class on the following Tuesday, and that if they missed that second deadline, they could bring it to her office the following Friday—a full week past the original deadline. Later she discovered that some of the students who scored high on the procrastination questionnaire hadn't even bothered to write down the first two deadlines. As far as they were concerned, the double-extended due date was the only one that counted.

The papers were graded by instructors who didn't know when the work had been submitted, but Tice and Baumeister kept track of that information so that they could compare the students' performance. The procrastinators—as measured both on the questionnaire and by how late they turned in their papers—did worse by every academic measure: lower grades on their papers, lower scores on their midterm and final exams. But might they have benefited in other ways? As a separate project in this health psychology class, the students kept records of their own health, including all the symptoms and illnesses they had and how often they went to the campus clinic or other health-care provider. When Tice reviewed the findings from the first semester's study, she found a stunning result: The procrastinators were healthier! They reported fewer symptoms and fewer physician visits. It looked as if there were a trade-off: Sure, the early birds had gotten their work in on time and had gotten better grades than the procrastinators, but the latter had enjoyed better health. Exercising self-control ahead of the deadline seemed to take some sort of toll, perhaps by diverting glucose from the immune system. But as Baumeister and Tice pondered this result, they remembered that the students' assignment to keep health records had ended before the final week of the semester—just when the procrastinators were doing their last-minute papers. They might have been healthier when they were not working, but what happened to them at the end of the term, when the deadlines came due?

So the experiment was repeated another semester with another class, and this time the students continued to keep track of illnesses, symptoms, and physician visits right up through final exams. Once again the procrastinators got lower grades and enjoyed better health early in the semester, when some of the early birds in the class were sniffling with colds as they worked on their papers. The procrastinators may have been out playing Frisbee, relaxing at parties, getting plenty of sleep. For a procrastinator whose deadlines are far off, life is pretty good. But eventually the bill comes due. At the end of the semester, the procrastinators suffered considerably more stress than the others. Now they had to pull themselves together to do the overdue work, and they reported a sharp rise in symptoms and illnesses. In fact, the procrastinators were so much sicker than other students at the end of the semester that it more than canceled out their better health from the early weeks. Their all-nighters took a toll, and they had more health problems overall.

The worst procrastinators didn't even manage to meet the third and final deadline. They fell back on the sop that many universities offer procrastinating students, which is to take an "Incomplete" grade, thus postponing the work until the next semester. The university allowed incomplete grades but had a firm policy that all work had to be made up and handed in so that grades could be turned in to the registrar by 5:00 P.M. on a particular Friday late in the following semester. This Friday, then, was a hard-and-fast deadline, with no wiggle room, for the students of Tice who took an Incomplete—a group that included, inevitably, the female student who had scored highest on the procrastination questionnaire at the start of the term. According to university policy, it was up to her to work out a schedule with her teacher for completing the work so that there was time for it to be read and graded. Weeks went by, but there was no word from her. Finally, on the afternoon of that fatal Friday, barely two hours before the grade was due at the registrar's office, the student telephoned.

"Hi, Dr. Tice," she said, sounding nonchalant. "Can you remind me, what was this about a term paper for your class last semester?"

As you might have guessed, she didn't get the paper done in time. There comes a point when no amount of willpower will save you. But most people, even chronic procrastinators, can avoid that fate by learning to play offense. So far in this book, we've discussed hundreds of self-control experiments and strategies. Now let's review them and put them to use.

Willpower 101, First Lesson: Know Your Limits

No matter what you want to achieve, playing offense begins by recognizing the two basic lessons from chapter 1: Your supply of willpower is limited, and you use the same resource for many different things. Each day may start off with your stock of willpower fresh and renewed, at least if you've had a good night's sleep and a healthy breakfast. But then all day things chip and nibble away at it. The complexity of modern life makes it difficult to keep in mind that all these seemingly unrelated chores and demands draw on the same account inside of you.

Consider some of the things that happen in a typical day. You pull yourself out of bed even though your body wants more sleep. You put up with traffic frustrations. You hold your tongue when your boss or spouse angers you, or when a store clerk says "Just one second" and takes six minutes to get back to you. You try to maintain an interested, alert expression on your face while a colleague drones on during a boring meeting. You postpone going to the bathroom. You make yourself take the first steps on a difficult project. You want to eat all the French fries on your lunch plate but you leave half of them there, or (after negotiating with yourself) almost half. You push yourself to go jogging, and while you jog you make yourself keep running until you finish your workout. The willpower you expended on each of these unrelated events depletes how much you have left for the others.

This depletion isn't intuitively obvious, especially when it comes to appreciating the impact of making decisions. Virtually no one has a gut-level sense of just how tiring it is to decide. Choosing what to have for dinner, where to go on vacation, whom to hire, how much to spend—these all take willpower. Even hypothetical decisions deplete energy. After making some tough decisions, remember that your self-control is going to be weakened.

Remember, too, that what matters is the exertion, not the outcome. If you struggle with temptation and then give in, you're still depleted because you struggled. Giving in does *not* replenish the willpower you have already expended. All it does is save you from expending any more. You may have spent the day succumbing to a series of temptations and impulses, but you could nonetheless have used up quite a bit of energy by resisting each one for a while. You can even use up willpower by partaking in indulgences that don't appeal to you. Forcing yourself to do something you don't really want to do at the moment—chug tequila, have sex, smoke a cigar—will leave you with less willpower. Similarly, the most tiring decisions are the ones that seem tough to you even though they may seem obvious to others. Your rational self might be fully convinced that you should rent the affordable apartment with the extra room, but it can still deplete you to pass up the impractical one with the spectacular view.

Watch for Symptoms

There's no obvious "feeling" of depletion. Hence you need to watch yourself for subtle, easily misinterpreted signs. Do things seem to bother you more than they should? Has the volume somehow been turned up on your life so that things are felt more strongly than usual? Is it suddenly hard to make up your mind about even simple things? Are you more than usually reluctant to make a decision or exert yourself mentally or physically? If you notice such feelings, then reflect on the last few hours and see if it seems likely that you have depleted your willpower. If so, try to conserve what's left while anticipating the effects on your behavior.

While you're depleted, frustrations will bother you more than usual. You'll be more prone to say something you'll regret. Impulses to eat, drink, spend, or do other things will be harder than usual to resist. As we said earlier, the best way to reduce stress in your life is to stop screwing up, but when you're depleted you're liable to make mistakes that will leave you with more bills to pay, more relationship damage to repair, more pounds to lose. Beware of making binding decisions when your energy is down, because you'll tend to favor options with short-term gains and delayed costs. Try to compensate by assigning extra weight to the long-range consequences of the decision. To avoid succumbing to irrational biases and lazy shortcuts, articulate your reasons for your decision and consider whether they make sense.

Your capacity for fairness and balanced judgment will suffer. You'll be more inclined to stick with the status quo and less inclined to compromise, particularly if the trade-offs involve much mental work. Like the depleted parole judges we discussed in chapter 4, you'll be inclined to take the safer, easier option even when that option hurts someone else. Being aware of these effects can help you resist some of the dangers of the depleted state.

And like Jim Turner, the actor we discussed in chapter 2, you may find yourself unable to make the simplest choices even when they help you. In his one-man show about his struggles with diabetes, Turner tells about a day at the beach when he felt his blood sugar falling dangerously low. He realized that he and his son, then four years old, had to leave quickly, and they started to gather up the boy's toys and put them into the two boxes he'd brought to the beach. It was a routine task, but with his glucose level so low, Turner was flummoxed by his options: which toy in which box? He desperately settled on the first rule that occurred to him—each toy had to go in *exactly the same box* that it had arrived in—and wasted time obsessively rearranging the toys as his blood sugar kept falling. Then, when they finally left and headed toward the beachside facilities—a snack bar and a public restroom—he was stymied by another decision.

"I stood there for fifteen minutes with this internal dialogue going on: pee first or eat first?" Turner recalls. "My son was tugging at me, but I couldn't decide. It was so exhausting I finally just sat down. My son was freaking out. We were there close to half an hour before I finally managed to get up and go eat."

You might keep in mind that image of Turner—a guy collapsed on the beach too exhausted to make a decision about going to the bathroom—the next time you find yourself struggling with a routine decision. That's what a shortage of glucose can do to you. "It feels like a part of your brain has been taken from you," Turner says. "You can't concentrate. You sit there staring knowing that something needs to be happening, and you wonder why you can't do it." You can't do

it until you make the same choice that finally saved Turner: Eat first.
Lab researchers replenish this basic fuel by giving sugar-filled drinks
because they work quickly, but it's better to use protein. Get some
healthy food into your body, wait half an hour, and then the decision
won't seem so overwhelming.

Pick Your Battles

You can't control or even predict the stresses that come into your life,
but you can use the calm periods, or at least the peaceful moments,
to plan an offense. Start an exercise program. Learn a new skill. Quit
smoking, reduce drinking, make one or two lasting changes toward
a healthy diet. These are all best done during times of relatively low
demand, when you can allocate much of your willpower to the task.
You can then sensibly pick your battles—and sensibly figure out
which ones are too much trouble. Even someone with David Blaine's
iron will and astonishing tolerance for pain knows his limits. When
we told him about Stanley's treks through the jungle, he recoiled upon
hearing about the constant swarms of mosquitoes and other bugs.

"*That* I can't do," Blaine said. "When there are mosquitoes
everywhere, I flee. It's just something I can't handle."

When you pick your battles, look beyond the immediate challenges and put your life in perspective. Are you where you want
to be? What could be better? What can you do about it? You can't
do this every day, of course, and certainly not during busy, stressful times, but you can set aside at least one day a year—maybe your
birthday—to do some reflection and write down notes on how well
you spent the previous year. If you make this an annual ritual, you
can look back over the notes from previous years to see what kinds
of progress you've made in the past: which goals were met, which
goals remain, which ones are hopeless. You should always have at
least a vague five-year objective along with more specific intermedi-

ate goals, like the monthly plans that we discussed in chapter 3. Have an idea of what you want to accomplish in a month and how to get there. Leave some flexibility and anticipate setbacks. When you check your progress at month's end, remember that you don't have to meet each goal every time — what matters is that your life gradually improves from month to month.

Aiming for huge and quick transformations will backfire if they seem impossible. If you can't bring yourself to quit smoking altogether, try cutting down to two or three cigarettes per day. If you're drinking too much but won't swear off alcohol, perhaps you can live with a weekly plan that limits alcohol to the weekends, or that specifies several nights each week of no drinking while allowing whatever you want on other nights. Are you someone who can interrupt an evening of drinking to have no alcohol for an hour, to see where you are, and then make a good decision about whether to resume drinking? If you are, that can be an effective way to limit the damage. But if you're not one of those people, don't kid yourself. Effective planning should even budget your willpower. How will you expend your willpower today, this evening, and the next month? If there are extra challenges ahead, like doing your taxes or traveling, figure out where you'll get the extra willpower, such as by cutting back on other demands.

When you're budgeting your time, don't give drudgery more than its necessary share. Remember Parkinson's Law: Work expands so as to fill the time available for its completion. Set a firm time limit for tedious tasks. "Clean out basement" or "Reorganize closets" could take up the whole day — if you ever got around to it, which you won't because you don't want to lose a day of your life to something so mundane. But if you set a clear limit of one or two hours, you might get something done this Saturday (and then, if necessary, plan another short stint of work for another weekend). Even David Allen, the guru of productivity, makes allowances for Parkinson's Law. When he travels for speeches on *Getting Things Done*, he doesn't start packing until thirty-five minutes before departure. "I know I can pack in thirty-five minutes," he says, "but if I start any earlier, I could spend six hours on it. Giving myself a deadline forces me to make decisions that I don't want to make ahead of time—and I've accepted that about myself. I've got bigger battles to fight."

Make a To-Do List—or at Least a To-Don't List

We devoted chapter 3 to the glorious history of the to-do list, but we realize that some readers might still not feel like drawing one up. It can sound dreary and off-putting. If so, try thinking of it as a to-don't list: a catalog of things that you *don't* have to worry about once you write them down. As we saw in our discussion of the Zeigarnik effect, when you try to ignore unfinished tasks, your unconscious keeps fretting about them in the same way that an ear worm keeps playing an unfinished song. You can't banish them from your brain by procrastinating or by willing yourself to forget them.

But once you make a specific plan, your unconscious will be mollified. You need to at least plan the specific next step to take: what to do, whom to contact, how to do it (in person? by phone? by e mail?). If you can also plan specifically when and where to do it, so much the better, but that's not essential. As long as you've decided what to do and put it on the list, your unconscious can relax.

Beware the Planning Fallacy

Whenever you set a goal, beware of what psychologists call the planning fallacy. It affects everyone from young students to veteran executives. When was the last time you heard of a highway or building being completed six months early? Late and over budget is the norm.

The planning fallacy was quantified in an experiment involving college seniors working on honors theses. The psychologist Roger Buehler and his colleagues asked these seniors to predict when they would probably finish, along with best-case and worst-case predictions. On average, the students predicted it would take thirty-four days to finish, but in fact they ended up taking nearly twice as long—fifty-six days. Only a handful finished by the date of their best-case prediction. The worst-case prediction, based on the assumption that everything would go as poorly as it possibly could, should have been easy to beat—after all, rarely does *everything* go wrong—but in fact it wasn't. Not even half the students finished by their worst-case predicted date. The planning fallacy can affect just about everyone, but it takes a special toll on procrastinators who expect to get the job done in one concentrated burst of effort at the last minute. This strategy might work if they left themselves a big enough chunk of time right before the deadline, but they won't do that. They'll underestimate how long the work will take, and then they'll discover that they don't have enough time left to do it well.

One way to avoid the planning fallacy is to force yourself to think about your past. If Tice's dilatory student had seriously considered how long it had taken her to write previous term papers, she might have allowed more than a couple of hours for the next one. In the honors-thesis experiment, when students were directed to base their future plans on their previous projects, they were much more realistic in predicting the completion date of their theses. Another finding was that students were also much more realistic and hence more accurate at predicting the completion dates for *other* students' theses. All of us, whether or not we're serious procrastinators, tend to have an optimistic bias toward our own work, so it makes sense to ask others to review our plans. You might write a quick e-mail outlining your plans, or just describe it briefly in a conversation. Or you can be a little more systematic (without getting too complicated) by following the management technique that Aaron Patzer used to guide

Mint.com from a small start-up to a company tracking the finances of millions of people.

"We simply ask our managers and other workers to set their top goals for the week," Patzer says. "You can't have more than three goals, and it's fine if you have less than three. Each week we go over what we did last week and whether we met those goals or not, and then each person sets the top three goals for this week. If you only get goals one and two done, but not three, that's fine, but you can't go off working on other goals until you've done the top three. That's it—that's how we manage. It's simple, but it forces you to prioritize, and it's rigorous."

Don't Forget the Basics (like Changing Your Socks)

As you start working toward your goal, your brain will automatically economize on willpower expenditures in other ways. Remember those college students at exam time whom we discussed in chapter 1—the ones who became lax about changing socks, washing their hair, cleaning up the dishes, and eating healthy food? To them, these cutbacks might have seemed a fair price to pay in order to channel all their energies into preparing for exams. But it probably didn't seem fair to some of the roommates who had to smell their socks and clean up the messes, and the resulting disputes may well have left everyone drained. In the long run, slovenliness can leave you with less energy—and fewer healthy relationships.

Forget the image of starving artists who do great things by working around the clock in filthy garrets. Self-control will be most effective if you take good basic care of your body, starting with diet and sleep. You can indulge yourself in rich desserts, but be sure to get enough healthy food on a regular basis so that your mind has adequate energy. Sleep is probably even more important than food: The more that researchers study sleep deprivation, the more nasty effects they keep discovering. A big mug of coffee in the morning is not an adequate substitute for sleeping until your body wakes up on its own because it has gotten enough rest. The old advice that things will seem better in the morning has nothing to do with daylight, and everything to do with depletion. A rested will is a stronger will.

Another simple old-fashioned way to boost your willpower is to expend a little of it on neatness. As we described in chapter 7, people exert less self-control after seeing a messy desk than after seeing a clean desk, or when using a sloppy rather than a neat and well-organized Web site. You may not care about whether your bed is made and your desk is clean, but these environmental cues subtly influence your brain and your behavior, making it ultimately less of a strain to maintain self-discipline. Order seems to be contagious.

Watch out for other kinds of cues, too, that can influence your behavior one way or the other. Bad habits are strengthened by routine: The doughnut shop you pass on the way to work, the midafternoon cigarette break or chocolate binge, the after-work drink, the late-night bowl of ice cream while watching the same TV show in the same easy chair. Changing your routine makes it easier to break these habits. Take a different route to work. Go for a midafternoon stroll. Schedule a session at the gym after work. Eat ice cream only at the kitchen table, and switch to doing sit-ups during that TV show. Do your Web surfing on a different computer from the one where you work. To break a really entrenched bad habit like smoking, do it on vacation, when you're far away from the people and places and events you associate with cigarettes.

The Power of Positive Procrastination

Procrastination is usually a vice, but occasionally—very occasionally—there is such a thing as positive procrastination. In the previous chapter we discussed experiments showing that people tempted by chocolate managed to avoid it by telling themselves they'd eat it some other time—a postponement strategy that worked better than trying to deny themselves altogether. This "I'll have it later" trick can work for other temptations, too. If a TV show is keeping you from getting back to work, record it and tell yourself you'll finish watching it later. You might discover, once you've finished work and don't need an excuse to procrastinate, that you don't really want to watch the show after all. Vice delayed may turn out to be vice denied.

A more dubious form of positive procrastination was identified by Robert Benchley, one of the deadline-challenged members of the Algonquin Round Table. (His colleague Dorothy Parker gave her editor at *The New Yorker* the all-time best excuse for an overdue piece: "Somebody was using the pencil.") In a wry essay, Benchley explained how he could summon the discipline to read a scientific article about tropical fish, build a bookshelf, arrange books on said shelf, and write an answer to a friend's letter that had been sitting in a pile on his desk for twenty years. All he had to do was draw up a to-do list for the week and put these tasks below his top priority—his job of writing an article.

"The secret of my incredible energy and efficiency in getting work done is a simple one," Benchley wrote. "The psychological principle is this: anyone can do any amount of work, provided it isn't the work he is supposed to be doing at that moment."

Benchley recognized a phenomenon that Baumeister and Tice also documented in their term-paper study: Procrastinators typically avoid one task by doing something else, and rarely do they sit there doing nothing at all. But there's a better way to exploit that tendency, as Raymond Chandler recognized.

The Nothing Alternative
(and Other Tricks of Offense)

Anthony Trollope's writing regimen is one path to self-discipline, as we mentioned in chapter 5. But what if, unlike Trollope with his watch at his side, you're incapable of producing 250 words every fifteen minutes? Fortunately, there's another strategy for ordinary mortals, courtesy of Raymond Chandler, who was bewildered by writers who could churn out prose every day.

Chandler had his own system for turning out *The Big Sleep* and other classic detective stories. "Me, I wait for inspiration," he said, but he did it methodically every morning. He believed that a professional writer needed to set aside at least four hours a day for his job: "He doesn't have to write, and if he doesn't feel like it, he shouldn't try. He can look out of the window or stand on his head or writhe on the floor, but he is not to do any other positive thing, not read, write letters, glance at magazines, or write checks."

This Nothing Alternative is a marvelously simple tool against procrastination for just about any kind of task. Although your work may not be as solitary and clearly defined as Chandler's, you can still benefit by setting aside time to do one and only one thing. You might, for instance, resolve to start your day with ninety minutes devoted to your most important goal, with no interruptions from e-mail or phone calls, no side excursions anywhere on the Web. Just follow Chandler's regimen:

"Write or nothing. It's the same principle as keeping order in a school. If you make the pupils behave, they will learn something just to keep from being bored. I find it works. Two very simple rules, a. you don't have to write. b. you can't do anything else. The rest comes of itself."

The rest comes of itself. That's the seeming effortlessness that comes from playing offense. Chandler was incorporating several of the techniques we discussed earlier. The Nothing Alternative is a bright-line rule: a clear, unmistakable boundary, like the no-drinking vow taken by Eric Clapton and Mary Karr. Chandler's particular rule—*If I can't write, I will do nothing*—is also an example of an implementation plan, that specific if-x-then-y strategy that has been shown to reduce the demands on willpower. It's easier to resist the temptation to go into debt if you enter the store with a firm implementation plan, like, *If I shop for clothes, I will buy only what I can pay for with the cash in my wallet.* Every time you follow this kind of rule, it becomes more routine, until eventually it seems to happen automatically and you have a lasting technique for conserving willpower: a habit.

Of course, it's even easier to avoid running up debt at a clothing store if you go there without a credit card. Precommitment is the ultimate offensive weapon. Buy junk food in small packages or keep them out of the kitchen altogether. Plan meals by the week, rather than on the spur of the moment when it's already past dinnertime and you're starving. If you're planning to have a child, set up an automatic payroll deduction plan to build up a nest egg of ten thousand dollars so you're not stressed out by money during those first sleep-deprived months of parenthood. If you have a gambling problem and are going someplace where there's a casino, sign up ahead of time for the self-exclusion list (which will prevent you from collecting any winnings). To precommit to the Nothing Alternative, use a software program (like the one named Freedom) that locks you off the Internet for a set period.

Precommitment helps you avoid the hot-cold empathy gap we discussed earlier: the common failure to appreciate, in moments of cool deliberation, how different you'll feel in the heat of later moments. One of the most common reasons for the self-control problem is overconfidence in willpower. In one recent study, smokers were invited to bet that they could hold an unlit cigarette in their mouths while watching a movie without succumbing to the temptation to smoke. Plenty took the bet, and they lost. Better to precommit by leaving the cigarette somewhere else.

Keep Track

Monitoring is crucial for any kind of plan you make—and it can even work if you don't make a plan at all. Weighing yourself every day or keeping a food diary can help you lose weight, just as tracking your purchases will help you spend less. Even a writer who doesn't share Trollope's ability to meet daily quota can still benefit just by noting the word count at the beginning and end of the day: The mere knowledge that you'll have to put down a number will discourage procrastination (or the kind of busywork that might feel virtuous but doesn't contribute to that word count). The more carefully you keep track, the better. Weighing yourself every week is good. Weighing yourself every day is better. Weighing yourself and recording it is even better.

Self-monitoring can be a bore, but it's easier than ever thanks to the new tools that do the grunt work for you. As we discussed in chapter 5, you can let Mint and other programs monitor your credit card and bank transactions, draw up a budget, and track your progress toward goals. You can track your cash spending by sending yourself messages via e-mail or Twitter with programs like Xpenser and Tweetwhatyouspend. Entrepreneurs are rushing to monitor just about every aspect of your life—your health, your moods, your sleep—and you can find dozens of their products by consulting Web sites like Quantified Self and Lifehacker.

Besides offering immediate encouragement, monitoring lets you improve your long-term planning. If you keep records, you can periodically check how far you've come so that you can set more realistic goals for the future. On days when you slack off and break the rules, when you might be tempted to write yourself off as a hopeless cause, you can see otherwise by looking back at your progress. Gaining a couple of pounds this week isn't so discouraging if you've got a chart for the last six months showing a line sloping downward.

Reward Often

When you set a goal, set a reward for reaching it—and then don't stiff yourself. If you just use willpower to deny yourself things, it becomes a grim, thankless form of defense. But when you use it to gain something, you can wring pleasure out of the dreariest tasks. We've criticized the everybody-gets-a-trophy philosophy of the self-esteem movement, but trophies for genuine accomplishments are fine. As we saw in the chapter on parenting, the most successful strategies for promoting self-control involve rewards, whether they're being offered by British nannies, Asian-American mothers, or computer-game designers. Young people who seem hopelessly undisciplined in school or on the job will concentrate for hour after hour on games that involve the same skills needed for more productive work at the computer: Look at information on a screen, balance short-term and long-term goals, make a choice, and click. The computer-game industry's astounding growth—by age twenty-one, the typical American has spent ten thousand hours playing computer games—occurred because its designers had an unprecedented opportunity to observe people's responses to incentives.

Online games became essentially the largest experiment ever conducted into motivational strategies. By getting instant feedback from millions of online players, the game designers learned precisely which incentives work: a mix of frequent small prizes with occasional big ones. Even when players lose battles or make mistakes or die, they remain motivated because of the emphasis on rewards rather than punishment. Instead of feeling as if they've failed, the players think that they just haven't succeeded yet.

That's the feeling we should aim for in the real world, and we can do it by steadily rewarding ourselves for successes along the way. Achieving a big goal, like quitting smoking for a year, deserves a big reward—at the very least, use the money you would have spent on cigarettes for some extraordinary indulgence, like a meal at a hideously expensive restaurant. But it's just as important to have lots of little rewards for little feats. Never underestimate how little it takes to motivate. How do you get people to devote a full two minutes to brushing their teeth and gums? Sell them an electric toothbrush that displays a smiley face after two minutes of brushing, as some of Braun's models do. Dopey drawings may not work for you, but something else will. Esther Dyson likes to tell how, after years of failing to floss regularly, she finally hit on the proper incentive. As we mentioned earlier, she was quite disciplined in most other parts of her life, including forcing herself every day to do an hour of swimming. One evening she had an epiphany: "If I floss my teeth tonight, I'll let myself take five minutes off the swimming tomorrow. That was four years ago, and I've flossed just about every night since. It's incredibly silly but amazingly effective. Everybody needs to find their own little thing. It's got to be a reward that's relevant."

The Future of Self-control

Until fairly recently, most people relied on a traditional method for maintaining self-control: They outsourced the job to God. Or at least to the fellow members of their religion. Divine precepts and social pressure from the rest of the congregation made religion the most powerful promoter of self-control for most of history. Today, even though the influence of religion is waning in some places, people are learning other ways to outsource self-control—to friends and to smartphones, to Web sites that monitor behavior and enforce bets, to neighbors meeting in church basements and to social networks linked electronically. We have new tools for quantifying just about everything we do and sharing it with new congregations. Meanwhile, more and more people have come to recognize that weak self-control is central to personal and social problems. When societies modernize, the newly affluent people at first tend to gorge themselves on previously forbidden (or unaffordable) fruit, but eventually they look for a more satisfying way to live.

The point of self-control isn't simply to be more "productive." People today don't have to work as hard as Ben Franklin and the Victorians did. In the nineteenth century, the typical worker had barely an hour of free time per day and didn't even think about retiring. Today we spend only about a fifth of our adult waking hours on the job. The remaining time is an astonishing gift—an unprecedented blessing in human history—but it takes an unprecedented type of self-control to enjoy it. Too many of us tend to procrastinate even when it comes to pleasure because we succumb to the planning fallacy when we estimate "resource slack," as behavioral economists term it. We assume we'll magically have more free time in the future than we do today. So we say yes to a work commitment three months from now that we'd never accept if it were next week—and then discover too late that we still don't have any time for it. Researchers term this the "Yes . . . Damn!" effect.

And we keep putting off present pleasures, like visiting the zoo or getting away for the weekend. There's so much of this procrastination that airlines and other marketers save billions of dollars annually from frequent flyer miles and gift certificates that go unredeemed. Like pathological tightwads who end up with saver's remorse, procrastinators of pleasure wind up regretting the trips not taken and the fun forgone. Whether you're working or playing, you'll find more happiness and less stress by going on offense. Your ideal of paradise might be three weeks of doing nothing on a tropical island, but you can't get there without making plans in advance—and maybe, in the case of workaholics, establishing some bright-line rules against working in paradise.

Self-control is ultimately about much more than self-help. It's essential for savoring your time on earth and sharing joy with the people you love. Of all the benefits that have been demonstrated in Baumeister's experiments, one of the most heartening is this: People with stronger willpower are more altruistic. They're more likely to donate to charity, to do volunteer work, and to offer their own homes as shelter to someone with no place to go. Willpower evolved because it was crucial for our ancestors to get along with the rest of the clan, and it's still serving that purpose today. Inner discipline still leads to outer kindness.

That's why, despite all the foibles and failings described in this book, there's reason to be bullish on self-control. Willpower is still evolving. Lots of us have succumbed lately to new temptations, and there will be plenty of unexpected challenges ahead. But no matter what new technologies arise, no matter how overwhelming some of the new threats seem, humans have the capacity to deal with them. Our willpower has made us the most adaptable creatures on the planet, and we're rediscovering how to help one another use it. We're learning, once again, that willpower is the virtue that sets our species apart, and that makes each one of us strong.

Acknowledgments

We wish to thank the many people who made this book possible and who contributed in so many ways to make it better. We'll start with Kris Dahl, our literary agent extraordinaire, who helped us develop the idea and delivered us to the expert hands of our editor, Ann Godoff. We deeply appreciate the support and guidance from Ann, who never lost perspective and never lost her patience either. We're also grateful to the rest of the team at The Penguin Press, especially Lindsay Whalen and Yamil Anglada, and to Laura Neeley of ICM, all of whose willpower seemed similarly inexhaustible.

We owe special thanks to the many colleagues who discussed their work with us and offered suggestions for the book, starting with Dan Ariely, who originally suggested the project. Kathleen Vohs was particularly helpful in pointing us to specific findings and developments in the fast-moving research literature on self-regulation. We're grateful to George Ainslie, Ian Ayres, Jack Begg, Warren Bickel, Benedict Carey, Christopher Buckley, Ruth Chao, Pierre Chandon, Alexander Chernev, Stephen Dubner, Esther Dyson, Stuart Elliott, Eli Finkel, Catrin Finkenauer, Winifred Gallagher, Daniel Gilbert, James Gorman, Todd Heatherton, Wilhelm Hoffman, Walter Isaacson, Dean Karlan, Ran Kivetz, Gina Kolata, Jonathan Levav, George Loewenstein, Dina Pomeranz, Michael McCullough, William Rashbaum, Martin Seligman, Piers Steel, June Tangney, Gary

Taubes, Dianne Tice, Jean Twenge, Christine Whelan, and Jim and Phil Wharton.

We're indebted to the people whose stories are told in this book, including Amanda Palmer, Jim Turner, David Allen (whose GTD system is still being used by Tierney), Drew Carey, David Blaine, Eric Clapton, Mary Karr, Deborah Carroll, Cyndi Paul and her family, and Oprah Winfrey. We owe a special debt to Tim Jeal, the masterly biographer, who generously provided information about Henry Morton Stanley and reviewed our chapter for historical accuracy. Aaron Patzer, Martha Shaughnessy, and the rest of the team at Mint .com — including Chris Lesner, Jacques Belissent, T. J. Sanghvi, David Michaels, and Todd Manzer — kindly provided us with a painstaking analysis of more than two billion financial transactions.

Baumeister's work was facilitated by a sabbatical leave from Florida State University, by the host university for his sabbatical (the University of California, Santa Barbara), and especially by the opportunities associated with his Francis Eppes Eminent Scholar professorial position at FSU. Some of his time was supported by the grant "Self-Control and Stress," 1RL1AA017541, from the National Institutes of Health. He also acknowledges that many previously published works that are covered here were supported by his earlier research grant, "Ego Depletion Patterns and Self-Control Failure," MH-57039, also from the National Institutes of Health.

Tierney's research was aided by the endlessly resourceful Nicole Vincent-Roller, a graduate student in Columbia University's creative writing program, who worked with him as part of the school's MFA research internships program. Thanks to her and to the program's director, Patricia O'Toole.

Finally, we want to thank our families — especially Dianne and Athena, Dana and Luke — for putting up with our own moments of depleted willpower during the writing of this book. Their strength has been a continuing inspiration.

Notes

INTRODUCTION

1 **Charles Darwin:** *The Descent of Man* (New York: American Home Library, 1902), 166.

2 **international survey on character strengths:** Values in Action project (see C. Peterson and M. Seligman, eds., *Character Strengths and Virtues* [Washington, DC: American Psychological Association, 2004]); the statistics on frequency of listing were done by Neal Mayerson specifically for this project.

3 **German beeper study:** W. Hoffman, K. Vohs, G. Förster, and R. Baumeister (completed in 2010 and to be submitted for scientific publication in 2011). Hoffman is now at the University of Chicago.

4 **Victorians and morality:** For particular coverage of the Victorian concerns about morality and religion, see W. E. Houghton, *The Victorian Frame of Mind, 1830–1870* (New Haven, CT: Yale University Press, 1957). Also relevant: P. Gay, *Bourgeois Experience: Education of the Senses* (New York: Oxford University Press, 1984).

5 *Self-Help:* Samuel Smiles, *Self-Help; with illustrations of Character, Conduct, and Perseverance* (London: John Murray, 1866), 104.

5 *The Power of Will:* Frank Channing Haddock, *Power of Will* (Meriden, CT: Pelton, 1916), 7.

6 **new self-help bestsellers:** See C. B. Whelan, "Self-Help Books and the Quest for Self-Control in the United States, 1950–2000" (Ph.D. dissertation, University of Oxford, 2004), http://christinewhelan.com/wp-content/uploads/Self-Help_Long_Abstract.pdf; and P. Carlson, "Let a Thousand Gurus Bloom," *Washington Post Magazine,* February 12, 1995, W12.

6 **Dale Carnegie:** *How to Win Friends and Influence People* (New York: Gallery Books, 1998), 63-70.

7 **"realizable wish":** Norman Vincent Peale, *The Power of Positive Thinking* (New York: Simon & Schuster, 2003), 46.

7 **"believe yourself already in possession of the money":** N. Hill, *Think and Grow Rich* (Radford, VA: Wilder Publications, 2008), 27.

7 **Allen Wheelis:** *The Quest for Identity* (New York: Norton, 1958).

8 **B. F. Skinner:** *Beyond Freedom & Dignity* (New York: Knopf, 1971).

9 **U.S. math students:** J. Mathews, "For Math Students, Self-Esteem Might Not Equal High Scores," *Washington Post,* October 18, 2006, http://www.washingtonpost.com/wp-dyn/content/article/2006/10/17/AR2006101701298.html.

10   **Mischel's studies of delayed gratification:** A good recent summary of Mischel's studies, including the famous "marshmallow test," is W. Mischel and O. Ayduk, "Willpower in a Cognitive-Affective Processing System: The Dynamics of Delay of Gratification," in R. Baumeister and K. Vohs, eds., *Handbook of Self-Regulation: Research, Theory, and Applications* (New York: Guilford, 2004), 99–129. An earlier summary, probably more extensive and closer to the original work, was W. Mischel, "Processes in Delay of Gratification," in L. Berkowitz, ed., *Advances in Experimental Social Psychology* (San Diego, CA: Academic Press, 1974), 7:249–92. For the follow-ups showing how childhood performance predicted adult outcomes, see W. Mischel, Y. Shoda, and P. Peake, "The Nature of Adolescent Competencies Predicted by Preschool Delay of Gratification," *Journal of Personality and Social Psychology* 54 (1988): 687–96; also, Y. Shoda, W. Mischel, and P. K. Peake, "Predicting Adolescent Cognitive and Self-Regulatory Competencies from Preschool Delay of Gratification: Identifying Diagnostic Conditions," *Developmental Psychology* 26 (1990): 978–86.

10   **childhood experiences and adult personality:** M. E. P. Seligman, *What You Can Change and What You Can't: The Complete Guide to Successful Self-Improvement* (New York: Alfred A. Knopf, 1993).

11   *Losing Control:* R. F. Baumeister, T. F. Heatherton, and D. M. Tice, *Losing Control: How and Why People Fail at Self-Regulation* (San Diego, CA: Academic Press, 1994).

11   **scale for measuring self-control:** The self-control trait scale (along with predictive findings) was published in J. P. Tangney, R. F. Baumeister, and A. L. Boone, "High Self-Control Predicts Good Adjustment, Less Pathology, Better Grades, and Interpersonal Success," *Journal of Personality* 72 (2004): 271–322.

11   **self-control predicts college grades:** R. N. Wolfe and S. D. Johnson, "Personality as a Predictor of College Performance," *Educational and Psychological Measurement* 55 (1995): 177–85. Also see A. L. Duckworth and M. E. P. Seligman, "Self-Discipline Outdoes IQ in Predicting Academic Performance of Adolescents," *Psychological Science* 16 (2005): 939–44.

12   **self-control and prisoners:** J. Mathews, K. Youman, J. Stuewig, and J. Tangney, "Reliability and Validity of the Brief Self-Control Scale among Incarcerated Offenders" (presented at the annual meeting of the American Society of Criminology, Atlanta, Georgia, November 2007).

12   **New Zealand study:** T. Moffitt and twelve other authors, "A Gradient of Self-Control Predicts Health, Wealth, and Public Safety," *Proceedings of the National Academy of Sciences* (January 24, 2011), http://www.pnas.org/content/early/2011/01/20/1010076108.

14   **evolution of brain for self-control:** The social brain theory was discussed and compared with the fruit-seeking brain theory and others in several of Dunbar's works. One key source is R. I. M. Dunbar, "The Social Brain Hypothesis," *Evolutionary Anthropology* 6 (1998): 178–90.

15   **animals cannot project into the future:** W. A. Roberts, "Are Animals Stuck in Time?" *Psychological Bulletin* 128 (2002): 473–89.

16   **connecting across time:** See M. Donald, *A Mind So Rare: The Evolution of Human Consciousness* (New York: Norton, 2002); applied specifically to the will, G. Ainslie, *Breakdown of Will* (New York: Cambridge University Press, 2001).

CHAPTER 1: IS WILLPOWER MORE THAN A METAPHOR?

19   **Amanda Palmer:** See her Web site: http://amandapalmer.net/afp/. The many videos of her on YouTube include some during her early career as a living statue. Photos of her as a living statue are at http://brainwashed.com/amanda/.

22   **ego-depletion experiments:** The radish and chocolate experiment was originally published in R. F. Baumeister, E. Bratlavsky, M. Muraven, and D. M. Tice, "Ego Depletion: Is the Active Self a Limited Resource?" *Journal of Personality and Social Psychology* 74

(1998): 1252–65. Other early ego-depletion experiments covered in this chapter (including the emotion control, handgrip, and white bear studies) were reported in M. Muraven, D. M. Tice, and R. F. Baumeister, "Self-Control as Limited Resource: Regulatory Depletion Patterns," *Journal of Personality and Social Psychology* 74 (1998): 774–89. For a recent overview of the research program, see R. F. Baumeister, K. D. Vohs, and D. M. Tice, "Strength Model of Self-Control," *Current Directions in Psychological Science* 16 (2007): 351–55.

25 **suppressing thoughts:** For the early studies on suppressing thoughts (e.g., of white bears, as well as not thinking about your mother) see D. M. Wegner, *White Bears and Other Unwanted Thoughts* (New York: Vintage, 1989).

27 **no evidence for Freudian sublimation:** R. F. Baumeister, K. Dale, and K. L. Sommer, "Freudian Defense Mechanisms and Empirical Findings in Modern Social Psychology: Reaction Formation, Projection, Displacement, Undoing, Isolation, Sublimation, and Denial," *Journal of Personality* 66 (1998): 1081–1124.

28 **Michael Inzlict:** M. Inzlicht and J. N. Gutsell, "Running on Empty: Neural Signals for Self-Control Failure," *Psychological Science* 18 (2007): 933–37.

30 **meta-analysis on ego depletion:** M. S. Hagger, C. Wood, C. Stiff, and N. L. D. Chatzisarantis, "Ego Depletion and the Strength Model of Self-Control: A Meta-Analysis," *Psychological Bulletin* 136 (2010): 495–525.

30 **intensification of feelings during depletion, and the broader question of what depletion feels like:** See K. D. Vohs, R. F. Baumeister, N. L. Mead, S. Ramanathan, and B. J. Schmeichel, "Engaging in Self-Control Heightens Urges and Feelings" (manuscript submitted for publication, University of Minnesota, 2010).

31 **A. P. Herbert:** Quoted in S. A. Maisto, M. Galizio, G. J. Connors, *Drug Use and Abuse* (Belmont, CA: Wadsworth, 2008), 152.

31–32 **the quotations from Daryl Bem:** From personal conversations and from his conference presentations on that work.

32 **on students' self-control deteriorating during exam times:** See M. Oaten and K. Cheng, "Academic Examination Stress Impairs Self-Control," *Journal of Social and Clinical Psychology* 24 (2005): 254–79.

33 **German beeper study:** See citation in Introduction notes.

34 **on conserving willpower for later demands:** M. Muraven, D. Shmueli, and E. Burkley, "Conserving Self-Control Strength," *Journal of Personality and Social Psychology* 91 (2006): 524–37.

36 **pulse becomes more erratic:** S. C. Segerstrom and L. Solberg Nes, "Heart Rate Variability Reflects Self-Regulatory Strength, Effort, and Fatigue," *Psychological Science* 18 (2007): 275–81.

36 **chronic physical pain leaves people with a perpetual shortage of willpower:** L. A. Solberg Nes, C. R. Carlson, L. J. Crofford, R. de Leeuw, and S. C. Segerstrom, "Self-Regulatory Deficits in Fibromyalgia and Temporomandibular Disorders," *Pain* (in press).

36 **four broad categories of self-regulation:** Adumbrated in R. F. Baumeister, T. F. Heatherton, and D. M. Tice, *Losing Control: How and Why People Fail at Self-Regulation* (San Diego: Academic Press, 1994).

CHAPTER 2: WHERE DOES THE POWER IN WILLPOWER COME FROM?

40 **"Twinkie defense":** Carol Pogash, "Myth of the 'Twinkie defense,'" *San Francisco Chronicle,* November 23, 2003, http://www.sfgate.com/cgi-bin/article.cgi?f=/c/a/2003/11/23/INGRE343501.DTL.

40 **Melanie Griffith divorce filing:** "Rocky Mountain Low," *People,* March 28, 1994, http://www.people.com/people/archive/article/0,20107725,00.html.

41 **glucose and ego depletion:** The main source for the first set of studies on glucose and

depletion is the Gailliot et al. 2007 article; however, the milkshake study was deleted
before the final package was published because he thought the paper was long and other
experiments made the point more strongly. M. T. Gailliot, R. F. Baumeister, C. N. DeWall,
J. K. Maner, E. A. Plant, D. M. Tice, L. E. Brewer, and B. J. Schmeichel, "Self-Control
Relies on Glucose as a Limited Energy Source: Willpower Is More Than a Metaphor,"
Journal of Personality and Social Psychology 92 (2007): 325–36.

44   **glucose and self-control literature:** The research on literature on glucose and self-
control was reviewed and summarized by M. T. Gailliot and R. F. Baumeister, "The
Physiology of Willpower: Linking Blood Glucose to Self-Control," *Personality and
Social Psychology Review* 11 (2007): 303–27. That article contains original sources and
summaries for many of the studies mentioned here. Additional experiments were reported in the Gailliot et al. (2007) *JPSP* paper.

46   **Jim Turner:** Information on his one-man show, "Diabetes: My Struggles with Jim
Turner," can be obtained by writing to jim@jimturner.net. More material is at Dlife
(http://www.dlife.com/diabetes/information/dlife_media/tv/jim_turner_index.html)
and in a profile of him by G. Brashers-Krug, "Laughing at Lows," *Voice of the Diabetic*
23, no. 3 (Summer edition 2008), http://www.nfb.org/images/nfb/Publications/vod/
vod_23_3/vodsum0801.htm.

48   **aggression during computer games:** Gailliot and Baumeister (*PSPR*, 2007).

49   **self-control in dogs:** H. C. Miller, K. F. Pattison, C. N. DeWall, R. Rayburn-Reeves,
and T. R. Zentall, "Self-Control Without a 'Self'?: Common Self-Control Processes in
Humans and Dogs," *Psychological Science* 21 (2010): 534–38.

50   **the findings on glucose counteracting the effects of depletion in dieters' brains:**
Reported by Heatherton in his presidential address at the Society for Personality and
Social Psychology, San Antonio, Texas, in January 2011. See K. Demos, C. Amble,
D. Wagner, W. Kelley, and T. Heatherton, "Correlates of Self-Regulatory Depletion in
Chronic Dieters" (poster presented at Society for Personality and Social Psychology,
San Antonio, Texas, 2011).

51   **craving sweet things to eat:** Masicampo and Baumeister conducted these experiments
in 2011, and as of this writing their manuscript has been submitted for publication.

51   **Jennifer Love Hewitt:** "That time of the month again," *OK!*, September 22, 2009,
http://www.ok.co.uk/posts/view/14355/That-time-of-the-month-again.

52   **"It ruins a large portion of my life":** "The worst PMS on the planet," NoPeriod
.com, http://www.noperiod.com/stories.html. Other comments on PMS are at PMS
Central, http://www.pmscentral.com/.

52   **Marg Helgenberger's PMS Pink:** D. R. Coleridge, "CSI Star's Emmy Thrill," *TV
Guide,* July 20, 2001, http://www.tvguide.com/news/CSI-Stars-Emmy-36572.aspx.

53   **physiological explanation for PMS:** M. T. Gailliot, B. Hildebrandt, L. A. Eckel, and
R. F. Baumeister, "A Theory of Limited Metabolic Energy and Premenstrual Syndrome
(PMS) Symptoms: Increased Metabolic Demands During the Luteal Phase Divert Metabolic Resources from and Impair Self-Control," *Review of General Psychology* 14
(2010): 269–82.

58   **Mary J. Blige:** "Oprah Talks to Mary J. Blige," *O*, May 15, 2006, http://www.oprah
.com/omagazine/Oprah-Interviews-Mary-J-Blige/3.

59   **driving a car when sick:** http://www.yell.com/motoring/blog/having-a-cold-or-the
-flu-can-affect-your-driving/ contains secondary source; link to study at http://www
.insurance.lloydstsb.com/personal/general/mediacentre/sneeze_and_drive.asp.

60   **workers who were not getting enough sleep; unethical behavior:** C. M. Barnes,
J. Shaubroeck, M. Hugh, and S. Ghumman, "Lack of Sleep and Unethical Conduct,"
Organizational Behavior and Human Decision Processes (in press; publication is likely
in late 2011 or early 2012). In contrast, a recent paper found no effect of sleep deprivation
on self-control of aggression: K. D. Vohs, B. D. Glass, W. T. Maddox, and A. B. Markman,

"Ego Depletion Is Not Just Fatigue: Evidence from a Total Sleep Deprivation Experiment," *Social Psychological and Personality Science* 2 (2011): 16–173.

CHAPTER 3: A BRIEF HISTORY OF THE TO-DO LIST

63 **course of moral perfection:** Benjamin Franklin, *The Autobiography of Benjamin Franklin* (Philadelphia: Henry Altemus, 1895), 147–64.

65 **Franklin's showing off booklet:** W. Isaacson, *Benjamin Franklin: An American Life* (New York: Simon & Schuster, 2003), 92.

66 **studies on conflicting goals:** R. A. Emmons and L. A. King, "Conflict among Personal Strivings: Immediate and Long-Term Implications for Psychological and Physical Well-being," *Journal of Personality and Social Psychology* 54 (1988): 1040–48. Also see H. W. Maphet and A. L. Miller, "Compliance, Temptation, and Conflicting Instructions," *Journal of Personality and Social Psychology* 42 (1982): 137–44.

68 **addicts thinking of the future:** W. Bickel and M. W. Johnson, "Delay Discounting: A Fundamental Behavioral Process of Drug Dependence," in G. Loewenstein, D. Read, and R. Baumeister, eds., *Time and Decision* (New York: Russell Sage, 2003), 419–40.

70 **proximal versus distal goals:** A. Bandura and D. H. Schunk, "Cultivating Competence, Self-Efficacy, and Intrinsic Interest Through Proximal Self-Motivation," *Journal of Personality and Social Psychology* 41 (1981): 586–98.

71 **Dutch study on distal goals:** M. L. De Volder and W. Lens, "Academic Achievement and Future Time Perspective as a Cognitive-Motivational Concept," *Journal of Personality and Social Psychology* 42 (1982): 566–71.

72 **daily versus monthly plans:** D. S. Kirschenbaum, L. L. Humphrey, and S. D. Malett, "Specificity of Planning in Adult Self-Control: An Applied Investigation," *Journal of Personality and Social Psychology* 40 (1981): 941–50. Also see D. S. Kirschenbaum, S. Malett, L. L. Humphrey, and A. J. Tomarken, "Specificity of Planning and the Maintenance of Self-Control: 1 Year Follow-up of a Study Improvement Program," *Behavior Therapy* 13 (1982): 232–40.

73 **Napoleon on improvising:** O. Connelly, *Blundering to Glory: Napoleon's Military Campaigns* (Lanham, MD: Rowman & Littlefield, 2006), p. ix.

73 **Prussian military planning:** H. Koch, *A History of Prussia* (New York: Dorset, 1978).

73 **D-day schedule:** "First U.S. Army Operations Plan 'Neptune,'" 1944, reprinted at Primary Source Documents, Encyclopedia Britannica, http://www.britannica.com/dday/table?tocId=9400221.

73 **Robert S. McNamara:** G. M. Watson Jr. and H. S. Wolk, "'Whiz Kid': Robert S. McNamara's World War II Service," *Air Power History*, Winter 2003, http://findarticles.com/p/articles/mi_hb3101/is_4_50/ai_n29053044/?tag=content;col1. See also Tim Weiner, "Robert S. McNamara, Architect of a Futile War, Dies at 93," *New York Times*, July 6, 2009, http://www.nytimes.com/2009/07/07/us/07mcnamara.html?_r=1&sq=Robert%20McNamara%20obituary&st=nyt&scp=4&pagewanted=all.

75 **David Allen:** For details on GTD, see Allen's *Getting Things Done* (New York: Penguin Books, 2001); *Making It All Work* (New York: Penguin Books, 2008); and the David Allen Company Web site, http://www.davidco.com/. For biographical material, see Gary Wolf, "*Getting Things Done:* Guru David Allen and His Cult of Hyperefficiency," *Wired*, June 25, 2007, http://www.wired.com/techbiz/people/magazine/15-10/ff_allen?currentPage=all; and Paul Keegan, "How David Allen Mastered Getting Things Done," *Business 2.0 Magazine*, July 1, 2007, http://money.cnn.com/magazines/business2/business2_archive/2007/07/01/100117066/index.htm. For research into GTD, see F. Heylighen and C. Vidal, "Getting Things Done: The Science behind Stress-Free Productivity," *Long Range Planning* 41, no. 6 (2008): 585–605, http://dx.doi.org/10.1016/j.lrp.2008.09.004.

80 **Danny O'Brien survey:** C. Thompson, "Meet the Life Hackers," *New York Times*

Magazine, October 16, 2005, http://www.nytimes.com/2005/10/16/magazine/16guru
.html?scp=1&sq=zeigarnik&st=nyt.

80   **Zeigarnik effect:** E. J. Masicampo and R. F. Baumeister, "Consider It Done!: Making a
Plan Eliminates the Zeigarnik Effect" (manuscript submitted for publication, Tufts
University).

CHAPTER 4: DECISION FATIGUE

89   **Eliot Spitzer scandal:** See W. K. Rashbaum and C. Moynihan, "At a Sentencing, Details
of Spitzer's Liaisons," *New York Times,* June 1, 2009, http://www.nytimes.com/
2009/06/02/nyregion/02emperor.html?_r=2. See also in the case *United States of America
v. Mark Brener, et al.,* "Affidavit in Support of Application for Arrest Warrants,
Search Warrants and Seizure Warrants, Section II: The Emperors Club's Prostitution
Crimes: Payment" (United States District Court Southern Court of New York, March 5,
2008); "Emperors Club: All About Eliot Spitzer's Alleged Prostitution Ring," *Huffing-
ton Post,* October 18, 2008; and M. Dagostino, "Ex-Call Girl Ashley Dupré," *People,*
November 19, 2008.

90   **on choice as ego depleting:** See K. D. Vohs, R. F. Baumeister, B. J. Schmeichel,
J. M. Twenge, N. M. Nelson, and D. M. Tice, "Making Choices Impairs Subsequent
Self-Control: A Limited Resource Account of Decision Making, Self-Regulation, and
Active Initiative," *Journal of Personality and Social Psychology* 94 (2008): 883–98.

93   **the Rubicon model of action phases:** There are many sources, but the best introduc-
tion is in Å. Achtziger and P. M. Gollwitzer, "Rubicon Model of Action Phases," in
R. F. Baumeister and K. D. Vohs, eds., *Encyclopedia of Social Psychology,* vol. 2 (Los
Angeles, CA: Sage, 2007), 769–71.

96   **the data on the judges' parole decisions:** From S. Danziger, J. Levav, and L. Avnaim-
Pesso, "Breakfast, Lunch, and Their Effect on Judicial Decisions," *Proceedings of the
National Academy of Sciences* (in press).

97   **on postponing decisions and other effects of depletion on decision making:** A. Pocheptsova, O. Amir, R. Dhar, and R. F. Baumeister, "Deciding Without Resources: Resource
Depletion and Choice in Context," *Journal of Marketing Research* 46 (2009): 344–55. The
studies on postponing decisions were central to early versions of the paper, but reviewers
objected, and so they are described only briefly, in the Discussion section.

100 **sampling of personal ads in the city magazines:** John Tierney, "The Big City: Picky,
Picky, Picky," *New York Times Magazine,* February 12, 1995.

101 **Rigorous analysis of people's romantic pickiness:** G. J. Hitsch, A. Hortacsu, and
D. Ariely, "What Makes You Click: An Empirical Analysis of Online Dating," 2005
(unpublished manuscript, available online at http://docs.google.com/viewer?a=v&q=c
ache:TvqMaYnA544J:www.aeaweb.org/annual_mtg_papers/2006/0106_0800_0502
.pdf+Hortacsu+Ariely&hl=en&gl=us&pid=bl&srcid=ADGEESi38lvapp1EsKKrnIz2
vihtfNCfFYHwND0063fj76Ll84elqD_raDLhoQ9-dLiXLhZKN4uc5mJ41_AgiXH
bnLePsQlcvcors0nx_ZCe5OLH3rEuuTNWfaFsSbgQoKJ5OWhaCTEw&sig=AHIE
tbSk0_weqgMh_LCtbhvPolj-yx6_fg).

101 **Closing a door:** J. Shin and D. Ariely, "Keeping Doors Open: The Effect of Unavail-
ability on Incentives to Keep Options Open," *Management Science* 50 (2004): 575–86.

103 **Hoarding your energy by avoiding compromises:** A. Pocheptsova, O. Amir, R. Dhar,
and R. F. Baumeister, "Deciding Without Resources: Resource Depletion and Choice
in Context," *Journal of Marketing Research* 46 (2009): 344–55. E. J. Masicampo and
R. F. Baumeister, "Toward a Physiology of Dual-Process Reasoning and Judgment:
Lemonade, Willpower, and Expensive Rule-Based Analysis," *Psychological Science* 19
(2008): 255–60.

103 **car dealers and choice fatigue:** J. Levav, M. Heitmann, A. Herrmann, and S. Iyengar, "Order of Product Customization Decisions: Evidence from Field Experiments," *Journal of Political Economics* 118 (2010): 274–99.

104 **the negative reaction to having too many choices:** Shown in S. S. Iyengar and M. R. Lepper, "When Choice Is Demotivating: Can One Desire Too Much of a Good Thing? *Journal of Personality and Social Psychology* 79 (2105): 996–1006. Barry Schwartz has elaborated this theme in articles and a book titled *Tyranny of Choice.*

105 **glucose in soft drinks can counteract short-term thinking:** X. T. Wang and R. D. Dvorak, "Sweet Future: Fluctuating Blood Glucose Levels Affect Future Discounting," *Psychological Science* 21 (2010): 183–88.

105 **Ingenious study by Margo Wilson:** M. Wilson and M. Daly, "Do Pretty Women Inspire Men to Discount the Future?" *Biology Letters* (proceedings of the Royal Society London, B; Suppl., DOI 10.1098/rsbl. 2003.0134, online 12/12/2003).

106 **DNA research shows men's reproductive odds were lower:** This work and its implications are discussed at length in R. Baumeister, *Is There Anything Good About Men? How Cultures Flourish by Exploiting Men* (New York, Oxford University Press, 2010) as "most underappreciated fact" about gender differences. See also J. A. Wilder, Z. Mobasher, and M. F. Hammer, "Genetic Evidence for Unequal Effective Population Sizes of Human Females and Males," *Molecular Biology and Evolution* (2004), 2047–57.

CHAPTER 5: WHERE HAVE ALL THE DOLLARS GONE?

108 **Darwin letter to son:** F. Burkhardt, S. Evans, and A. M. Pearn, eds., *Evolution: Selected Letters of Charles Darwin, 1860–1870* (New York: Cambridge University Press, 2008), 248.

108 **MRI test at Stanford:** J. Tierney, "The Voices in My Head Say 'Buy It!'" *New York Times,* January 16, 2007.

109 **Aaron Patzer and Mint:** See http://www.mint.com/.

110 **mirror test:** A classic paper on the mirror test with primates was G. G. Gallup, "Chimpanzees: Self-Recognition," *Science* 167 (1970): 86–87.

111 **early self-awareness studies:** Those by Wicklund and Duval were published in the 1970s and most are covered in their book, S. Duval and R. A. Wicklund, *A Theory of Objective Self-Awareness* (New York: Academic Press, 1972).

112 **Carver and Scheier book with coverage of many experiments:** C. S. Carver and M. F. Scheier, *Attention and Self-Regulation: A Control Theory Approach to Human Behavior* (New York: Springer-Verlag, 1981).

113 **the Halloween studies:** A. L. Beaman, B. Klentz, E. Diener, and S. Svanum, "Self-Awareness and Transgression in Children: Two Field Studies," *Journal of Personality and Social Psychology* 37 (1979): 1835–46.

113 **alcohol and self-awareness:** J. G. Hull, "A Self-Awareness Model of the Causes and Effects of Alcohol Consumption," *Journal of Abnormal Psychology* 90 (1981): 586–600.

114 **Trollope's quantified self:** Anthony Trollope, *An Autobiography of Anthony Trollope* (New York: Dodd Mead, 1912), 104–5, 237.

116 **statistics from RescueTime:** T. Wright, "Information Overload: Show Me the Data!" The RescueTime Blog, June 14, 2008, http://blog.rescuetime.com/2008/06/14/information-overload-show-me-the-data/. See also S. Scheper, "RescueTime Founder, Tony Wright, on Life and Focus," *How to Get Focused,* http://howtogetfocused.com/chapters/rescue time-founder-tony-wright-on-life-and-focus/.

117 **quantified self:** See QuantifiedSelf.com, http://quantifiedself.com; and Gary Wolf, "Know Thyself: Tracking Every Facet of Life, from Sleep to Mood to Pain," *Wired,* June 22, 2009, http://www.wired.com/medtech/health/magazine/17-07/lbnp_knowthyself.

118 **Thomas Jefferson:** *Jefferson's Memorandum Books,* July 1776; April–July 1803.

118 **Mint.com analysis of spending trends:** It is possible to compare a person's behavior before and after using Mint because several months of past transaction history are generally available when people join Mint. For this study, two billion transactions from three million anonymous users were aggregated and analyzed by Chris Lesner, a member of Intuit's Technology Innovation Group, with support from Jacques Belissent, the leader of data and research for Intuit Personal Finance Group and Mint. Resources were also provided by T. J. Sanghvi, the engineering manager directly overseeing Mint's data team; David Michaels, the head of the engineering department for Intuit Personal Finance Group (which includes Mint.com and Quicken); and Todd Manzer.

120 **Experiments by Ayelet Fishbach:** M. Koo and A. Fishbach, "Climbing the Goal Ladder: How Upcoming Actions Increase the Level of Aspiration," *Journal of Personality and Social Psychology* 99 (2010), 1–13.

121 **Moodscope:** http://www.moodscope.com/.

121 **benefits of comparing self to others:** See P. Wesley Schultz et al., "The Constructive, Destructive, and Reconstructive Power of Social Norms," *Psychological Science* 18, no. 5 (May 1, 2007): 429–34; also R. H. Thaler and C. R. Sunstein, *Nudge: Improving Decisions About Health, Wealth, and Happiness* (New Haven, CT: Yale University Press, 2008), and C. Thompson, "Desktop Orb Could Reform Energy Hogs," *Wired,* July 24, 2007.

121 *Public information has more impact than private:* See R. F. Baumeister and E. E. Jones, "When Self-Presentation Is Constrained by the Target's Knowledge: Consistency and Compensation," *Journal of Personality and Social Psychology* 36 (1978): 608–18. For a literature review, see R. F. Baumeister, "A Self-Presentational View of Social Phenomena," *Psychological Bulletin* 91 (1982): 3–26. For multiple relevant sources, see R. F. Baumeister, ed., *Public Self and Private Self* (New York: Springer-Verlag, 1986).

122 **neurotic pennypinching:** S. I. Rick, C. E. Cryder, and G. Loewenstein, "Tightwads and Spendthrifts," *Journal of Consumer Research* 34 (April 2008): 767–82.

122 **hyperopia:** A. Keinan and R. Kivetz, "Remedying Hyperopia: The Effects of Self-Control Regret on Consumer Behavior," *Journal of Marketing Research* (2008).

CHAPTER 6: CAN WILLPOWER BE STRENGTHENED?

124 **David Blaine:** Facts and quotations are drawn from interviews with Blaine; from his memoir, *Mysterious Stranger: A Book of Magic* (New York: Random House, 2003), and his Web site, http://davidblaine.com/; from John Tierney's reporting in the *New York Times* on Blaine's breath-holding training (April 22, 2008) and record attempt (April 30, 2008); and from Glen David Gold's article, "Making a Spectacle of Himself," *New York Times Magazine,* May 19, 2002.

129 **the original studies on building self-control strength through exercise:** Reported in M. Muraven, R. F. Baumeister, and D. M. Tice, "Longitudinal Improvement of Self-Regulation Through Practice: Building Self-Control Through Repeated Exercise," *Journal of Social Psychology* 139 (1999): 446–57.

132 **subsequent studies with handedness exercises and speech modification:** Reviewed in R. F. Baumeister, M. Gailliot, C. N. DeWall, and M. Oaten, "Self-Regulation and Personality: How Interventions Increase Regulatory Success, and How Depletion Moderates the Effects of Traits on Behavior," *Journal of Personality* 74 (2006):1773–1801.

133 **The fade-out effect of Head Start and other interventions is common knowledge among intelligence researchers:** See D. K. Detterman, "Intelligence," Microsoft Encarta Encyclopedia (2001), http://encarta.msn.com/find/Concise.asp?z=1&pg=2&ti=761570026.

133 **The papers on building self-control strength by Oaten and Cheng are as follows:** M. Oaten and K. Cheng, "Improved Self-Control: The Benefits of a Regular Program of Academic Study," *Basic and Applied Social Psychology* 28 (2006): 1–16; M. Oaten and

K. Cheng, "Longitudinal Gains in Self-Regulation from Regular Physical Exercise," *British Journal of Health Psychology* 11 (2006): 717–33; M. Oaten and K. Cheng, "Improvements in Self-Control from Financial Monitoring," *Journal of Economic Psychology* 28 (2006): 487–501.

136 **study of domestic violence:** E. J. Finkel, C. N. DeWall, E. B. Slotter, M. Oaten, and V. A. Foshee, "Self-Regulatory Failure and Intimate Partner Violence Perpetration," *Journal of Personality and Social Psychology* 97 (2009): 483–99.

CHAPTER 7: OUTSMARTING YOURSELF IN THE HEART OF DARKNESS

142 **"Self-control is more indispensable":** Henry Morton Stanley, *The Autobiography of Sir Henry Morton Stanley* (Breinigsville, PA: General Books, 2009), 274.

142 **Henry Morton Stanley:** Details of Stanley's life and expeditions are drawn chiefly from Tim Jeal's masterly biography, *Stanley: The Impossible Life of Africa's Greatest Explorer* (New Haven, CT: Yale University Press, 2007), and from personal communications with Jeal. Other sources include Stanley's *Autobiography;* Stanley's *In Darkest Africa, or the Quest, Rescue, and Retreat of Emin Governor of Equatoria* (Kindle, 2008), his account of the 1887–89 expedition; and a modern account by D. Liebowitz and C. Pearson, *The Last Expedition: Stanley's Mad Journey through the Congo in Darkest Africa* (New York: Norton, 2005).

143 **Kurtz lacked restraint:** Joseph Conrad, *Heart of Darkness* (Boston: Bedford Books, 1996), 74.

144 **maimed and killed, and sometimes eaten:** "They harassed the land column on a daily basis, killing and maiming men, women, and children with spears and poisoned arrows and, more often than not, dragging their victims into the forest to eat them." *The Last Expedition,* 236 (describing the 1888 march through forest).

144 **"For myself, I lay no claim":** Stanley, cable to *The Times* (London), December 8, 1890, reprinted in *Autobiography,* 274.

144 **"When I contrast what I have achieved":** Mark Twain, *Mark Twain's Speeches* (New York: Harper & Brothers, 1910), 157. See Jeal's *Stanley,* p. 468, for Twain's prediction of Stanley's enduring fame.

145 **"stubborn, invincible striving":** Rosamund Bartlett, *Chekhov: Scenes from a Life* (London: Free Press, 2004), 163.

146 **tales concocted of adoptive father:** Jeal concludes that while in New Orleans, the young Welshman never even met the American cotton broker Henry Hope Stanley, whom he would later claim as his adoptive father (34).

147 **"I rose at midnight":** Stanley, *Autobiography,* 24.

148 **"At home these men had no cause":** Stanley's January–June 1889 notebook, quoted in Jeal, 358.

148 **"hot-cold empathy gap":** D. Ariely and G. Loewenstein, "The Heat of the Moment: The Effect of Sexual Arousal on Sexual Decision Making," *Journal of Behavioral Decision Making* 19 (2006): 87–98.

150 **"I have taken a solemn, enduring oath":** Stanley, *How I Found Livingstone* (London: Sampson Low, Marston, Low, and Searle, 1872), 308–9.

152 **"Public Humiliation Diet":** D. Magary, "The Public Humiliation Diet: A How-To," Deadspin.com, http://deadspin.com/5545674/the-public-humiliation-diet-a-how+to?skyline=true&s=i.

152 **Covenant Eyes:** http://www.covenanteyes.com/.

152 **stickK.com:** Information is drawn from http://www.stickk.com/; and from I. Ayres, *Carrots and Sticks: Unlock the Power of Incentives to Get Things Done* (New York: Bantam, 2010).

153 **economists offered Philippine smokers:** X. Giné, D. Karlan, and J. Zinman, "Put Your Money Where Your Butt Is: A Commitment Contract for Smoking Cessation," *American*

Economic Journal: Applied Economics 2 (2010): 213–35. See also D. Karlan and J. Appel, *More Than Good Intentions* (New York: Dutton, 2011).

156 **messy room and sloppy Web site:** R. Rahinel, J. P. Redden, and K. D. Vohs, "An Orderly Mind Is Sensitive to Norms" (unpublished manuscript, University of Minnesota, Minneapolis, MN, 2011).

157 **meta-analysis with Dutch researchers:** D. De Ridder, G. Lensvelt-Mulders, C. Finkenauer, F. M. Stok, and R. F. Baumeister, "Taking Stock of Self-Control: A Meta-Analysis of How Self-Control Affects a Wide Range of Behaviors" (submitted for publication in 2011).

158 **Boice's studies of professors:** A good overview is provided in R. Boice, *Advice for New Faculty Members* (Needham Heights, MA: Allyn & Bacon, 2000).

162 **"For my protection against despair":** Stanley, *Autobiography,* 281.

163 **Navy SEAL Hell Week:** E. Greitens, "The SEAL Sensibility," *Wall Street Journal,* May 7, 2011.

164 **lofty thoughts:** K. Fujita, Y. Trope, N. Liberman, and M. Levin-Sagi, "Construal Levels and Self-Control," *Journal of Personality and Social Psychology* 90 (2006): 351–67.

CHAPTER 8: DID A HIGHER POWER HELP ERIC CLAPTON AND MARY KARR STOP DRINKING?

167 **"Holy Mother":** Eric Clapton and Stephen Bishop, "Holy Mother," *Live at Montreux, 1986* (DVD, Eagle Rock Entertainment, 2006). Lyrics used by permission of Eric Clapton and Stephen Bishop.

167 **Eric Clapton:** Details and quotations are from his book, *Clapton: The Autobiography* (New York: Broadway Books, 2007).

167 **Mary Karr:** Details and quotations are from her books, *Lit: A Memoir* (New York: HarperCollins, 2009) and *The Liars' Club* (New York: Viking Penguin, 1995).

172 **the fallacy of comparing alcoholism to physical diseases:** Noted by multiple authors, including a particularly vivid version in J. A. Schaler, *Addiction Is a Choice* (Chicago, IL: Open Court/Carus, 2000).

172 **some evidence that AA works:** For a review of theoretical and empirical obstacles to drawing firm conclusions, as well as evidence for benefits of attending AA meetings, see J. McKellar, E. Stewart, and K. Humphreys, "Alcoholics Anonymous Involvement and Positive Alcohol-Related Outcomes: Cause, Consequence, or Just a Correlate? A Prospective 2-Year Study of 2,319 Alcohol-Dependent Men," *Journal of Consulting and Clinical Psychology* 71 (2003): 302–8.

173 **Project MATCH:** Has been discussed extensively in many writings. See coverage by J. A. Schaler, *Addiction Is a Choice* (Chicago, IL: Open Court/Carus: 2000). Also see G. M. Heyman, *Addiction: A Disorder of Choice* (Cambridge, MA: Harvard, 2009).

174 **desire for peer approval is often what got them in trouble :** C. D. Rawn and K. D. Vohs, "People Use Self-Control to Risk Personal Harm: An Intra-personal Dilemma," *Personality and Social Psychology Review* (in press).

175 **One of the newest and most ambitious alcoholism studies:** This study by lead investigator Carlo DiClemente is currently being prepared for publication. Baumeister served as consultant on the grant and this material is from his discussions with the researchers regarding the project in progress.

176 **history of drinking in America and the "barbecue law":** See W. J. Rorabaugh, *The Alcoholic Republic: An American Tradition* (New York: Oxford University Press, 1979).

177 **Resolutions more kept if made in presence of others, especially lovers:** This also emerged from the DiClemente-led study of alcoholics in Baltimore (see note above).

177 **Chilean street vendors:** F. Kast, S. Meier, and D. Pomeranz. "Under-Savers Anonymous: Evidence on Self-Help Groups and Peer Pressure as a Savings Commitment Device," working paper, November 2010.

178 **self-control is contagious:** On smoking, see N. A. Christakis and J. H. Fowler, "The Collective Dynamics of Smoking in a Large Social Network," *New England Journal of Medicine* 358 (2008): 2249–58. For obesity, see N. A. Christakis and J. H. Fowler, "The Spread of Obesity in a Large Social Network over 32 Years," *New England Journal of Medicine* 357 (2007): 370–79; and E. Cohen-Cole and J. M. Fletcher, "Is Obesity Contagious: Social Networks vs. Environmental Factors in the Obesity Epidemic," *Journal of Health Economics* 27 (2008): 1382–87.

179 **on religion and longevity:** M. E. McCullough, W. T. Hoyt, D. B. Larson, H. G. Koenig, and C. E. Thoresen, "Religious Involvement and Mortality: A Meta-Analytic Review," *Health Psychology* 19 (2000): 211–22.

179 **overview of religion and self-control:** M. R. McCullough and B. L. B. Willoughby, "Religion, Self-Regulation, and Self-Control: Associations, Explanations, and Implications," *Psychological Bulletin* 135 (2009): 69–93.

180 **Meditation activates the same brain centers used for self-regulation:** J. A. Brefczynski-Lewis, A. Lutz, H. S. Schaefer, D. B. Levinson, and R. J. Davidson, "Neural Correlates of Attentional Expertise in Long-Term Meditation Practitioners," *Proceedings of the National Academy of Sciences* 104, no. 27 (2007): 11483–88.

180 **subliminal exposure to religious words:** A. Fishbach, R. S. Friedman, and A. W. Kruglanski, "Leading Us Not into Temptation: Momentary Allurements Elicit Overriding Goal Activation," *Journal of Personality and Social Psychology* 84, no. 2 (2003): 296–309, http://dx.doi.org/10.1037/0022-3514.84.2.296.

180 **"anaerobic workout for self-control":** J. Tierney, "For Good Self-Control, Try Getting Religious About It," *New York Times,* December 30, 2008.

181 **study with photograph of pope:** M. W. Baldwin, S. E. Carrell, and D. F. Lopez, "Priming Relationship Schemas: My Advisor and the Pope Are Watching Me from the Back of My Mind," *Journal of Experimental Social Psychology* 26 (1990): 435–54.

183 **Bright Lines and "hyperbolic discounting":** G. Ainslic, *Breakdown of Will* (New York: Cambridge University Press, (2001).

CHAPTER 9: RAISING STRONG CHILDREN

187 **Deborah Carroll and the Paul family:** Details and quotations from Carroll and the Pauls are drawn from interviews; from "The Little House of Horrors" episode of *Nanny 911* (on DVD, *Nanny 911: The First Season,* Fox Broadcasting Company, released 2008); and from the book by Deborah Carroll and Stella Reid with Karen Moline, *Nanny 911: Expert Advice for All Your Parenting Emergencies* (New York: Harper Entertainment, 2005).

188 **Branden on self-esteem:** See N. Branden, *The Six Pillars of Self-Esteem* (New York: Bantam Books, 1994). The quotation was from N. Branden, "In Defense of Self," *Association for Humanistic Psychology* (August–September 1984): 12–13.

189 **Mecca quotation:** From I. Davis, "Ministry for Feeling Good," *The Times* (London), January 22, 1988.

189 **Smelser quotation:** From p. 1 of N. J. Smelser, "Self-Esteem and Social Problems: An Introduction," in A. M. Mecca, N. J. Smelser, and J. Vasconcellos, eds., *The Social Importance of Self-Esteem* (Berkeley, CA: University of California Press, 1989), 1–23.

190 **the big self-esteem report:** R. F. Baumeister, J. D. Campbell, J. I. Krueger, and K. D. Vohs, "Does High Self-Esteem Cause Better Performance, Interpersonal Success,

Happiness, or Healthier Lifestyles?" *Psychological Science in the Public Interest* 4 (2003): 1–44. The following year a condensed version was published in *Scientific American* and later reprinted in *Scientific American Mind.*

190 **the experiment on students and grades:** D. R. Forsyth, N. A. Kerr, J. L. Burnette, and R. F. Baumeister, "Attempting to Improve the Academic Performance of Struggling College Students by Bolstering Their Self-Esteem: An Intervention That Backfired," *Journal of Social and Clinical Psychology* 26 (2007): 447–59.

192 **narcissists' popularity in groups:** D. L. Paulhus, "Interpersonal and Intrapsychic Adaptiveness of Trait Self-Enhancement: A Mixed Blessing?" *Journal of Personality and Social Psychology,* 74 (1998): 1197–1208.

193 **increase in narcissim:** J. M. Twenge and W. K. Campbell, *The Narcissism Epidemic: Living in the Age of Entitlement* (New York: Free Press, 2009).

193 **narcissism in song lyrics:** C. N. DeWall, R. S. Pond Jr., W. K. Campbell, and J. M. Twenge, "Tuning In to Psychological Change: Linguistic Markers of Psychological Traits and Emotions over Time in Popular U.S. Song Lyrics." *Psychology of Aesthetics, Creativity, and the Arts* (2011), online publication, March 21.

194 **Chinese and American toddlers:** M. A. Sabbagh, F. Xu, S. M. Carlson, L. J. Moses, and K. Lee, "The Development of Executive Functioning and Theory of Mind," *Psychological Science* 17 (2006): 74–81.

195 **Asian-American IQs:** J. R. Flynn, *Asian Americans: Achievement Beyond IQ* (Hillsdale, NJ: Erlbaum, 1991).

195 **Kim sisters:** Dr. S. K. Abboud and J. Kim, *Top of the Class: How Asian Parents Raise High Achievers—and How You Can Too* (New York: Berkley Books, 2005).

196 **Confucian concepts of *chiao shun* and *guan*:** See S. T. Russell, L. J. Crockett, and R. K. Chao, eds., *Asian American Parenting and Parent-Adolescent Relationships* (New York: Springer, 2010), especially chapter 1.

196 **study of Chinese mothers in Los Angeles:** R. K. Chao, "Chinese and European American Mothers' Beliefs about the Role of Parenting in Children's School Success," *Journal of Cross-Cultural Psychology* 27 (1996): 403.

197 **Amy Chua:** *Battle Hymn of the Tiger Mother* (New York: Penguin Press, 2011), 9.

199 **Cotton Mather:** E. S. Morgan, *The Puritan Family* (New York: Harper & Row, 1966), 103.

200 **On parental discipline mistakes:** S. O'Leary, "Parental Discipline Mistakes," *Current Directions in Psychological Science* (4), (1995): 11–13.

203 **on children and money:** A. M. C. Otto, P. A. M. Schots, J. A. J. Westerman, and P. Webley, "Children's Use of Saving Strategies: An Experimental Approach," *Journal of Economic Psychology* 27 (2006): 57–72.

204 **Children who have bank accounts are more likely to become savers:** See B. D. Bernheim, D. M. Garrett, and D. M. Maki, "Education and Saving: The Long-Term Effects of High School Financial Curriculum Mandates," *Journal of Public Economics* 80 (2001): 436–67. For parental influence on children's saving, see P. Webley and E. K. Nyhus, "Parents' Influence on Children's Future Orientation and Saving," *Journal of Economic Psychology* 27 (2006): 140–64.

204 **overjustification effect:** There are many sources, but an early and authoritative one is M. R. Lepper and D. Greene, eds., *The Hidden Costs of Reward: New Perspectives of the Psychology of Human Motivation* (Hillsdale, NJ: Erlbaum, 1978).

205 **studies on paying students for grades and achievements:** R. G. Fryer Jr., "Financial Incentives and Student Achievement: Evidence from Randomized Trials" (working paper, Harvard University, EdLabs, and NBER, July 8, 2010), http://www.economics.harvard.edu/faculty/fryer/files/Incentives_ALL_7-8-10.pdf; see also A. Ripley, "Should Kids Be Bribed to Do Well in School?" *Time,* April 8, 2010.

206 **"Try to sleep, Bella":** Stephenie Meyer, *New Moon* (New York: Little, Brown and Company, 2006), 52.

206 **Mary Brunton's novels:** For a discussion of Brunton's career and her novels *Self-Control* (1811) and *Discipline* (1814), see H. J. Jackson, "Jane Austen's Rival," *Times Literary Supplement,* April 5, 2006.

206 **"I can never, never afford":** Stephenie Meyer, *Twilight* (New York: Little, Brown and Company, 2005), 310.

207 **another discovery about self-control:** W. Mischel, "Preference for a Delayed Reinforcement: An Experimental Study of a Cultural Observation," *Journal of Abnormal and Social Psychology* 56 (1958): 57–61.

207 **deficits on children of single parents:** One source is M. R. Gottfredson and T. Hirschi, *A General Theory of Crime* (Stanford: Stanford University Press, 1990).

208 **Joan McCord:** J. McCord, "Some Child-Rearing Antecedents of Criminal Behavior in Adult Men," *Journal of Personality and Social Psychology,* 37 (1979): 1477–86.

209 **meta-analysis on marijuana use among children; benefits of parental monitoring:** See A. Lac and W. D. Crano, "Monitoring Matters: Meta-Analytic Review Reveals Reliable Linkage of Parental Monitoring with Adolescent Marijuana Use," *Perspectives on Psychological Science* 4 (2009): 578–86.

209 **parental monitoring and diabetics:** A. Hughes, C. Berg, and D. Wiebe, "Adolescent Problem-Solving Skill and Parental Monitoring Moderate Self-Control Deficits on Metabolic Control in Type 1 Diabetics" (poster presented at Society for Behavioral Medicine meeting; manuscript in preparation).

210 **Mischel and the marshmallow studies:** See "Mischel's studies of delayed gratification" in the notes for the Introduction.

212 **on the Tools of the Mind preschool programs:** See A. Diamond, W. S. Barnett, J. Thomas, and S. Munro, "Preschool Program Improves Cognitive Control," *Science* 318 (2007): 1387–88.

212 **most children aren't being hurt by playing video games:** L. Kutner and C. Olson, *Grand Theft Childhood: The Surprising Truth About Video Games* (New York: Simon & Schuster, 2008).

213 **"gamification":** See J. McGonigal, *Reality Is Broken: Why Games Make Us Better and How They Can Change the World* (New York: Penguin Press, 2011), and *The Gamification Encyclopedia,* http://gamification.org/wiki/Encyclopedia.

CHAPTER 10: THE PERFECT STORM OF DIETING

215 **Oprah Paradox:** Material about Oprah Winfrey is drawn from her article "How Did I Let This Happen Again?" *O, The Oprah Magazine,* January 2009, and from her foreword to a book by her trainer, Bob Greene, *The Best Life Diet* (New York: Simon & Schuster, 2009).

216 **the King Henry VIII and Oprah Winfrey Effect:** John Tierney, "Fat and Happy," *New York Times,* April 23, 2005.

217 **meta-analysis of self-control studies:** D. De Ridder, G. Lensvelt-Mulders, C. Finkenauer, F. M. Stok, and R. F. Baumeister, "Taking Stock of Self-Control: A Meta-Analysis of How Self-Control Affects a Wide Range of Behaviors" (submitted for publication in 2011).

217 **study of overweight college students:** A. W. Crescioni, J. Ehrlinger, J. L. Alquist, K. E. Conlon, R. F. Baumeister, C. Schatschneider, and G. R. Dutton, "High Trait Self-Control Predicts Positive Health Behaviors and Success in Weight Loss," *Journal of Health Psychology* (in press).

218 **exercise doesn't necessarily shed pounds:** See G. Taubes, *Good Calories, Bad Calories:*

Challenging the Conventional Wisdom on Diet, Weight Control, and Disease (New York: Alfred A. Knopf, 2007), 298-99; and G. Kolata, "For the Overweight, Bad Advice by the Spoonful," *New York Times*, August 30, 2007.

218 **diets are ineffective and counterproductive:** T. Mann, A. J. Tomiyama, E. Westling, A.-M. Lew, B. Samuels, and J. Chatman, "Medicare's Search for Effective Obesity Treatments: Diets Are Not the Answer," *American Psychologist* 62 (2007): 220–33; and G. Kolata, *Rethinking Thin: The New Science of Weight Loss—and the Myths and Realities of Dieting* (New York: Picador, 2007).

219 **betting on weight loss:** N. Burger and J. Lynham, "Betting on Weight Loss . . . and Losing: Personal Gambles as Commitment Mechanisms," *Applied Economics Letters* 17 (2010): 12, 1161–66, http://dx.doi.org/10.1080/21836840902845442.

219 **"curvaceously thin" impossible dream:** K. Harrison, "Television Viewers' Ideal Body Proportions: The Case of the Curvaceously Thin Woman," *Sex Roles* 48, no. 5–6 (2003): 255–64.

220 **diets fail miserably in the long run:** C. Ayyad and T. Andersen, "Long-Term Efficacy of Dietary Treatment of Obesity: A Systematic Review of Studies Published Between 1931 and 1999," *Obesity Reviews* 1 (2000): 113–19.

220 **what-the-hell effect:** C. P. Herman and D. Mack, "Restrained and Unrestrained Eating," *Journal of Personality* 43 (1975): 647–60.

222 **monitoring stops after diet is broken:** J. Polivy, "Perception of Calories and Regulation of Intake in Restrained and Unrestrained Subjects," *Addictive Behaviors* 1 (1976): 237–43.

222 **studies with rigged clocks and shelled nuts:** Described in S. Schachter, "Some Extraordinary Facts about Obese Humans and Rats," *American Psychologist* 26 (1971): 129–44. See also S. Schachter and J. Rodin, *Obese Humans and Rats* (Hillsdale, NJ: Erlbaum, 1974). Schachter's other book from this period, *Emotion, Obesity, and Crime*, likewise covers much of that material.

227 **depletion in dieters:** K. D. Vohs and T. F. Heatherton, "Self-Regulatory Failure: A Resource-Depletion Approach," *Psychological Science* 11 (2000): 249–54.

227 **urges and feelings during depletion:** K. D. Vohs, R. F. Baumeister, N. L. Mead, S. Ramanathan, and B. J. Schmeichel, "Engaging in Self-Control Heightens Urges and Feelings" (manuscript submitted for publication, University of Minnesota, 2010).

228 **study of candy in desk drawer:** J. E. Painter, B. Wansink, and J. B. Hieggelke, "How Visibility and Convenience Influence Candy Consumption," *Appetite* 38, no. 3 (June 2002): 237–38.

229 **"implementation intention":** P. M. Gollwitzer, "Implementation intentions: Strong effects of simple plans," *American Psychologist* 54 (1999): 493-503.

230 **Obese people cluster together:** N. Christakis and J. Fowler, "The spread of obesity in a large social network over 32 years," *New England Journal of Medicine* 357 (2007): 370-79.

230 **members of Weight Watchers shed pounds:** S. Heshka, J. W. Anderson, R. L. Atkinson, et al., "Weight Loss with Self-Help Compared with a Structured Commercial Program: A Randomized Trial," *Journal of the American Medical Association* 289, no. 14 (2003):1792–98, http://jama.ama-assn.org/cgi/content/full/289/14/1792.

231 **daily weighings are best:** R. R. Wing, D. F. Tate, A. A. Gorin, H. A. Raynor, J. L. Fava, and J. Machan, "'STOP Regain': Are There Negative Effects of Daily Weighing?" *Journal of Consulting and Clinical Psychology* 75 (2007): 652–56.

231 **scales that transmit weight wirelessly:** Two of the better-known brands are Withings and LifeSource.

232 **weight gain among prisoners:** See B. Wansink, *Mindless Eating: Why We Eat More Than We Think* (New York: Bantam, 2006).

232 **people who kept food diary lost more weight:** J. F. Hollis, C. M. Gullion, V. J. Stevens,

et al., "Weight Loss during the Intensive Intervention Phase of the Weight-Loss Maintenance Trial," *American Journal of Preventive Medicine* 35, no. 2 (2008): 118–26.

232 **"health halo" effects:** See P. Chandon and B. Wansink, "The Biasing Health Halos of Fast Food Restaurant Health Claims: Lower Calorie Estimates and Higher Side-Dish Consumption Intentions," *Journal of Consumer Research* 34, no. 3 (October 2007): 301–14; and B. Wansink and P. Chandon, "Can 'Low-Fat' Nutrition Labels Lead to Obesity?" *Journal of Marketing Research*, 43, no. 4 (November 2006): 605–17.

232 **healthy labels create "negative calories":** A. Chernev, "The Dieter's Paradox," *Journal of Consumer Psychology* (scheduled for April 2011 issue; published online in September 2010). Informal study in Park Slope by Tierney, Chandon, and Chernev described in Tierney's Findings column, "Health Halo Can Hide the Calories," *New York Times*, December 1, 2008.

233 **eating in front of the television increases consumption:** See B. Wansink, *Mindless Eating*.

233 **on effects of eating with others:** See C. P. Herman, D. A. Roth, and J. Polivy, "Effects of the Presence of Others on Food Intake: A Normative Interpretation," *Psychological Bulletin* 129 (2003): 873–86.

233 **the studies with perpetually refilling soup bowl and uncleared chicken bones:** See B. Wansink, *Mindless Eating*.

233 **underestimates of food volume:** P. Chandon and N. Ordabayeva, "Supersize in 1D, Downsize in 3D: Effects of Spatial Dimensionality on Size Perceptions and Preferences," *Journal of Marketing Research* (in press). For a look at an online experiment involving this effect, see J. Tierney, "How Supersizing Seduces," TierneyLab, *New York Times*, December 5, 2008.

235 **on telling yourself you can have the treat later:** N. L. Mead and V. M. Patrick, "In Praise of Putting Things Off: How Postponing Consumption Pleasures Facilitates Self-Control (manuscript submitted for publication).

CONCLUSION: THE FUTURE OF WILLPOWER

238 **St. Augustine:** *Confessions,* trans. R. S. Pine-Coffin (New York: Penguin Books, 1961), 169.

239 **German beeper study:** See citation in Introduction notes.

239 **Dutch study:** D. De Ridder, G. Lensvelt-Mulders, C. Finkenauer, F. M. Stok, and R. F. Baumeister, "Taking Stock of Self-Control: A Meta-Analysis of How Self-Control Affects a Wide Range of Behaviors" (submitted for publication in 2011).

239 **U.S. studies showing less stress:** A. W. Crescioni, J. Ehrlinger, J. L. Alquist, K. E. Conlon, R. F. Baumeister, C. Schatschneider, and G. R. Dutton, "High Trait Self-Control Predicts Positive Health Behaviors and Success in Weight Loss," *Journal of Health Psychology* (in press). This study contained a large data set and not all analyses are reported in the final version of the paper, but the relationship was clear.

239 **Cicero:** "The Sixth Phillipic," *The Orations of Marcus Tullius Cicero*, trans. C. D. Yonge (London: George Bell & Sons, 1879), 119.

239 **Jonathan Edwards preached an entire sermon:** "Procrastination; or, The Sin and Folly of Depending on Future Time," *The Works of President Edwards*, vol. 5 (London: James Black & Son, 1817), 511.

239 **prevalence of procrastination:** P. Steel, *The Procrastination Equation* (New York: Harper, 2011), 11, 67, 101.

240 **perfectionism and impulsiveness:** P. Steel, "The Nature of Procrastination: A Meta-Analytic and Theoretical Review of Quintessential Self-Regulatory Failure," *Psychological Bulletin* 133, no. 1 (January 2007): 67.

241 **Deadline Test:** D. M. Tice and R. F. Baumeister, "Longitudinal Study of Procrastina-

tion, Performance, Stress, and Health: The Costs and Benefits of Dawdling," *Psychological Science* 8 (1997): 454–58.

248 **Parkinson's Law:** C. N. Parkinson, *Parkinson's Law, or the Pursuit of Progress* (London: John Murray, 1958), 4.

250 **The planning fallacy:** R. Buehler, D. Griffin, and M. Ross, "Exploring the "Planning Fallacy": Why People Underestimate Their Task Completion Times," *Journal of Personality and Social Psychology* 67 (1994): 366–81.

253 **Dorothy Parker's excuse:** James Thurber, *The Years with Ross* (New York: Harper-Collins, 2000), 19.

253 **Robert Benchley's psychological principle:** Robert Benchley, "How to Get Things Done," *The Benchley Roundup* (Chicago: University of Chicago Press, 1954), 5.

254 **Nothing Alternative:** T. Hiney and F. MacShane, eds., *The Raymond Chandler Papers: Selected Letters and Nonfiction, 1909–1959* (New York: Atlantic Monthly Press, 2002), 104.

255 **software to block Internet access:** http://macfreedom.com/.

256 **monitoring of spending:** Mint, http://www.mint.com/; Xpenser, http://xpenser.com/; TweetWhatYouSpend, http://www.tweetwhatyouspend.com/.

256 **monitoring of computer usage:** RescueTime, https://www.rescuetime.com/; Slife, http://www.slifeweb.com/; ManicTime, http://www.manictime.com/.

256 **Quantified Self and Lifehacker:** http://quantifiedself.com/; http://lifehacker.com/.

257 **rewards in computer games:** T. Chatfield, "7 Ways Games Reward the Brain," TED Talk, TedGlobal 2010. See also his book *Fun Inc.: Why Games Are the 21st Century's Most Serious Business* (London: Virgin Books, 2011).

259 **trends in free time:** J. H. Ausubel and A. Grübler, "Working Less and Living Longer: Long-Term Trends in Working Times and Time Budgets," *Technological Forecasting and Social Change* 50 (1995): 113–31.

259 **"resource slack":** G. Zauberman and J. G. Lynch Jr., "Resource Slack and Propensity to Discount Delayed Investments of Time Versus Money," *Journal of Experimental Psychology* 134, no. 1 (2005): 23–37.

259 **procrastinating pleasure:** S. B. Shu and A. Gneezy, "Procrastination of Enjoyable Experiences," *Journal of Marketing Research* (2010).

260 **willpower and altruism:** M. Gailliot, R. Baumeister, C. N. DeWall, J. Maner, E. Plant, D. Tice, L. Brewer, and B. Schmeichel, "Self-Control Relies on Glucose as a Limited Energy Source: Willpower Is More Than a Metaphor," *Journal of Personality and Social Psychology* 92 (2007), 325–36. Also see C. N. DeWall, R. Baumeister, M. Gailliot, and J. Maner, "Depletion Makes the Heart Grow Less Helpful: Helping As a Function of Self-Regulatory Energy and Genetic Relatedness," *Personality and Social Psychology Bulletin* 34 (2008): 1663–76.

Index

Hofmann, Wilhelm, 3
"Holy Mother" (Clapton), 167, 168
honors-thesis experiment, 250
Hopkins, Anthony, 51
hot-cold empathy gap, 148–50, 255–56
hotornot.com, 105–6
Houdini, Harry, 127
Houston, Whitney, 189, 190, 193
How to Win Friends and Influence People (Carnegie), 6–7
hunter-gatherers, 53
hyperbolic discounting, 183–86
hyperopia, 122–23
hypertension, 171–72
hypoglycemia, 44–46, 56

ice water test, 91–92
immune system, 44, 59, 242
implementation intention strategy, 229–30, 231, 255
impulse control, 37, 52, 53, 122, 180, 206, 245
  absent fathers and, 208
  Chinese imposition of, 194
  procrastination and, 240–41
In Darkest Africa (Stanley), 159
Industrial Revolution, 45
infants, human, 110–11, 202–3, 222
  Ferberization technique for, 202
information-processing model, 17, 42
intelligence, 1, 11–12, 13, 14, 43, 133
  artificial, 110
  of Asian-Americans, 194–95
Intuit, 110, 270n
investment opportunities, 99, 105, 117, 153–54
Inzlicht, Michael, 28–29
IQ (intelligence quotient), 11, 195
Iraq War, 74
Islam, 181
Israeli prisons, 96–99
Iyengar, Sheena, 103–4

Japanese-Americans, 195
Jeal, Tim, 145–46, 152, 155–56, 162, 271n
Jefferson, Thomas, 118
Jewish holidays, 181, 182
Johnson, Don, 40, 56
Journal of Personality and Social Psychology, 70–71
judges, 90, 96–99, 102, 246
juvenile delinquents, 45, 209

Karlan, Dean, 152–54
Karr, Mary, 167, 169–71, 175, 176–77, 182, 255
Kast, Felipe, 177–78
Kelly, Kevin, 117
Kim family, 195–96, 197, 204
King, Laura, 66–68
King Henry VIII and Oprah Winfrey Effect, 216
Koo, Minjung, 120
Korea, 120
Korean-Americans, 195–96
Kutner, Lawrence, 212

labels, food, 232–33
Lady Alice (boat), 160, 161
Lady Gaga, 187, 189, 190
legal realists, 96–97
legal system, 8, 96–97
  see also judges; prisons
Lent, 40–42, 181
Leopold II, king of Belgium, 145
Lesner, Chris, 270n
Levav, Jonathan, 97, 103
Lewin, Kurt, 81
Liars' Club, The (Karr), 169–70
licensing effect, 136
Lifehacker, 256
Lit (Karr), 167, 170
living statues, 20–21, 35, 39, 55
Livingstone, David, 142, 145, 150–51, 155–56, 159, 160, 162, 165
Loewenstein, George, 148, 149
loneliness, 175–76
Losing Control (Baumeister, Tice, and Heatherton), 11
loss, sense of, 101–2
luteal phase, 53–56

McCord, Joan, 209
McCullough, Michael, 179–80, 182
McKellar, John, 172
McMaster University, 105
McNamara, Robert S., 73–74
Madonna, 107
Magary, Drew, 152
management planning, 77–78
Manzer, Todd, 270n
Mardi Gras Theory, 40–42
marijuana use, 54, 69
  parental monitoring and, 209
marital counseling, 23–24